# Neville Chamberlain

*The Passionate Radical*

# NEVILLE CHAMBERLAIN

## THE PASSIONATE RADICAL

WALTER REID

BIRLINN

For Lachlan

First published in 2021 by
Birlinn Limited
West Newington House
10 Newington Road
Edinburgh
EH9 1QS

*www.birlinn.co.uk*

ISBN 978 1 78027 674 8

Typeset by Hewer Text UK Ltd, Edinburgh

Printed and bound by Clays Ltd, Elcograf S.p.A.

# Contents

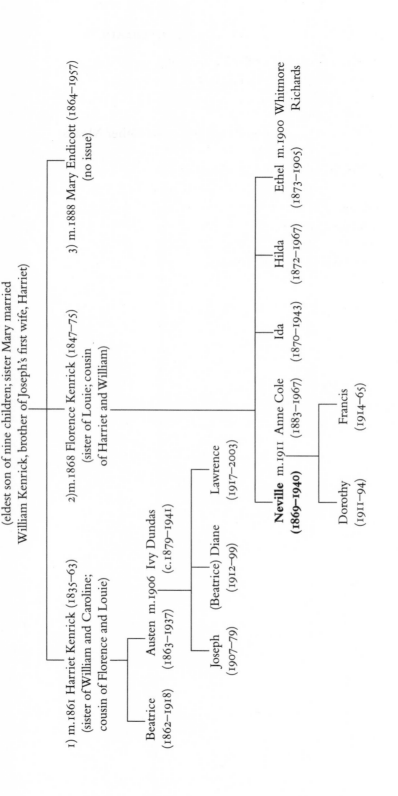

Joseph Chamberlain (1836–1914)
(eldest son of nine children; sister Mary married
William Kenrick, brother of Joseph's first wife, Harriet)

1) m.1861 Harriet Kenrick (1835–63)
(sister of William and Caroline;
cousin of Florence and Louie)

2) m.1868 Florence Kenrick (1847–75)
(sister of Louie; cousin
of Harriet and William)

3) m.1888 Mary Endicott (1864–1957)
(no issue)

Beatrice
(1862–1918)

Austen  m.1906  Ivy Dundas
(1863–1937)      (c.1879–1941)

Neville  m.1911  Anne Cole
(1869–1940)       (1883–1967)

Ida
(1870–1943)

Hilda
(1872–1967)

Ethel  m.1900  Whitmore
(1873–1905)        Richards

Joseph
(1907–79)

(Beatrice) Diane
(1912–99)

Lawrence
(1917–2003)

Dorothy
(1911–94)

Francis
(1914–65)

*Prologue*

# A Puzzle

As the nineteenth century moved into the twentieth, a young man, subsequently to be a Prime Minister of Great Britain, lived rough for five years, a pioneer on the edge of the Empire. He rarely saw another European face. He spent long days labouring under the tropical sun. He tested his strength against that of the native labourers, who idolised him, and taught himself to sail single-handed. Who was he?

Some hints. He never went to university. He spent his frontiersman evenings educating himself, reading widely, coming to love Shakespeare more than any other politician of his time. Despite the rigours of this early life he was a man who enjoyed his pleasures. He was far from teetotal and would suffer from gout. He loved his cigars as well as his wine. He entered politics overshadowed by the reputation of a great parliamentary father, whose last days had been marred by cruel incapacity. He venerated his father's memory and, an emotional man, his voice shook when he spoke of him. Could this be Churchill?

Given the title and subject of this book, this tease was never going to work; but in other circumstances it might have taken some time before the penny dropped and the hardbitten colonial pioneer was identified as Neville Chamberlain, the funny man with an umbrella who capitulated to Hitler and came back from Munich flapping a piece of paper and talking about peace in our time: the point I want to make right at the outset is just how misleadingly history remembers Neville Chamberlain.

The crass caricature has persisted. How can it be reconciled with the kind of young man who lived the life I've just described? That's what this book is about: unpacking a very private man and showing how very far his reality was from the way in which he is remembered: 'the undertaker', 'the coroner', 'the man with the umbrella'.

What emerges is just how human and susceptible – how *passionate* – he was. It was to some extent his very humanity and vulnerability that's to blame for the bloodless image. In his shyness he constructed a shell to conceal what he thought demeaning. The fact that he was a man of flesh and blood does not of course mean that he was wholly likeable. He was far from that, very far indeed. He didn't feel it necessary to fight against his shyness. Indeed he was rather proud of his reserve, and behind it, like not a few shy people, he had a good opinion of his own abilities. Thus he could be high-handed and dismissive of those he felt to be his intellectual inferiors. Perhaps he should have resolved to master that shyness. Maybe not doing so was a kind of arrogance. Certainly, in the last half of his adult life, arrogance was his dominant characteristic.

But it's worth understanding what made him tick, because he's much more complicated and interesting than the moustache and umbrella matchstick man. After his return from the tropics he was a businessman and a very good accountant (which doesn't help the image), but what truly animated him were not the intricacies of finance, but emotions and ideals – emotions and ideals for which he worked through the medium of politics.

Not many 1930s politicians have images so fixed in the popular imagination as Chamberlain. Even people who have little interest in the politics of the interwar years will have, many of them, an image of this fussy little man (actually he was quite tall), almost a Charlie Chaplin lookalike, with his wing collar, an irritating moustache and an unbelievable capacity for credulity as far as Hitler was concerned. In the popular view, he was a tiresome presence which had to be disposed of before Churchill could get on with winning the war and bringing out the greatness of Great Britain.

The irony is that not only is the caricature so well defined, but also that it's so wrong. The first paragraph of this section was a puzzle which didn't come off very well: 'Who was this man?' The rest of the book is an attempt to answer the bigger and more difficult question: 'Who was the real Neville Chamberlain?', and we'll start by returning to a minor island in the Bahamas.

# Chapter 1

# Andros

Our first meeting with Arthur Neville Chamberlain is not with a foolish-looking elderly gentleman clutching a piece of paper at Heston aerodrome, but with a bronzed hunk, his shirt open to the waist, splashing through the Caribbean on the beach of the island of Andros.

He was a good-looking young man. At home, in a suit, he looked not unlike a youthful Anthony Eden. Here, in tropical gear, on the edge of the Empire, he looked more like Errol Flynn, or Douglas Fairbanks, or even Daniel Craig. His moustache was perhaps a bit on the bushy side (ahead of his marriage, years later, his wife advised him to trim it), but it was far from a walrus.

It was indeed a swashbuckling existence which young Neville led. Just a year earlier, when the enterprise was in preparation and his father has told him to sail from England to the Bahamas, Neville had said, 'The idea of travelling across the Atlantic all by myself was appalling, but I never thought of hesitating to obey,' and he adapted immediately to the lifestyle of this frontier existence on islands which had been the home of the pirates Captain Kidd and Blackbeard.

It was a truly rugged existence. At first he lived in the simple home of a local resident, and one day he got by on two biscuits for breakfast and nothing else for the rest of the day.[1] He had few baths, and no haircuts. He grew a beard and that moustache developed into full-blown side-whiskers. In the early days he and his men made their way around the island on foot, his shoes shredded by the stony ground. In temperatures which were occasionally as high as 50° Celsius they suffered badly from thirst which they tried to satisfy from any filthy water they could find: they looked for crabholes which they enlarged with their fingers. Neville slept in a hammock slung from poles, but the mosquitoes got through his net and there was little sleep. The following night he slept on the ground, on pinecones. 'The mosquitoes were not so numerous as the night before but bad enough to worry.'

Why was he here? As with almost all he did in his life – indeed with everything that mattered – he did it because of his father, Joseph Chamberlain, who was not only arguably the most influential politician of his age, but also a phenomenally successful businessman. But by the time that Neville was sent out to Andros in the Bahamas, Joe was getting short of money. Short in a relative sense. He still maintained an immense establishment at Highbury in Birmingham together with a substantial house in London, but the expectation, when he had sold off his business interests, that he could live on the income from his capital had proved to be over-optimistic. He had not received a ministerial salary since 1886, and although he was a Member of Parliament, parliamentarians in those days were unpaid. Furthermore, his investments had declined in value.

In 1890 Joe was in Montreal. He had gone there to meet his third wife's American family, but he also met there a man of great vigour and powers of persuasion, Sir Ambrose Shea. Joe Chamberlain's improbable decision to diversify from engineering in the Midlands to growing sisal in the Bahamas was the result of these powers of persuasion.

Ambrose Shea's father had emigrated from County Tipperary, Ireland, to Newfoundland in Canada around 1784. Young Shea worked on the family's newspaper, *The Newfoundlander*, before employing his indefatigable energies in business, insurance, the transatlantic steamer trade and finally politics. In 1885, and over the age of seventy, he lobbied for appointment as governor of Newfoundland. Although he was well qualified for the appointment, he had made enemies in political life, and despite having gone all the way to London to press his case, in 1887 he was obliged to settle for governorship of the Bahamas instead. There he remained until his retirement in 1894. Even then, now aged seventy-nine, he went back to London to press again for the governorship of Newfoundland, but again failed in his bid. At last, this prodigy of energy and ambition retired from public life. He died in London in 1905 at the age of ninety, but his body was returned to Newfoundland, always the focus of his ambitions, where he was given a state funeral. He was known as the father of Canadian Confederation – indeed, it had been his less federally minded colleagues in Newfoundland who had blocked his claim to be their governor.

However persuasive Shea was, it is remarkable how readily Joe Chamberlain, the shrewdest and most calculating of men, was taken in. Shea told him that sisal would grow like a weed in the benevolent climate of the Bahamas.* Its fleshy leaves were used to produce hemp fibre for ropes, matting, carpets and so forth. To be fair, Joe didn't entirely rely on Shea's salesmanship. His elder son, Austen, Neville's half-brother, was already in America, making his own enquiries, and it was he who telegraphed Birmingham to suggest that Neville should join him.

During his time in the Bahamas, Shea applied his drive and energy to the welfare of what was then a British Crown Colony by stimulating its development in all sorts of ways. Having been involved in selling and chartering ships during his mercantile career, he saw the scope for capitalising on the strategic position of the islands through expansion of trade by way of steamship cargo. He built up both steamship routes and telegraphic communications. He himself earlier had experience of the sisal trade, and believed that it was the key to the improvement of the poor rural prospects in some of the islands, bringing some kind of organised employment for the islanders. So when Austen and Neville arrived in Nassau, they were faced by a man of great energy and charm who was determined to sell the opportunities for the production of sisal to potential investors. He courted the Chamberlains assiduously, and they were a great draw at the balls and social events which he laid on in their honour.

The two young men reached Sir Ambrose and Lady Shea at their residence in Nassau on 10 November 1890. We know quite a lot about the efforts the Sheas took to sell the dream as Neville was a prolific diary-writer. In addition, one of the endearing aspects of his character was his fondness for his sisters, Ida, Hilda and Ethel, to whom he wrote at great length and very regularly throughout his life, documenting his reaction to events from these early days in the Bahamas to the high drama of the Munich crisis.

---

* *Agave sisilana* or sisal is processed to produce a fibre which is used in the ways mentioned above.

The governor's house was a large bungalow. Neville and Austen were encouraged to pick oranges and guavas from the garden, and from his bedroom Neville could see the sisal growing luxuriantly in Nassau, as alas it never would do in Andros. The Sheas laid on elaborate entertainments. There was a dance: 'Some of the girls were fairly bright but the standard of beauty was not what we were led to expect.' One wonders what the false prospectus consisted of. After he was established in Andros, Neville came back on business to Nassau from time to time and was increasingly disenchanted by the charms of local society.

Shea confidently assured the boys that although sisal did not bear a crop until its fourth year, cuttings could be taken in advance of that and used to extend the original planting area exponentially. It was an enticing pyramid scheme, but Austen was not entirely convinced and warned his father that all this should be taken with a pinch of salt.

Austen and Neville explored the islands on a small sailing ship, the *Bonny Jean*. They ran into gales almost immediately and both boys were violently sick. Water poured into their cabin through a leaking porthole; their baggage fell onto them. Neville was soaked not just with rainwater but with thick paint which fell from the deckhead onto his face and hair. On the way back to Nassau the dinghy was capsized and had to be abandoned. Neville was unfazed. He excitedly told his sisters about life on Nassau, eating oranges from trees, watching hummingbirds sucking from brilliantly coloured flowers, seeing octopus and fishing for sharks by moonlight.

Back at Nassau and the unappealing charms of what Austen describes as its not-very-interesting white society, they faced again Sir Ambrose's uncritical appraisal of the future of sisal production. Its first crop would recoup all the initial capital expenditure: future crops would be clear profit after the (unquantified) expenses. The brothers asked Shea why, if the profits were so enormous, he was prepared to subsidise exports. The problem was the 'sluggishness' of the inhabitants. Neville agreed with Austen that Shea was unrealistic. There wasn't a history of hemp production in the Bahamas, so the promised market price of £25 per ton was no more than a guess. They did their own sums. They concluded that capital expenditure of £12,000 would be required over the first three years. Their own calculations, based in part on a manual about sisal production in Mexico, were about as amateurish as Shea's. Inevitably, it was the older Austen who took the main part in assessing the venture. His evaluation was based on unproved assumptions, not least regarding the cost of getting the cut leaf out of the bush, but somehow or other he arrived at the view that a net profit in excess of 50 per cent on the capital employed was attainable. That projection of £6,000 *per annum* after three years proved wildly over-optimistic.

But the responsibility for Andros lay with the experienced capitalist to whom he reported: Austen had his reservations, and advised his father that it would be unfair to expect Neville to live out in the islands for five years. (In the event he was there for six.) He conceded that he would have to be there for six months or a year but thought that the most that would be required after that would be an annual visit by one or other of them. Neville had his own reservations – not about the demands on his constitution, but about the problems of the soil quality. He had done enough research to know that rich soil would produce a low fibre percentage, whereas poor soil would discourage adequate growth.

Joseph Chamberlain received with insouciance the reports from his sons on issues on which they were not competent to judge. His own brothers, seasoned men of business, warned him that the project was a crazy gamble. They told him that even an experienced man could not do what Neville was being asked to do and that it was unfair to put him into the physical and moral perils that he would face. Joe simply said that he had complete confidence in his son.

Neville was no doubt pleased enough to escape from the parties and receptions that the Sheas laid on for him. He was also fed up listening to Sir Ambrose talking nonsense about the Irish Question and repeating his stories. Neville, who was far from deficient in his sense of humour, could see the funny side of things and had to pinch himself to avoid giggling at the absurd breakfast conversation. He and Austen escaped from it as soon as they could. 'Not for long though! We hear a snort outside and in comes that old man of the sea, the Governor, under pretext of showing us a paper, and there he sits and discusses Mr Parnell till we get up and say we are going for a walk ... Shan't I be glad to go off to Andros!'

The decision to go ahead with the Andros venture had now been made. On 1 April 1891 *The Times* reported that Joseph Chamberlain had bought the island of Mayaguana, planning to grow sisal at the cost of £12 a ton and then selling it at £34 per ton. On the following day the paper admitted that the story had been an April Fool's trick. It wasn't a funny one (though it's interesting that newspapers were already trying to trick their readers in 1891) and the joke was really on the paper, because just a month later at the age of just twenty-two, Neville was left, more or less alone, on the island of Andros to establish a sisal plantation: the 1 April 'joke' had been accurate about everything except the name of the island.

Joe Chamberlain told his brothers that Neville was off to Andros because of his own appraisal of the enterprise. That wasn't the case. Neville went off simply because he was a dutiful son. The Andros experiment was to be a disastrous one. It was to hurt Neville and haunt him for many years, and it was a minor tragedy that of the three Chamberlains who decided on the venture he was the one with the least input.

Andros may have looked a propitious site for a sisal plantation but the research that had been carried out on the prospect had been remarkably scanty and superficial. The island is still known as 'the sleeping giant' and it certainly slumbered in 1891. Seventy-seven miles by boat from Nassau, the Bahamas capital, Andros is flat and heavily forested, about a hundred miles by forty-five. The coast is heavily indented. In Chamberlain's time that coastline was occupied largely by mangrove swamps. Inland was bush, dense scrub that made movement across the island very difficult. Although the Bahamas climate favoured growth, the possibility of agriculture or commercial forestry was hugely inhibited by extensive wetlands which even today make the extraction of timber expensive or even impossible. Some of these wetlands were associated by a very large number of 'blue holes', essentially entrances to underground cave systems. Today these are a major tourist draw, but then they were yet another hindrance to the development of a sisal economy.

The climate which encouraged the luxuriant plant growth was more benevolent to vegetables than to humans. Although the temperature range was mostly moderate – from a night-time low of 5° Celsius in the winter season to a daytime summer maximum of around 30° (with a few significant spikes well above that) – relative humidity was often 100 per cent. A hurricane arrived on average every two and a half years.

The island was inhabited by a population of about 2,000 people who lived mostly on a narrow strip on the east coast, fishing and harvesting sponges. A significant part of the population was descended from freed slaves liberated by British merchantmen and settled on the island. In 1807, Britain had abolished the slave trade (although not slavery). Thereafter the Royal Navy intercepted trading ships and thousands of liberated slaves were resettled in the Bahamas from US ships that had been intercepted or that were forced into the islands owing to bad weather. Even before slavery itself was abolished in the Bahamas in 1834, Britain insisted that any slave brought to the islands from outside the British West Indies was manumitted.

The Bahamas as a whole are associated with the Caribbean, even though they are geographically separated from the Caribbean islands by the Windward Passage, but as a result of the settlement of the liberated slaves, Andros was more akin to West Africa than to the West Indies.

Neville set off for Andros with Darwin's *On the Origin of Species* and *A Naturalist's Voyage Round the World*, books on botany, surveying and bookkeeping, Bagehot's *The English Constitution*, and Eliot's *Middlemarch* and *Adam Bede*. More reading material followed: the Bible, an atlas, a French dictionary, a set of Shakespeare, a work on orchids (an important matter for Joe and Neville) and *Robinson Crusoe*: he had a sense of the absurd.

Writing elsewhere in another connection I once recalled Chamberlain's referring to Jorkins, the absent and uncaring partner of nice Mr Spenlow in *David Copperfield*, who's blamed for any unpleasant decisions that have to be made. I said that this was a surprising reference for a pretty unliterary type. How wrong and careless I was – as indeed I would have been at that time in almost any judgement I made about Chamberlain. He was a prodigiously literary type. At our cost, we now live in an age when few politicians, let alone Prime Ministers, find solace, inspiration and perhaps a sense of balance in the world of books. That wasn't always the case. Asquith, for instance, Churchill, Macmillan were all better people for the inner resources they found in literature. Chamberlain was surpassed by no other twentieth-century Prime Minister in his reading, both in its volume and in its range. That reading

continued throughout his life – indeed *Middlemarch*, which he took
with him to Andros was beside his bed when he died fifty-nine years
later. At the strangely named house he built for himself on Andros,
Mastic Point, he read and re-read the book.

He not only read widely; he read critically. On re-reading *Middlemarch*
he concluded that it wasn't as good a novel as he'd thought, not so good
for instance as *John Halifax*. It would be tedious to list all that he read in
these tropical surroundings. His books included Prescott's *Ferdinand and
Isabella*, Wallace's *Tropical Nature*, Carlyle's *Cromwell*, John Richard
Green's *A Short History of the English People*, books on political biography and mental evolution. He read not only in English but maintained
a steady progress in German. Far from being a tongue-tied Little-
Englander when he flew to meet Hitler, he had read far more German
literature than the Führer had ever done.

Chamberlain was from a strongly Unitarian background, and I'll
touch later on just how important this influence was on his character,
but this non-conformist background meant not that life was grim and
cheerless, as the caricature tends to suggest, but on the contrary that
life was important and enjoyable and therefore should not be wasted.
Books were not just for filling the time and entertaining, but were
there as a resource to enable life to be lived more fully. So Chamberlain
thought about what he read and treasured and remembered the poetry
which meant so much to him. His education had not been on the
classical side, so his hinterland was not of Greece and Rome, as was
the case for Asquith and Macmillan. Like Churchill, who also read
self-consciously for improvement, Chamberlain's literary education
was based on the glories of English literature. But where Churchill, as
a subaltern in India, read Gibbon and Macaulay and the *Annual Review*
to fit himself for a life in politics, Chamberlain's reading was wider,
perhaps more critical and certainly more broadly educational. He
never had the creative command of English which Churchill so
signally enjoyed, but the resources and pleasure to be derived from
English literature were always with him.

The tropical climate and the lack of agricultural disturbance meant
that the island had an outstanding range of plants and animals. Joe
Chamberlain's hobby ('You must find a hobby,' he told Austen. 'You
must have something else to think about or you won't sleep, and then

you will get ill') was the cultivation of orchids, and he could only have been impressed by the spectacular profusion of orchids on Andros. No less than fifty species have been counted. Neville was to have many hobbies. To Joe's delight, one of them was a shared interest in the orchid family. He was already a keen ornithologist and there was a vast range of species for him to examine on the island. The rare Kirtland's Warbler had been discovered there just a few years earlier.

He visited Cuba. His diary records the trip in lyrical terms: royal palms with 'smooth white stems looking like pillars, blue and scarlet convolvuli, deep indigo mountains, light-green cane fields'. In Cuba he placed orders and came back to blow up hills, lay tracks and order rails. All of this was a delight for the man who had inspired the whole exercise: Sir Ambrose Shea. He came out in person to inspect, to be greeted by native music and to make a speech. He was impressed, as was the rector of Andros: 'You ought to see the place, new houses springing up by the dozens everywhere, fine roads in all directions . . . railways being laid down seven miles into the forest, and a long jetty stretching out into the deep water.'[2]

But despite Sir Ambrose Shea's delight, things were not going any better than they deserved to on the basis of an ill-sketched business plan. One of the great attractions of the islands, it had been thought, was that the islanders were said to embrace enthusiastically a tradition of piecework; but right from the start this tradition proved to be an imagined one. In Neville's very first week there was a strike against piecework payment. Only one man came to work; all the others having struck for day labour. Having encountered what his official biographer described as 'this feckless, childlike native labour', he had endless difficulties.[3] From then on, he decided to import labour, and he told his father he was tightening the reins of discipline.

Everything was entrusted, as Neville described himself later, 'solely to a boy just out of his teens with no experience of the world whatever'. But he faced his responsibilities both cheerfully and ably. In the course of the preliminary exploration when he battled with the mosquitoes, in three days and two nights he and his companions had covered no more than twenty miles. 'When we emerged we were in a sorry plight. Our feet were black and blue, our shins were scarred and bruised from knee to ankle, our hands were covered in scratches and mosquito bites, our boots were in shreds, and our clothes were as

black as an engine driver's.' Not quite the man with the umbrella.
Neville returned to Nassau and engaged another planter's manager,
Michael Knowles, as his own manager. He also tightened his contract
with Shea. The Chamberlains would have an option on 20,000 acres,
the first 10,000 at five shillings an acre and the second 10,000 at
sixteen shillings and eight pence an acre.

He and Knowles then embarked on a schooner to take them to
Andros. The whole crew was asleep and the master mariner was dead
drunk, so Knowles himself had to take charge. As he did so, Chamberlain
saw they were being followed in the water by a dog which he had
adopted in Nassau. It was duly taken aboard.

Once Neville and Knowles were established on Andros, they set
themselves to the task of clearing the ground. It was hard work in
very hot conditions. Neville rose at 5 a.m., often working with an axe
alongside his men. They worked for six days a week. Self-pity or
complaint was foreign to the Chamberlain code, but although his
upper lip was always stiff, he enjoyed impressing his sisters with
accounts of the toughness of his life. A long letter was sent home
every Sunday which gives a reasonably full picture of his life for his
first unbroken stretch of fourteen months on Andros. He didn't allow
himself to complain, but occasionally he is honest enough to describe
reality: 'Suffering much from having sat on a poisonwood-tree ...
black blisters on my leg ... skin came off leaving it quite raw.'

His heaviest burden, because he was a sociable man, was the lack of
personal contact. At one stage he wrote, 'I see myself condemned to a
life of total solitude, mentally if not physically.' He wrote to an
acquaintance some fifty miles away, 'I do indeed wish you were nearer:
it is mental starvation here.' Again, 'evenings are weary and long ...
hard to read from 8 to 12'. But he enjoyed the reading, annotating bits
of Bagehot for example in the evenings and longer chunks on Sundays
– 'wish it contained less argument and more description'. He loved
dogs, and they loved him. His first canine companion was the dog
which had swum out in the dark to be with him, a Cuban blood-
hound called Don Juan. When another dog died, poisoned as Neville
believed, he was 'much afflicted at his painful death for he was a very
faithful dog and much attached to me'.

There were, however, compensations. His great interest in flowers
meant that at an early point he started to create a garden and he wrote

to his sisters for seeds not just for vegetables but for flowers too. To his delight he discovered a rare orchid – 'I think *Epidendrum nemorale*, but I have never seen ... [the] species in flower, sepals clear brownish yellow, petals similar but speckled with purple at the end, lip, three-lobed lateral lobes pale purple enclosing the column, the central lobe whitish with five purple streaks. Flowers two feet across, very fragrant, borne on a spike. Does this answer the description?' He enjoyed swimming, despite the risk of sharks. A rubber bath arrived so that he could occasionally wash and relieve the irritation of the mosquitoes and the sandflies.

Initially an important part of his efforts related to the logistics of setting up his base. To begin with he and Knowles had shared a very basic three-roomed wooden house, but he set himself to build more substantial houses both for Knowles and himself, and to establish a basic store for the workforce. The store stocked everything: flour, sugar, pork, biscuits, boots, corsets, trimmed hats and pink satin boots. His sense of fun was self-deprecating, and he reported to his sisters his reincarnation as a small shop keeper: 'Pork? Yes, sir. Anything else today? Thank you. *Good* day.' By the end of 1890 his house was progressing – though at a cost. He told his half sister, Beatrice, 'I have worn out ten pairs of boots ... a terrible lot of fever about ... I am tired out.' Six months later Mastic Point was pretty well complete. It was a large house with a cream-coloured exterior and a red roof, and a 'piazza' running round it.\* He delighted in its view of the sea and its airy interior.

In the fields he worked in cotton trousers tied with string, but at home everything was done as it would have been in Birmingham. He had a cook and a houseboy, and a garden full of flowers grown from Highbury seeds. The rooms were decorated with photographs and flowers. A flag flew from the flagpole and the sponge ships that sailed past dipped their ensigns to it. He had his own little schooner, *Pride of Andros*, on which he sailed himself through the dangerous shoal waters.

He had adapted well and employed his energies efficiently. He had suppressed liquor shops, opened a school and even organised a savings

---

\* In those days, in the United States, 'piazza' was used to describe what we would call a verandah.

bank – very Birmingham, very Chamberlain. He was a de facto magistrate and even a doctor: 'I have three patients now ... the girl with the mutilated fingers, a man with an abscess and another who slashed his finger to the bone.' He was well liked by the little community over which he presided, and on his birthday unmusical bands serenaded him from his piazza. On Christmas Day 1891 the residents and workers on the estate wrote to him in fulsome terms: 'It is with pleasure that we welcome you on our shores and we do feel already that your presence here has caused as it were a new light to shine among us. Accept our hearty thanks for the indefatigable exertions you have made here.'[4]

He directed operations to clear as much land as possible – ideally up to 10,000 acres. Roads and wharves had to be made and labour engaged. By the end of 1893 the Andros Fibre Company was a substantial presence in Andros, supported by agents on other islands. Fifteen hundred acres had been cleared in the first year, 4,350 acres planted in December 1893 and over 6,000 by April 1895. At their maximum there were 800 labourers. By 1895, nearly £13,000 (about £2 million today) had been invested.

In October 1893, Joe himself paid a fleeting regal visit which Neville described to Beatrice: 'An immense crowd yelled and waved their hats and let off guns ... [Y]ou will imagine that Father has not been here without having some ideas. His general vision is to push the tramways and machinery at once ... and for this I am going to Cuba.'

While he never complained, the physical burden he shouldered was immense. To replace the work-shy men of Andros, with their aversion to piecework, Neville set to building a house for immigrant labourers from Nassau. When Michael Knowles went there to collect the men, he was asked how the young Englishman was coping. They could not imagine that he was not about to go home in the face of the heat and the mosquitoes and the walking. Knowles replied that 'Chamberlain could beat him hollow any day at walking or heat or mosquitoes.'[5]

But even at a distance, and despite Neville's stoicism, back in Birmingham Joe was concerned for his younger son's health. Endearingly, he repeatedly wrote to him full of solicitude: 'I feel that this experience, whatever its ultimate result on our fortunes, will have had a beneficial and formative effect on your character ... I am inclined to envy you the opportunity you are having to show your manhood. Remember, however, now and always that I value your health more than anything and that you must not run any unnecessary risks either on land on sea.'[6] Austen, continuing Joe's line, told him to take care. A couple of weeks later his father wrote again, expressing his confidence in his son's judgement, but also, again, his concern: 'Do not overdo yourself . . . As to food – you must have good plain food and regular meals . . . Please understand that I regard this as of most serious importance and shall be worrying unless I hear of a more satisfactory state of things . . . Your superintendence and brain work are the valuable things – therefore spare your strength as much as possible.'[7] Maybe Joe had been listening to his wife: Neville was much more revealing to his stepmother than he was to his father. He wrote to her at the end of November 1891, 'I have been through enough roughing to last a lifetime and I am heartily sick of it and long for civilization and comfort.'[8]

Out in the bush, Neville was inclined to be amused by these fatherly concerns. When Joe suggested that a houseboy should take a healthy lunch out to him in the fields every day, he pointed out to his sister how impractical it would be to carry this wholesome fare miles into the jungle. 'Hire a boy,' Joe had written, 'and let him carry out a bowl of something (such as rice and molasses or canned meat) to the field where you are. It is really *very* bad for you to go without food for so long even when you seem not to want it.'[9] The advice reduced Neville to such helpless laughter that his surveyor, Forsyth, thought he would have a fit.

He rather liked the macho image and the risks of life on the frontiers of civilisation. Although in later life he suffered from various ailments – gout, improbably for a moderate man, affected him very badly – he was physically (and indeed morally) strong, and proud of it. Thanks to a well-thumbed copy of *The Culture of the Abdomen*, he kept in good shape throughout his life.*

---

* *The Culture of the Abdomen: The Cure of Obesity and Constipation* was a best-seller in its time. The author, F. A. Hornibrook, was such a successful product of the Sandow system of physical training that he was known as 'Brawnibrooks', and his book went through eighteen editions. He was particularly concerned about constipation, which he held was due to 'the white man's burden': an overloaded colon. He is quite carried away by the plight of 'the unfortunate sufferer' and 'the stagnant morass which is fermenting in his belly. His digestion is a mockery, gurgling and groaning in helpless disability, his breath reminiscent of a Limburger cheese, and his outlook in life a pessimistic wail.'

He made hair-raising journeys by boat, frequently running aground; he killed a tarantula in front of Knowles; he walked prodigious distances in the toughest of conditions and accepted uncomplainingly privations that would have incommoded a soldier on the North-West Frontier. But what he found more difficult to deal with was the continuing lack of congenial company. His nearest neighbour was a red-bearded Scot, kindly but eccentric, who only just scratched a subsistence living. He was only three miles away, but even if Neville had sought his company, the three miles involved half a day pushing a punt through shallow water with a pole. Knowles was not easy company. His wife seemed to have been more congenial, but her health was far from good. She was well bred, but not too well bred to mend Neville's socks, which he described as a labour of Hercules (socks did not cope well with the long hard walks). He also appreciated her as a buffer between him and his cook, Mrs Pinder, 'as black as your hat and as ugly as sin who regards me with a passionate admiration not unmixed with tenderer feelings. The other day she told Mrs Knowles that she was going to kiss me and I have carefully avoided her ever since for fear she should carry out this amiable intention.'[10]

When Knowles was away and Mrs Knowles was unwell, the young Neville nursed her. Eventually, after a premature birth, she died. Her death was a huge blow to Neville, who had become devoted to her. Her death prompted him to write to his sister saying that he saw himself condemned for an indefinite period to a life of total solitude: 'I miss Mrs Knowles very much indeed; she was a most unselfish and warm-hearted woman and it is very sad to think that she is gone. Constantly I think of something to tell her that will amuse her and then remember . . .'[11] These moving words reveal how much, even at a platonic level, this reserved and emotionally repressed young man craved for affection.

In view of the later idea that Chamberlain was a desiccated and robotic leader, it's salutary to record, alongside his painful reaction to Mrs Knowles' death, how sensitive and vulnerable he was when his mother's twin sister, Aunt Louie, died at the beginning of 1892. Neville's mother, Florence, Joe's second wife, had died in stillborn childbirth when Neville was only six – a double tragedy for Joe, whose first wife had died in the same circumstances just a few years earlier – and Florence's twin sister, Louie, had come close to taking her place. Neville was devoted to her and she regarded him almost as her own son. When she died, his sisters took infinite care to break the news to him, at the far end of the world, as delicately as they could. The bonds between these siblings were of the utmost sensitivity and the care which they took to respect each other's feelings is revealing of the sensibility that pervaded the family, however disciplined they might appear in public. Ida was always closest to Neville and it was she who had to be first to break the news. For her part, Beatrice stressed how aware they were that their brother had to receive the news alone and so far away. Neville replied that he could hardly bear to think of coming home to Aunt Louie's absence.

The death of Mrs Knowles hit her husband even harder than it hit Neville. Michael Knowles had already been drinking heavily, and Neville had been worried about the consequences if anything happened to Mrs Knowles. Now he persuaded Knowles to go on holiday and not to return to Andros until he felt strong again. This was a generous and selfless action, because he knew how difficult it would be to manage on his own. In Nassau, Ambrose Shea had heard that Neville was overdoing things and sent an assistant to help.

In London, as in Nassau, it was increasingly obvious that Neville was being asked to do too much. The family was concerned for Neville. 'Cast iron,' said Beatrice, 'I am sure would not stand it.' Joseph Chamberlain echoed her views: 'Remember, my dear boy, that my first interest is in you and Andros is only second. Do not risk your health whatever happens; I would sooner give up the whole concern.'[12] Shea, still concerned for Neville, wrote from Nassau to tell him not to overdo things. All the same, his gubernatorial responsibilities required him to point out the huge fortunes which the Andros Fibre Company would shortly be making. Back in Birmingham, Joe wryly wondered where the vast profits were going to come from when sisal was at £13 on the London Market as opposed to the £25 which had originally been budgeted for. Despite his caring injunctions, he never told Neville to close down the enterprise. It was Neville who bit the bullet and stopped the manufacturing process, the separation of the fibre from the leaf.

# Chapter 2

# The Cost of a Dream

At the start, the Chamberlains had been assured that sisal could be extracted from the plants in their fourth year – perhaps even in their third. In the meantime, cuttings from the trees, real magic money trees, would be propagated, to create an ever-enlarging perpetual supply of new stock. But by now it was becoming clear that the fibre would not be available for all of seven years and that the plants would produce nothing more thereafter. Neville could see that this critically affected the viability of the scheme and recommended to his father that they should stop cutting at 3,000 acres. Joe Chamberlain, who made his state visit at this point, remained perversely optimistic although he was far from well during his stay; but by the time he had returned home to Highbury he had to recognise that whatever he thought of Andros, the rest of his financial empire was in a poor state. His investments were uniformly decreasing in value and although he wanted to plough in more capital to Andros, he could not do so from his own resources. The decision was to transform the business into a limited liability company. A prospectus said that the enterprise was likely to be highly profitable and on that debatable premise a further £20,000 was obtained.*

Neville was the most dutiful of sons and he never criticised his father. He was, however, in an increasingly difficult situation. He, on the spot, had serious reservations about the viability of the scheme which Joe seemed determined to brush aside. Joe's response was to reiterate in ringing tones how much confidence he reposed in his son. It left Neville

---

* At the cost of some controversy and a libel action to bother Joe around the time of the general election of 1900.

in a false position. He was aware that his father's and his half-brother's political careers and their positions in society depended principally on his efforts, and he was being represented as having a confidence in the outcome of these efforts which did not exist.

A catalogue of the technical stages in the further downhill spiral at Mastic Point would make gloomy reading. What is most poignant is how bitterly Neville felt his sense of failure – not for himself, but for his family. The following letter to Beatrice in January 1898 touches on the impact of failure for him; but the most telling part of the letter is in the final sentence of the quotation:

> What is to become of me in the future if this thing fails I don't know. The mere sense of failure after so much hard work and sacrifice in other ways is enough to crush a man by destroying self-confidence.
>
> It will probably occur to you that I am suffering from overwork, overstrain or loneliness. Don't believe it: I wish that *were* all, but these considerations have been vaguely floating about in my mind for a long time though it is only lately that I have faced them fully. It is on this account that I am so dead against further assistance. I know that it is not necessary, I see that we can't afford the salary and I shrink from bringing in another fellow to this business which has such an unfavourable outlook.
>
> It is not Mrs Knowles' death or my own loneliness, though I have felt both, that weigh me down, it is the haunting dread of the future. Sometimes when I think of what failure means for Father and Mary I can hardly hold up my head.[1]

He told his brother that he couldn't acquit himself of responsibility for failure because he would have claimed chief credit if the enterprise had worked out, and he acknowledged that he had allowed himself to be deluded into thinking that the poor land could truly support sisal. In reality it had always been Joe, and to an extent Austen, who had been taken in by Shea's powerful salesmanship.

In March 1896, approaching his twenty-seventh birthday, he cleared off the last of the crop and told Joe that he could not go on throwing the family's good money after bad. At last, and only after a delay, Joe seemed prepared to face reality. For a hard-headed realist, he was extraordinarily slow to do so. The purchase of Andros had cost him about £50,000 – very roughly £1 million in today's money. The loss was so serious that he contemplated giving up public life altogether. There must have been an element of pride and deliberate blindness. The investment had been made against the advice of his very astute brothers, experienced men of business. Then when the enterprise lost money he had put more into it; finally he had sold debentures in the limited company.

Now he wrote to Neville, saying that his letters indicated the possibility of an outcome worse than he had feared: he seems to have clung to the hope, even at this stage, that somehow or other the magic money trees were going to fruit. Abandoning the undertaking 'would indeed be a catastrophe although it is one which must be faced courageously, if there is no alternative ... Whatever others might do, we cannot pass over to others at any price a speculation which we know is doomed to failure.' Even less – far, far less, in fact – than Neville, was Joe a man to show his emotions in public. While he didn't blame Neville, and treated the decision as a collective one, he didn't go much out of his way to lighten his son's burden: 'I can easily understand how disappointing and depressing the prospect is to you, but if the worst comes to the worst we will all make the best of it and remember our motto, *Je tiens ferme* ['I stand firm'].'[2]

Neville had always felt a responsibility for his workers – a significant trait in the Chamberlain family. When he left Mastic Point for the last time, the estate workers were in tears. Seventy of them saw him off. The Roman Catholic priest, who had admired all Neville had achieved, made a long voyage to say goodbye.

Thus Neville Chamberlain left Andros, 'seven thousand acres of worthless land', which he sold in 1921 for £200. He invested most of it in the purchase of a French cabinet. What else did he gain from these five years, punctuated by the occasional return home? He had already been a committed countryman. That part of his character, which was to prove a hinterland of enormous value to him in the difficult political days that lay ahead, was powerfully reinforced by closeness to the land in Andros. His interest in ornithology, taxidermy and above all horticulture had developed. He had pursued a constructive curriculum of reading which supplied him with the benefits of the liberal education which his father's preferences had denied to him. That was a benefit that was to last with him throughout his life, and in the world of literature he found another reserve to fall back on when philosophical support was needed. At a very early age he had enjoyed far greater responsibilities and had exercised much more initiative than he could conceivably have done in any other situation. The demands on him were far greater than he would have faced, say, as an army officer or in the colonial service. He was aware of this at the time; when things were starting to move distinctly in the wrong direction he wrote to Austen: '[E]ven if it turns out a failure I am not sure that I should regret the years I have spent here. The responsibility and independence have certainly called out whatever was in me and shown me that I was worth more than I thought.'[3] He said that at the time, and he later felt it even more strongly. As one historian put it: '[A]s the distance lengthened, he said the same, that Andros had made him. Initiative had become a habit, for with him alone it had rested, and confidence in his own judgement, since there had been no one else to judge.'[4]

That is very true; indeed the distinct self-contained confidence which became too marked a feature of his personality when he was Prime Minister would perhaps never have developed if it had not been for the Andros years – though of course the Andros years built on attitudes which were inherent in the Chamberlain tradition. Beatrice sent her brother off to the island with a quotation that their Aunt Louie had liked to repeat to them: ''Tis not in mortals to command success, / But we'll do more, Sempronius – we'll deserve it.' A very stoic sentiment, very much part of the Chamberlain philosophy. The quotation is from Joseph Addison's *Cato*. The lines from the same work, 'Better to die ten thousand deaths / Than wound my honour', would have appealed equally.

But along with the positive, character-forming benefits of Andros, Neville Chamberlain sailed home with another legacy of his time on the island: a profound and haunting sense of failure. He *had* indeed failed. His role had been to rescue the family finances. Joe and Austen had a destiny in politics. At this stage no one thought that was where Neville's destiny lay: he was to be the man of business who would provide the means for the expansive lifestyle on which the other two depended to project their careers. Instead of rescuing their position, he had made it worse. Of course, he could say, but didn't, that it wasn't his fault, and neither it was. But he had been part of the team that had assessed the venture, even if his were the minor part and he was being asked to do something which he was patently unqualified to do. Another man would have found excuses for himself and shrugged off any sense of failure, but Neville Chamberlain was not that kind of man. He was a shy and timid man at this stage in his life who pushed forward only as a duty. Failure was all the more painful.

And so, while the sharpness of the Andros failure diminished as the years passed, the experience of it never wholly left him. Moreover it would be reinforced in the course of the Great War, when again he accepted an impossible position out of a sense of duty. So, in looking at the kind of man Chamberlain was and the influences which made him that kind of man, Andros must always be kept in mind.

The impact of Andros was internal. For Chamberlain it would have been cheap and degrading to parade his personal experiences for political advantage. Advancement was to be achieved by hard work and application, not by self-advertisement. He was no Theodore Roosevelt. Nor was he a Winston Churchill, of whom Lloyd George said that he would use his grandmother's skin to make a drum to beat. Churchill's *My Early Life*, his account of *Boy's Own Paper* exploits such as escaping from the Boers in South Africa, was certainly written partly for the money – Churchill always needed that – but he also and quite frankly sought fame. He admitted that he wanted medals when he was in the army, and *My Early Life* was part of a consistent campaign of self-promotion. Chamberlain never used the Andros experience and the frontiersman image to promote himself. Scarcely anyone heard of the Andros years.

When Chamberlain appointed Churchill First Lord of the Admiralty in 1939 the two men had known each other for virtually all of their political lives. They had sat together in Parliament. They had even sat in Cabinet together for most of five years. And yet it was only when the Churchills invited the Chamberlains to dine at Admiralty House in October 1939 that Churchill heard properly about the Andros adventure and reflected how differently Hitler might have viewed Chamberlain if he had known about

> his six years' struggle to grow sisal on a barren West Indian islet near Nassau [at the behest of] [h]is father, the great 'Joe' . . . living nearly naked, struggling with labour difficulties and every other kind of obstacle . . . At the end of five years he was convinced that the plan could not succeed. He came home and faced his formidable parent,

who was by no means contented with the result. I gathered that in the family the feeling was that though they loved him dearly they were sorry for the lost £50,000 ...

I was fascinated by the way Mr Chamberlain warmed as he talked, and by the tale itself, which was one of gallant endeavour. I thought to myself, 'What a pity Hitler did not know when he met this sober English politician with his umbrella at Berchtesgaden, Godesberg and Munich, that he was actually talking to a hard-bitten pioneer from the outer marches of the British Empire!'

If Churchill had earlier been aware of this story (which he summarised slightly unfairly in regard to Joe's reaction), it might have affected his view of Chamberlain, just as he imagined it affecting Hitler's. Chamberlain's exploits were exactly the sort of manly endeavours to which Churchill, always an admirer of the man of action, readily warmed. Churchill was never going to be Chamberlain's best friend, but he might have thought twice about saying that Mr Chamberlain viewed everything 'through the wrong end of a municipal drainpipe'.[5]

Neville always believed that his Andros years had made a man of him. It might be truer that they deprived him of youth. But the most poignant aspect of the Andros failure for Neville was that he had let his father down. Joe Chamberlain was by any judgement a massive figure, marmoreal, creating visions beyond the imaginings of workaday politicians. He was admired and feared rather than loved, but Neville *did* love him, as well as admire him. Joe's vision was so elevated that he was in a way above party politics. All the same, Joe Chamberlain influenced politics more than any other man of his generation and there can be no argument that he influenced Neville profoundly. A titanic figure, the stormy petrel of British politics.

*Chapter 3*

# Radical Joe

In his middle age, Chamberlain said that like Hamlet he had been haunted by 'Father's Ghost'. The influence of Joe's politics on Neville was immense and no one can understand the son without understanding the father. The seismic ending of the era of free trade was begun by Joe, but completed by Neville in a poignant and deliberately staged moment of filial piety which would surprise anyone who persists in seeing Neville Chamberlain as a figure without feelings. But Joe's influence on his son's character and politics went far beyond that.*

Joe Chamberlain was never Prime Minister. Nowadays he is not remembered as are his contemporaries who held that office, but his stature and influence in his time was unparalleled. Churchill began his political career as Chamberlain senior ended his, and was fascinated by him. Joe was:

> [I]ncomparably the most live, sparkling, insurgent, compulsive figure in British affairs ... He was the man the masses knew. He it was who had solutions for social problems; who was ready to advance, sword in hand if need be, upon the foes of Britain; and whose accents rang in the ears of all the young peoples of the

---

* His influence persists. He was said in 2016 to be Theresa May's 'new lodestar' (John O'Sullivan, the *Spectator*, 16 July 2016). Joe's great achievement was to split two great political parties from top to bottom, and Theresa May likewise did her best. Her predecessor took the first steps to split the Conservative Party over Europe, but she finished the job. It remains to be seen how deep and enduring her fissure will be, but a split's a split for all that, and she did succeed in following her lodestar. Theresa May's enthusiasm for Joe probably came from her co-chief of staff, Nick Timothy, who admires him to the extent of publishing a pamphlet, *Our Joe*.

Empire and of lots of young people at its heart ... He lighted
beacon-fires which are still burning; he sounded trumpet-calls
whose echoes still call stubborn soldiers to the field. The fiscal
controversies which Chamberlain revived are living issues not only
in British but in World Politics today. The impetus which he gave
to the sense of Empire, in Britain and even more by repercussion
throughout the world, is a deep score on the page of History. Those
who met him in his vigour and hey-day are always conscious of his
keenly-cut impressions; and all our British affairs today are tangled,
biased or inspired by his action.[1]

Some allowance must be made for Churchillian extravagance, but Joe
Chamberlain was indeed still remembered as a towering political
figure when Churchill wrote these words in 1933 in a review of J. L.
Garvin's biography; they were later published in Churchill's biograph-
ical round-up, *Great Contemporaries*. Some of these contemporaries
can't remotely be considered to have been 'great', but Joe Chamberlain
was.[*]

Joe Chamberlain was born on 8 July 1836, the first son of another
Joseph Chamberlain. Joseph senior was a cordwainer, a maker of boots
and shoes, as his ancestors had been since the middle of the previous
century. Joe senior wasn't robust, a delicate eater. The writer Harriet
Martineau, who was related to the Chamberlains, said that he took his
lunch every day at the Dolphin tavern in Milk Street, London (where
the family shoemaking business was to be found), and where 'he paid
extra for his special cut of beef' washed down with several glasses of
port wine for the benefit of his constitution.[†] The Chamberlains were

* The only other contender, Franklin Roosevelt, hadn't yet done enough to qualify.
The choice of some of the other subjects was bizarre. The piece on the 'Ex-Kaiser'
begins with what is a distinct challenge for most people: 'No one should judge the
career of the Emperor William II without asking the question, "What should I have
done in his position?" ' It does, however, contain one good story: ' "Where is your
King now?" he asked one day of an English visitor; "At Windsor, Sir"; "Ah, I thought
he was boating with his grocer [Sir Thomas Lipton]." '
† The Dolphin was managed by Samuel Powell Beeton. His son, also Samuel
Beeton, became a publisher and brought out the first edition of Harriet Beecher
Stowe's *Uncle Tom's Cabin*. Young Sam married Isabella Mayson (whose family lived
in Milk Street), and her cookery book, *Household Management*, was published in 1852.

described in 1829 as 'the highest sort of tradesmen, plain, honest and sincere'.

Neville's half-brother, Austen, researched the family history and concluded a little unfairly that the Chamberlains had been honest and decent, but rather boring.[2] Caroline Harben, Joe's mother, came from a more expansive culture and brought to the more modest existence of the Chamberlains, who lived over their shop in the centre of London until just before young Joe's birth, interests in food and drink, books and amateur theatricals and entertainments for what they called *holydays*.

Even before her arrival, the family had not lived a confined existence. For many years the members of the family had been freemen or liverymen of the Cordwainers Company, and several members had been its Master. In the political world, young Joe's great grandfather had managed the constituency interests of the Duke of Newcastle, the elder Pitt's Whig colleague, and then those of the Duke of Richmond. The family was comfortably off.

The Chamberlains were Unitarians. Many Unitarians, including Joseph Priestley, opposed the war against revolutionary France, but the Chamberlains supported it. Young Joe's grandfather was a captain in the Honourable Artillery Company, and the family made money out of war: soldiers needed boots. As a result, Joe senior was able to take his family from the City to the leafy suburb of Highbury in North London.

To modern minds a Victorian non-conformist upbringing sometimes suggests a cold, narrow and loveless existence. It's doubtful if that is remotely accurate even as a generalisation. It certainly wasn't true for the Chamberlains. It was perhaps from his mother that young Joe acquired his social skills, his wit and his aesthetic interests, but his father was not a severe paterfamilias. He disapproved of corporal punishment and none of his children went to a school which permitted this sanction. He beat young Joe just once, when the boy had borrowed two pence, bought some gunpower and blown up his mother's garden. Having beaten him, Joe senior told him, 'Now, my boy, I have thrashed you not because you have blown up your mother's rockery, but because you have borrowed money which you have no means of repaying. In future when you require money you will come and borrow it from me.' His advice on the conduct of life was simple: 'Tell the truth and pay cash.'

The Unitarian tradition is very important to an understanding of the Chamberlain clan. Unitarians rejected the Trinity and saw God as one person. Indeed they went much further than that, rejecting for instance the theory of original sin and predestination. Membership of any non-conformist body, certainly until the end of the nineteenth century, powerfully affected adherents, but Unitarians occupied a much more extreme position than other dissident branches of the Reformed Church. Indeed, their entitlement to be regarded as Christians could be challenged, since they held that Jesus was not God. Until 1813 it was a criminal offence to deny the doctrine of the Trinity.

The character of Unitarianism in the period in which young Joe was growing up is demonstrated by the names of some of the prominent Unitarians of the time, from Sir Isaac Newton to Elizabeth Gaskell, through Mary Wollstonecraft, Joseph Priestley, the Luptons of Leeds, Florence Nightingale, Samuel Taylor Coleridge, Josiah Wedgewood and the Nettlefold family, whom we shall meet again shortly.

There were different theological positions within Unitarianism, but at a cultural level there were constants. There was a tradition of anti-clericalism, and of suspicion about the establishment and the upper classes, a feeling of being apart from society, almost indeed of being persecuted. Some of these persisting views were shared by many of the non-conformist churches, but in the case of Unitarians they were particularly strong in view of the criminal designation that attached to them until the passing of the Unitarian Relief Act in 1813.

In addition to these particular influences, the Unitarians were fully invested with the usual range of dissenting virtues (and surely they must be accounted virtues?): a consciousness that they had been given life for a purpose and it was their privilege to live it to the full. This meant living *good* lives, *useful* lives, and not in a vacuum: there was a duty to provide practical benefit not only to their own community, but also to the wider world. They were accountable for their lives and for what they did with them and had constantly to look at the state of their moral balance sheet. Unitarians did not divorce themselves from the realities of life. They informed themselves. They read. One of Neville's cousins said, '[F]rom early days [they] threw themselves into politics and social work. We always understood as children that as our lives have fallen in pleasant places it behoved us all the more to do what we could to improve the lot of those less happily placed.'[3]

Unitarians tended, possibly more than members of other non-conformist sects, to concentrate their social life – and indeed their marriages – within their own community. There was much intermarriage and cousinage within what they called the 'click' rather than the 'clique'.* In fact, they were so interrelated that Neville and his relative Cecily were first, second and third cousins.

The fact that the Chamberlains and their Unitarian friends and relatives chose to cut themselves off from the broader stream of social and political life tended of course to strengthen and intensify the habits of thought of their sub-culture and to sustain their religious beliefs. Historically non-conformists like the Unitarians had been left outside the mainstream of society. They, reciprocally, had little time for the established Church, the aristocracy or the Crown. In pursuance of the promotion of the popular as opposed to the privileged interest, Joe Chamberlain welcomed the expansion in the electorate in the 1867 Reform Act and saw it as a way of harnessing the energy of the people to advance social reform, especially in education and advanced levels of literacy.

When young Joe left the parental home, at just eighteen, he took with him, then, a strong Unitarian conviction. He grew older, richer and more important, but none of that deterred him from continuing to teach in the Sunday School. He lost his faith with the death of his second wife, but remained, as he told his son Neville, 'a very reverend agnostic'. Neville was not a Unitarian at a religious level to the extent that his father and ancestors had been, but it is important to remember how informed he was by the cultural influence of Unitarianism – and not just the cultural influence: even as an adult he, too, taught in the Sunday School.

One of the Nettlefold family, mentioned above, was Joseph Sutton Nettlefold, the father-in-law of Joe senior. The Nettlefolds were not cordwainers; they made screws. Indeed, they held the patent for a

---

* Caroline Squire, Joe Chamberlain's great-granddaughter, reports (Conservative Home website, 7 August 2016) that the family still use the expression, but in its French form, toasting themselves when they meet as 'the clique'. It's important to get these things right: the significance is always in the *nuances*, another French word.

machine which could turn out screws more efficiently than any other system. In 1854 Nettlefold had spotted an opportunity when the licence for the patent came on the market. Joe Chamberlain senior decided to get involved in this enterprise. What was novel about the woodscrew which he would be able to manufacture was that it came with a pointed end, so that it acted as its own gimlet. Like many great inventions, it seems, in hindsight too obvious to need to be invented. The investment required was £30,000. The Chamberlains put in £10,000. The factory was to be in Birmingham, at Smethwick, and not in London.

Who was to represent the Chamberlain interest on the spot? Joe senior had no doubt about the ability of his eighteen-year-old son, who had never left home before: 'Why, we'll send Joe.' Similar to Andros, the business was owned by the fathers but managed by the sons; in this case John Nettlefold and Joe Chamberlain senior owned, and Edward and Joe junior managed.

It could have been an experiment which led nowhere. Instead 'Nettlefold and Chamberlain' was the best investment the Chamberlains ever made. It put them at the heart of a huge and immensely prosperous commercial enterprise. It moved them from mere respectability to respectability plus wealth and the opportunities that wealth could bring. What is equally surprising, however, and what this book seeks to bring out, is that the change in their fortunes did not change their outlook. The Chamberlains severed their connection with the business when they had amassed enough money for their purposes: the pointless accumulation of wealth was not part of their philosophy. After their time the company went through various incarnations. In 2017 its gross revenue was £9.671 million and it employed 58,000 people.*

So, still a minor according to the law of the time, Joe Chamberlain was implanted in the Midlands. The fact that his adult life began there, rather than in London, is of the utmost importance. Religious life in

---

* One of the incarnations through which GKN, formerly Guest, Keen and Nettlefolds, went through was 'Guest, Keen, Baldwins', the Baldwins being the family of Stanley Baldwin, Neville's predecessor as Prime Minister. The two formed an important team within the Conservative Party between the wars, a team not without elements of rivalry.

Birmingham strengthened in the course of the nineteenth century and its most influential strand was of course non-conformism. There he was surrounded by dissenting families, Quakers and Unitarians, enterprising manufacturers many of them, like Cadburys, Lloyds, Albrights, Nettlefolds, of course, and the Kenricks, from whom Joe's mother came. It was an important time for the provinces. The industrial revolution had established centres of capital and industry in the Midlands and the north that were entitled to regard themselves not as mere provinces but almost as independent city-states like those of Renaissance Italy. In Manchester, Glasgow, Huddersfield or Birmingham people could take pride in their individualism, their prosperity, their lack of dependence on London. They were for the most part Liberals who looked down on the exclusiveness of the metropolis. The justification for their satisfaction in themselves lay to a large extent in their prosperity. Glasgow could call itself the Second City of the Empire and produced more than half of Britain's tonnage of shipping and a quarter of all locomotives in the world. Birmingham contested the title of 'Second City' and in time became the largest centre of manufacturing in Europe. The growth in its population in the nineteenth century, from 73,670 in 1801 to 400,774 in 1881, together with the cross-fertilisation and reciprocal stimulation of industrial and technological development, was dizzying. It isn't surprising that the inhabitants of the great Victorian provincial cities felt, like California today, that they could look the world in the face. And each of these great conurbations had its own characteristics. Manchester was the home of free trade. Birmingham was the cradle of political reform. Perhaps because of that, there remained a sense of classlessness in the city and relations between employer and employee were good.

In this world, Joe and his family were able to turn themselves into the 'Screw Kings', as he called them. He consciously educated himself in the industry, starting on the accounting side and moving to marketing, while Edward Nettlefold dealt with production. Joe's approach was paternalistic. He took a shrewd interest in his employees and found that shortening the day resulted, unexpectedly, in increased productivity. Accordingly he introduced a nine-hour day. He was proud of his good relations with the unions and that no time was lost through industrial disputes. He recognised that the economy of the region depended on its different strands. He became a director of the Midland Railway and worked on turning Lloyds Bank into a public company. Nettlefold and Chamberlain became such an effective force that competitors in the United States, despite tariff protection and the fact that they too had access to the woodscrew patent, paid him significant annual subventions to stay out of their market.

Although Joe Chamberlain was an exotic implant in Birmingham, he really did put his roots down. He saw himself, and continued to do so to the end of his life, as a Birmingham man. He put on no airs – an essential part of the Chamberlain persona. He walked to and from work, meeting the people of Birmingham, seeing both the leafy suburbs and the narrow lanes and open sewers. Birmingham was at heart, as it still is, a compact city, and many of the substantial villas in which the industrialists lived were no more than a mile and a half from the city centre. Chamberlain was proud that he knew his city and its people. Many years later, as he travelled the world, people would come to him and introduce themselves as Birmingham men. Some of them he had employed or taught or known in other ways; others simply felt themselves part of the freemasonry of the city. Chamberlain was proud to be greeted in this way and that 'none of those who approached him had ever appealed to him to do him a favour'.[4] His residence of choice was always in Birmingham, rather than the London house he acquired for parliamentary purposes in Princes Gardens, Knightsbridge.

His extensive property in Birmingham, known as Southbourne, was replaced three years after he went to Westminster by an even grander property on the south of the city and overlooking rural countryside. He named this new home Highbury, after the part of London in which he had been brought up. The wealth that he had accumulated in business sustained Highbury, with its eighteen acres and outstanding gardens where he entertained constituents at enormous garden parties. He built extensive greenhouses in which to house the orchids he so loved, as Neville too would do, building on the flowers he had identified in Andros.

Joe Chamberlain was – self-evidently – ambitious. His physical presence, his monocle, an orchid (or two) in his buttonhole, everything spoke of assurance and superiority. But it would be a mistake to think that his ambition was simply for personal advancement.

From the point of view of personal political advancement both his break with Gladstone over Home Rule and with the Conservative Party over Tariffs, which we shall come to later, were near fatal. If he had, in either case, stayed aboard he would have been a contender for party leadership. He sacrificed that for the sake of principle. In the case of tariff reform, his arguments were not unconfused but he *believed* in them and, for the sake of that belief, effectively sacrificed his career.

Joe may have looked like a quintessential establishment figure, but it is therefore important to remember that he was a radical. When the Prince of Wales, the future Edward VII, visited Birmingham, Chamberlain was doubtful whether he, as a republican, could share a carriage with the heir apparent.* Churchill described him as 'Chamberlain the Radical Mayor – far worse than any naughty socialist of today – who questioned whether he could condescend to drive as Mayor in the carriage which received the Prince of Wales ... on his visit to Birmingham'.[5]

In a series of speeches, his 'Unauthorised Programme' of 1885, he set himself out, as Churchill put it, as 'The Champion of the Radical or, as we should now call them, the Socialist Masses. No one ever in our modern history made so able an appeal to the ill-used, left-out millions.'[6] Neville too in garb and appearance may have looked conventional, but the animating passions, the desire for an improved society, were the same.

Joe's business success was a means to an end and not an end in itself. He worked hard, first in London, where he grasped the unexciting essentials of bookkeeping and accounting controls before he was sent north. In Birmingham, he mastered every detail of the business. His success was not achieved by chance or solely because of that wood-screw patent. In business, as later in Parliament, he worked himself hard – ultimately to death. Systems were analysed and adapted for efficiency. Cash flow was crucial and an important system of discounts was offered to stimulate it.

If financial success was not the aim, what was? The answer is the practical amelioration of the life of the people. The way to achieve

---

* And yet he became one of Queen Victoria's favourite ministers and the last to see her in January 1901.

that was through *local* politics. Joe Chamberlain always believed that more good could be done at a municipal level than in Parliament.

Just as the great provincial cities were seen as stars in their own right, and not as subordinate planets circling London, so, at this time, many grandees found nothing demeaning about involvement in local politics. Lord Rosebery, Joe's colleague before the latter left the Liberal Party, was about as grand a grandee as you could get. In 1889 he saw nothing odd about taking on the chairmanship of the London County Council after having been Foreign Secretary under Gladstone. At a time when it seemed that great things could be done by powerful local authorities, serving in them was not regarded as axiomatically inferior to serving in Westminster.

Joe stood for the Town Council of Birmingham in 1869. By 1874 he considered that he had secured sufficient financial resources to leave aside his business career. He retired from business in June, just before his thirty-eighth birthday. He had accumulated capital amounting to some £100,000. For a variety of reasons, it's impossible to calculate a true equivalent in today's money, but it might be in the region of £100 million. On what appeared to be a very firm financial basis (though things had changed a bit by the time of Andros) he now proceeded to get on with the real work of his life, saying, 'There is no nobler sphere for those who have not the opportunity of engaging in imperial politics than to take part in municipal work, to the wise conduct of which they owe the welfare, the wealth, the comfort and the lives of 400,000 people.'[7]

He was elected mayor of Birmingham after just four years, inaugurating 'the most famous mayoralty in British History' – an image partly promoted by his group of supporters which included John Thackray Bunce, the influential editor of the *Birmingham Daily Post*. Under Joe's direction, Birmingham became the largest local authority in England apart from London.*

His claim, which was fully justified in its performance, was, 'In twelve months by God's help the town shall not know itself.' The change that he effected is staggering enough to think of today, but for those who lived through it, the speed of the change must have been disorientating. Health and sanitation were crucial. Some councillors

---

* Glasgow, however, was rather larger at this time.

were sceptical about what he called his sagacious audacity. But he delivered on his promise. He secured the purchase by the city of the gas undertakings. The council spread itself abroad. It brought from the Elan Valley in Mid Wales a soft water which was chemically suited to the metal processes. After three years he allowed himself to reflect with pride that in these three years' active work he had 'almost completed my municipal programme and may sing *nunc dimittis*. The Town will be parked, paved, assessed, marketed, gas-and-watered and *improved*.'[8]

In the process, he impressed the people of Birmingham with the *effectiveness* of his politics. The politics of the city followed the politics of Chamberlain. Birmingham became a stronghold of Liberal Unionism and an example of municipal socialism that was admired throughout the world. Slums were replaced with forty acres of healthy housing and broad commercial avenues. The changes improved the health and the business climate of the city.

In changing the face of Birmingham, Chamberlain had become very well-known far beyond the bounds of his city. By 1876 his job in Birmingham was largely done. He was loath to leave municipal life but his talents were appreciated and he was ready to move to the world of imperial politics to which he had referred. In 1876 he entered Parliament. It's an interesting reflection on the importance of provincial politics that he remained on the Birmingham Council for four years, until he joined the Cabinet in 1880.

His dazzling public successes in Birmingham were, however, paralleled by personal tragedies, tragedies which he bore bravely and faced with a developing stoicism, a determination not publicly to be overwhelmed which informed his character and that of both his sons.

Joe followed the tradition of marrying into 'the family': 'On the Kenrick side, two brothers had married two first cousins, of the Paget family. Joseph Chamberlain's first wife, Harriet, was the daughter of one brother, and his second wife, Florence, daughter of the other. Chamberlain's sister married Harriet's brother. His favourite brother Arthur married the twin sister of Florence Kenrick.'[9]

Joe's marriage to Harriet was happy. She was not in awe of him and their partnership was a real one. She introduced him to gardening, which was to become his dominating hobby. 'I don't know after all', he said later, 'that any flowers ever gave me more pleasure than the first six pennyworth of red daisies that I bought in a market stall and carried home to plant with your mother in our little garden in the Harborne Road.'[10] Their first child, Beatrice, was born in 1862. Eighteen months later, Harriet died in childbirth. The baby, Austen, survived. The little family moved to the home of Harriet's father where, in accordance with Harriet's dying wish, her sister, Caroline, looked after the children.

In Arthur Kenrick's house, Joe had his own apartment and he threw himself into work. In his loss he could not sleep, and he now developed the practice he would follow for the rest of his life of working in the very early hours of the morning. Years later he revealed to Austen, only tangentially, how he had withdrawn himself from his children in order to conceal his desolation. Tough as he was, Joe could not bring himself to speak of Harriet to his children. It was only when Austen was twenty-five and his father about to marry for the third time that Joe revealed that fact. He said that until happiness had come again into his life he did not dare speak of Harriet and that even then the tears were coming into his eyes.

Nearly five years after Harriet's death, Joe married her cousin, Florence Kenrick. She was shy and diffident, just twenty, well read, a teacher in the Sunday School. Joe's loss of Harriet had left him with a feeling of insecurity, a fear of what the future might hold, and the inexperienced Florence must have needed a big heart to take him on along with her two stepchildren.

But she matured very rapidly. At a domestic level she was very good for the family. Beatrice and Austen were treated as her own children. She brought a liveliness into the household, and physical activities like walking, skating and riding. But she also saw the importance of public life for her husband. She worked for a number of charities, and she encouraged Joe to stand for the Town Council. The relationship between them was one of easy equality, and he discussed political affairs and valued her judgement and counsel. She was a remarkable woman in her energy. On top of her other duties, she found time to study botany, physiology and French, and, in just over five years, to bear four children, Neville was born on 18 March 1869, Ida in 1870, Hilda in 1872 and Ethel in 1873. A fifth child was expected in 1875.

Joe had always thought that Florence was not strong; she had a delicate expression which sometimes made him anxious. He had to preside at a meeting of the Town Council on Tuesday 9 February 1875, and

Florence decided in the event not to join him, but all seemed well, and the great Liberal statesman John Morley was invited to stay that night. At the end of the proceedings Chamberlain was handed a note – Florence had thoughtfully asked that it was not delivered until the proceedings were over in case it worried him. She thought the baby was coming early and asked him to cancel his visitors. Chamberlain returned home, where Florence looked unwell but was in good spirits.

By the following day she seemed better, and Chamberlain went off to London, returning late on the Thursday. Florence seemed a bit depressed but bravely said that it was good that everything would be over in time for Joe to have his Easter 'Holyday'. Two nights later, on the Saturday, the baby had still not arrived. That evening, Joe brought Neville and Ida to say good night. Florence kissed them with particular tenderness. Before midnight the baby was born. All seemed well, but remembering what had happened to Harriet, Joe asked the doctor to stay. On the following day, Florence fainted and died. The baby was also lost.

It was now that Joe Chamberlain lost his faith in formal religion. In his mind, the lives and premature deaths of his two wives fused together. Their characters, in particular their high moral commitment, seemed identical. Neville, the only one of Florence's children who remembered her as they grew up, wrote to *his* children forty years later, saying that their grandfather 'under an exterior that for many years was rather hard and cold, concealed intensely strong feelings. His love for my mother was not I think passionate – he had himself too much under control for that – but it was so profound that when she died it destroyed all his pleasure in life and altered his whole being.'[11] Joe only once brought himself to talk about Florence to Neville and Ida. He spoke very slowly, seeking to control his emotions: 'I think she was as perfect as a woman can be.'*

---

* Five years earlier there had been a brief thought of marriage to Beatrice Potter, who became much enamoured of Joe, unsettled by 'the deadly fight between the intellectual and the sensual' despite an age gap of twenty-two years. Beatrice Webb, née Potter, the austere sociologist, wife of Sidney Webb, founder of the Fabian Society and the London School of Economics, is not to be confused with Beatrix Heelis, née Potter, author of *The Tale of Peter Rabbit* and much else and President-elect at the time of her death of the Herdwick Sheepbreeders' Association, though it is hugely appealing to imagine Joe Chamberlain formulating his plans for imperial expansion surrounded by Benjamin Bunny, Mrs Tiggy-Winkle and Little Pig Robinson.

Joe was, however, to marry again. When Salisbury sent him on a mission to the United States in 1888 he fell in love with a girl from Massachusetts, Mary Endicott, and lost no time in becoming engaged.* Mary was younger than Beatrice and Austen, twenty-seven years younger than Joe and only five years older than Neville. They married in November 1888 in St John's Church in Washington, near the park in front of the White House. President Cleveland and most of the Cabinet were present, and army officers wore full uniform in honour of the bride's father, the Secretary of War. At the reception President Cleveland proposed the toast to the couple, referring to the bridegroom as 'England's man with a future'.

Mary was just twenty-four when she married Joe Chamberlain. She looked younger, though, and continued to look young for her age for all of a long life which ended in 1957 at the age of ninety-three. She was very beautiful and full of vitality.† Her ninety-third birthday was spent at the theatre, and when asked if she would like to go home afterwards, she said, 'I should hate that! I want to be taken to a large, loud, gay restaurant for supper!' Half a dozen young Conservative MPs dined with her. They rose to go at 11 o'clock. She exclaimed, 'You're not leaving now? I'm at my best till two in the morning.'[12]

---

* It was when Joe and Mary returned to the United States to visit her family that the meeting with Sir Ambrose Shea took place which would greatly affect Neville's future.

† She was painted by Millais, and Sargent also painted her very soon after her marriage. A friend, the journalist Collin Brooks, told her that in that picture there was a look of 'what could only be called impudence'. She replied that Sargent liked to talk as he painted, and she supposed that something impudent must have been said. She told Brooks that in Sargent's portrait of Joe, the papers on which the latter's hand is resting relate to the Jameson Raid. In 1895, Dr Leander Starr Jameson, a lieutenant of Cecil Rhodes, led a half-baked raid on the Transvaal in an attempt to replace Boer control for British. The raid failed and caused political embarrassment. There was a particular problem for Joe, who as Colonial Secretary had foreknowledge of the raid and had indeed facilitated it. He survived, and his role remained more or less secret because Rhodes needed to keep him. How many people other than Mary knew what he was toying with while Sargent painted his portrait? After Joe's death she married William Carnegie, the sub-dean of Westminster Abbey and chaplain to the House of Commons. He was only five years her senior. She regretted that she had not had children. At fifty-two Joe may have been reluctant to start a new family, and may have feared losing a third wife in childbirth.

The age differences between her and her stepchildren and the fact that she came to take over a household which Beatrice had been running for four years might have proved difficult, but she was gentle, assured and kind. Her stepchildren warmed to her. Neville knew her as 'Mary', a dear friend to whom he could confide. Under her influence some of Joe's self-protective reserve evaporated and he became closer to his children than he ever had been before.

To be brought up in Joe Chamberlain's household was to live in proximity to an immensely powerful force. He is repeatedly described as lively, witty and full of restless energy. He was personally brave – because of his hostility to Irish Home Rule, he was subjected to death threats from the Fenians. Neville said that his father never seemed to know what fear was. Although he was too imaginative for that to have been the case, the fact was that he never allowed fear to influence his actions. He was irritated by the presence of police protection, and refused to change his habits, driving to and from the Commons in an open cab. This, and the throwing away and ignoring of threatening letters, was of a part with the immense efforts he took to conceal the pain that the death of his first two wives caused him. Self-respect required a Roman indifference to the attacks of fate. This was what he meant when he wrote to Neville, after Andros, 'If the worst comes to the worst we will all make the best of it and remember our motto *Je tiens ferme.*' He set a high standard for his sons, but there was never any doubt that he or they would attain that standard.

## Chapter 4

# A Party Disabled

Joe Chamberlain is the most influential politician the United Kingdom has known since the death of Gladstone. He arrived in Westminster in 1876, and it was very much as a radical MP that he entered the House, 'the Brummagem Robespierre' as he was known. 'Radical Joe' was for 'Free Church, Free Schools, Free Land, Free Labour'. His mission was to change the nature of the Liberal Party and his election demands included free education, a sensitive issue both with the Church of England and non-conformists. He wanted the enfranchisement of the rural poor and to give them their three acres and a cow. Britain was 'too long a peer-ridden nation'. He was unpopular at the time with the Queen and rebuked by Gladstone (his position was rather like that of Lloyd George a decade later). He was dynamic and electrifying: his aggressive passion matched by emotion and sensitivity. Both loyal to his friends and a dangerous enemy, he could not be ignored.

He came after all to Westminster after an immensely successful career first in business and then in civil politics in Birmingham. There he had exercised more political power than most backbenchers and some Cabinet ministers would ever do. His network of political connections was known as the Duchy; he himself was 'the Great Elector'. He was forty but looked as if he were in his twenties. Indeed, he looked very different from a standard-issue Victorian politician. He was clean-shaven where most of his colleagues were bearded and shaggy, and was said to be the most handsome man of his generation in public life. He was exactly the same height as Neville, five feet and ten inches. Joe's gaze was dominating, all the more penetrating because, being short sighted, he wore an eyeglass

over one of his piercing blue eyes. Disraeli approvingly noted that he
wore the monocle like a gentleman. As a younger man he had
disconcerted provincial sensibilities in Birmingham by wearing seal-
skin topcoats and fur collars. In later life he dressed more circum-
spectly, but always beautifully. He wore a black or grey frock coat in
London, a tweed tailcoat in the country and a white waistcoat in the
summer. At Westminster, as elsewhere, he continued to wear an
orchid or two – occasionally three – in his buttonhole. He was not
beset by self-doubt.

Joe Chamberlain's political orientation was significant and determined Neville's affiliations. He had been a Liberal in provincial politics and was a Liberal at Westminster. The quilt of liberalism was,
however, made up of many patches and Joe's identity was on the radical side of the party. At Birmingham, the Liberal Association was
organised through a system of tiers of control, ultimately run by
Chamberlain and his associates. Now at Westminster he elaborated a
similar structure, establishing a National Federation of Liberal
Associations in 1877. Gladstone stayed with Chamberlain at
Southbourne for its inaugural meeting and recognised the value of
the Association and of what Chamberlain was doing, although relations between the two men were not close.

The Liberal Party won the 1880 general election and Gladstone,
back in power, formed his second administration. Joe Chamberlain
had played a part in organising victory, and he wanted his reward;
indeed, he threatened revolt if he didn't get it. He became President
of the Board of Trade

The Reform Act of 1884 and the Redistribution of Seats Act the
following year paved the way, as Joe and his Liberal radicals saw it, for
a change of direction, which he enunciated in 'The Radical
Programme', a series of speeches which was described in its own time
as socialism. Joe's role was more important than anyone else's in the
radicalisation of the Liberal Party, and in 1883 he had denounced the
aristocracy, 'who toil not, neither do they spin'.[1]

These were not Gladstone's politics, and Gladstone's politics were
not Joe's: on 17 December 1885 the Liberal Party, now in opposition,
was awakened to one of those very personal initiatives with which
Gladstone was inclined to reshape party policy. His son Herbert flew
'the Hawarden Kite', floating the suggestion that his father was

prepared to create an Irish parliament.* Home Rule would solve the Irish problem. A year later the Liberals were back in power. Despite his opposition to Home Rule, Chamberlain could not be ignored, and Gladstone had to invite him to join his administration even though he described Chamberlain to Rosebery as 'the greatest black-guard I ever knew', and to Granville as 'the prince of opportunists'.

So there was generalised antagonism, and there was Ireland. As the Kite had made clear, Gladstone's third premiership would be dominated by his desire to lay his axe to the root of the Irish upas tree by introducing Home Rule.† Chamberlain was against Home Rule, increasingly anxious to see the Empire consolidated, not broken up. What brought him to Westminster was the same concern for the amelioration of practical problems which had been the focus of his interest in local politics. But once he was there the imperial mission became increasingly important.

For the moment, Chamberlain remained an uneasy member of Gladstone's Cabinet, uncomfortable, but still within it. He remained in it because, despite the Kite, he didn't know what was in the old man's mind. The Gladstonian move had been tentative and largely concealed. It was only by leaked conversations that it became known to his colleagues and Chamberlain seems to have been one of the last to find out what was happening.

It was not until 26 March 1886 that the penny dropped. When it did, when he contemplated the dismemberment of the Empire, he and George Trevelyan, then Secretary of State for Scotland, dramatically walked out of the Cabinet Room in protest. As in the case of Michael Heseltine in the following century, there was some doubt about whether they were actually resigning, rather than absenting themselves for some more commonplace reason – although Chamberlain later wrote that he and Trevelyan had 'tendered our resignations'. When he got home, he certainly seems to have told Austen that he had resigned.

---

* Gladstone's son Herbert revealed to the National Press Agency that his father was in favour of Home Rule for Ireland. He also published a letter in *The Times* saying that if five-sixths of the Irish people wanted a parliament in Dublin then, 'in the name of Justice and Wisdom they should have it'. Hawarden was Gladstone's home in Flintshire, on the Welsh/English border.
† The upas is an East Asian tree of legendary toxicity. Gladstone used it as a metaphor for the Irish Problem.

The Home Rule Bill of 1886 failed, and the government fell. Joe
Chamberlain had changed the weather. He destroyed the Liberal
Party over Home Rule, taking many of its ablest members with him.
After 1886 and Chamberlain's resignation, the Liberals didn't form a
majority government until 1906. Later, he destroyed the Conservatives
over free trade. It took a pretty remarkable man to destroy one party
after another, depriving them of office for twenty years each: forty
years in total.

After the fall of the Liberals in 1886, Chamberlain moved from Radical
Liberalism to Liberal Unionism, the party that Neville would belong
to all his life. These were Liberals, many from the Whig tradition of
the party, who wanted to defend the Union, macho Liberals rather
than the wimpish majority. Liberal Unionism combined a still very
real radicalism with opposition to Home Rule and with, in due
course, a forward, aggressive policy for the Empire. That kind of imperial policy appealed to many Tories too. For the moment, Joe was no
Conservative – he was Radical Joe after all – but in 1891 he spoke at
a meeting of the National Union of Conservative Associations, and
said that he was prepared to associate with conservatism.

Joe Chamberlain was always muscular. He was physically tough and
fit, and fast on his feet. He was also muscular in a moral sense. He was
muscular in the way he got to grips with the social conditions of
Birmingham when he was in local government, and he had a similar
practical approach to getting things done when he reached Westminster.
The Liberal Unionists were the muscular wing of the Liberal Party.
The mainstream party could be too interested in abstract theories,
maybe even a little wet. Its creed was peace, retrenchment and reform.
The Liberal Unionists believed in imperial expansion, if necessary at
the cost of blood. Amongst its prominent members were Leo Amery,
Arthur Conan Doyle, A.V. Dicey, Ernest Shackleton and H. M. Stanley,
as well as John Bright and Chamberlain.

The new grouping was assumed to be temporary. Gladstone
referred to them as 'Dissension Liberals'. There was certainly a funda-
mental difference between the landed Whig element and the
Chamberlain radicals that was initially suggestive of impermanence.
But Liberal Unionism survived. In 1895, Liberal Unionists joined
Salisbury's new Conservative administration and it was from then that

the Conservative Party was regularly referred to as 'Unionist'. A few Liberal Unionists chose to forego their independence and join the Conservative Party, but the grouping in general maintained its separate identity until a formal merger in 1912, when the Conservative and Unionist Party was formed (the Scottish Liberal Unionists didn't finally merge until 1965). It is important to remember this Liberal Unionist tradition: Neville Chamberlain certainly did.

When Salisbury finally brought the Liberal Unionists aboard in June 1895 he offered them four places in Cabinet. Joe was offered anything except the Foreign Secretaryship and Leadership of the House. Everyone, including Salisbury, assumed that Chamberlain would wish to continue in the area of social reform, perhaps as Chancellor; to their surprise he chose the Colonial Office, what he had wanted from Gladstone but had not been given. Chamberlain and his place in history was defined by the appointment. It marked a move from domestic Liberal reform to a vision of modern imperialism. He had reached the position from which he could again destroy his party.

In the South African war he faced criticism because of the contracts which his arms manufacturing relatives received in wartime. A famous *Punch* joke ran: 'The more the Empire expands, the more these Chamberlains contract'. Chamberlain himself was largely unscathed by the war, but the cause of imperialism, the idea of a federated empire covering the globe, with London at its centre, was under threat.* The whole notion of Empire was challenged. Kipling had written *Recessional*, seen as acknowledging the end of Empire, in 1897. Henry Campbell-Bannerman, for the Liberal Party, was describing the steps that were being taken to crush the Boers as 'methods of barbarism'.

---

* Joe was for expansion and not contraction or scuttling from Empire. He gave Austen a brass milk can for use as a coal scuttle with this note:

The ways of Little England
Are hateful to us both;
And to adopt their policy
I know that you are loath.

But still I count upon you,
As your intellect is subtle,
To find excuse, and make a place
For this Aesthetic 'Scuttle'

Even the colonial premiers at a colonial conference in 1902 showed no tendency to coalesce around Chamberlain's vision or to espouse imperial free trade. The political world was not yet in step with him.

But his vision was understood even when it was not shared. He was described as 'the First Minister of the Empire' by Arthur Balfour, Salisbury's nephew, at a presentation in the Guildhall in 1902: 'a man who, above all others, has made the British Empire a reality'. That didn't mean that his colleagues accepted the principle of tariff reform; and tariff reform, for Joe, was an essential element of a forward imperial policy. Quite early as Colonial Secretary, he started thinking about a customs union amongst the self-governing colonies. The idea was not particularly popular with the colonies or with Britain, which was still wedded to free trade, both on dogmatic grounds and as a practical means of providing cheap food.

# Chapter 5

# Another Party Blown to Bits

In April 1902, Joe Chamberlain was invited to have dinner in the House of Commons with the young Winston Churchill and the group of parliamentarians known as 'The Hughligans', a play on the name of Lord Hugh Cecil, one of the group. The Hughligans were a bunch of young politicians who chose to make their names by being difficult, obstreperous critics of the Tory Party, and in particular of the urbane Arthur Balfour. As Chamberlain arrived, he looked critically at his hosts and said, 'I am dining in very bad company.' The Hughligans had reason to be grateful to Chamberlain for condescending to join the precocious band of troublemakers for dinner. In 1902, at the age of sixty-five, he was at the height of his powers, moving from the position of a committed radical, even republican, to promulgating the concept of the British Empire as a world-dominating influence on the world.

The Hughligans had, as usual, been critical of government policy, in this case about a journalist who was being denied entry to Britain because of an article he had written in the course of the South African War. Churchill and his friends weighed in, telling Chamberlain how wrong the government had been. 'What's the use,' he asked, 'of supporting your own government only when it is right?' But Churchill recorded that 'as he mellowed, he became most gay and captivating. I never remember having heard him talk better.' As he rose to leave, he paused at the door and, turning, said with much deliberation, 'You young gentlemen have entertained me royally, and in return I will give you a priceless secret. Tariffs! There are the politics of the future and of the near future. Study them closely and make yourselves masters of them, and you will not regret your hospitality to me'.[1] This was the penultimate paragraph in Churchill's account of his own early life.

In uttering that one word, 'tariffs', as he went out of the door, Chamberlain was pretty effectively singing for his supper. Tariff reform was for him an essential and positive element in promoting a customs union among the self-governing colonies. Its negative implication, which he was entirely happy to accept, was that in favouring the colonies, tariffs had to be erected against the rest of the world. This meant the abandonment of free trade.

Just a few months later, the war in South Africa over, Joe and Mary Chamberlain boarded a steamer bound for Durban. Joe wanted to see the country for himself and to meet Boer leaders. It was a remarkable journey, undertaken at times in covered wagons, sleeping under canvas. The trip was invigorating, and Chamberlain came back more than ever of the view that the movement for closer imperial cooperation was under way. The issue of tariff reform, the idea of tying the Empire together, replacing free trade with tariffs on non-imperial imports, was gestating in his mind.

But it was not an issue which found favour with his Cabinet colleagues. He returned to London to find that the Cabinet, under the weak control of Balfour, was backtracking on a tiny, but to Chamberlain immensely significant, hint of imperial preference in relation to Canadian imported corn and flour. Charles Ritchie, the Chancellor of the Exchequer and a keen free trader, threatened to resign.[*]

Chamberlain's response was one of those few political speeches which changed the landmark of politics for decades. On 15 May 1903, in Birmingham Town Hall, he declared that Britain would depend on its Empire in the twentieth century and that its Empire could only be bound together if the sacred doctrine of free trade were qualified to allow the use of tariffs to create imperial preference. He argued for a treaty of preference and reciprocity with the colonies and punitive tariffs against imperial competitors. 'You have an opportunity. You will never have it again.' He resigned from office four months later and was never again a member of any government.

To the Victorians, free trade meant cheap food, enlightenment, peace and almost everything that was good. To challenge it, to argue for a

---

[*] But ideas were in flux. Just a few months later Ritchie was dismissed by Balfour because of his antipathy to tariff reform.

return to protectionism, was cultural anathema. It is so very difficult, almost impossible, for us now, in the twenty-first century, to understand the almost mystical significance of the concept of free trade 150 years ago that the cult deserves a short section of its own. Both Joe and Neville were closely involved in the death of the cult, and to understand the scale of their aspirations, it's worth knowing a little about what they dared to attack.

From the beginning of the early modern period until about 1750, in so far as economic philosophies existed at all, what was called mercantilism was unchallenged. Mercantilism involved exporting products, selling them abroad and bringing home the proceeds in gold bullion. England, and Britain after the Union of the Crowns in 1707, particularly valued mercantilism. It was an economic way of life that suited an island, especially when the island had a strong maritime tradition. Some sea-edged regions of continental Europe, the Netherlands in particular, also espoused mercantilism. It was particularly appropriate for countries with colonial possessions because the idea was to export to the maximum to 'tame' purchasers – the client ports and the ports of the home nation therefore would be closed to competitors. It was an exclusive method of trade.

Britain not only grabbed at the opportunities presented, but saw ways of multiplying the profit opportunity. British India, for example, was discouraged from manufacturing her own textiles and metal products. Raw materials from India were shipped back to Britain and turned into manufactured goods which were then exported back to the subject continent. The profit opportunity was thus doubled. And the gearing was cranked up further when the proceeds gained by drawing on India's resources at negligible cost were reinvested in the developing Industrial Revolution. The products of that revolution were again multiplied: instead of simply exporting industrial products in a swap for cash, Britain devised the enormously effective and notorious triangular system of selling goods to West Africa, buying slaves there and selling them in the West Indies from where sugar and tobacco were brought back to be sold at home and in Europe.

So by the late eighteenth century, mercantilism was in practice increasingly challenged by its evolution from its crude original into a sophisticated economic model. The theoretical basis of mercantilism was also challenged by economists like Adam Smith and David

Ricardo, who provided an intellectual justification for the aggressive muscularity of the rough and tumble which was in effect free trade. In concord with the economic doctrines of the nineteenth century and the widespread belief in the importance of laissez-faire, Adam Smith said that '[i]f a foreign country can supply us with a commodity cheaper than we ourselves can produce, better buy it from them with some part of the produce of our own industry, employed in a way in which we have some advantage.'

Britain was now engaged in what was indeed *in effect* free trade; but few in England could quite bring themselves to admit that it was: one of the implications of accepting free trade as a doctrine rather than as an accident would be to attack one last but powerfully defended example of mercantilism – the tariffs and trade restrictions on imported food, particularly cereals, which were embodied in what were collectively known as the Corn Laws.

The Corn Laws were a set of measures that went back to the sixteenth century. Now, at the end of the eighteenth century, while great fortunes were made by stripping India of her wealth and by buying and selling slaves, they prevented the import of cheap foods and kept the price of domestically produced grain artificially high, even in times of famine. It was a system which persisted, and which was very vigorously defended because it worked to the advantage of the landed aristocracy. Specious arguments were, however, put forward: it would be dangerous for Britain to have to rely on imported food, cheap imported grain would reduce labourers' wages, and so on. The system was indefensible, but vested interest continued to defend it. A spectacular example of their selfish effect was given in 1815 when the Corn Law of that year, passed as corn prices fell with the end of the Napoleonic Wars, forced bread prices spectacularly high.

But the indefensible cannot be defended indefinitely. The end of the story is well known. There was increasing agitation for a totality of free trade and an abolition of protective duties. There were riots. The case for reform was adopted by the Anti-Corn Law League, which argued on the basis of morality and idealism. Finally, in 1845 and 1846, there was the start of the great Irish Famine. In the summer of the second of these years Peel in the House of Commons with the help of the Duke of Wellington in the Lords finally repealed the Corn Laws.

These two Tory statesmen accepted that there had to be change if things were to go on as before, but they took only half of their party with them. Robert Peel, though the founder of the modern Tory party, was from its manufacturing rather than its landed wing. He was capable of being persuaded to abandon tribal views in the case of Catholic Emancipation and parliamentary reform as well as the Corn Laws. But not all his party were so flexible. The measure was passed in the Commons with the votes of Whigs and radicals on 15 May 1846. By pressing for this challenge to social and economic convention, Peel ended his own career. He also pulled the Conservative Party apart; it did not form a majority government again until the 1870s.

Free trade in its broadest sense was now publicly unchallenged, but there were those in the Tory Party who looked to a return to the primitive charms of protectionism. For the moment they kept their counsel, because in polite political society the merits of free trade were not discussed. In Manchester, a Free Trade Hall was erected (not many public buildings have been named after an economic doctrine; not many Protectionist Palaces). Businessmen who had their doubts did not voice them. Richard Cobden, who had been so active in the Anti-Corn Law League, was now the voice of orthodoxy and Gladstone was the epitome of that orthodoxy: by 1860 he had removed duties on 400 different items of import.

And the thing was that free trade seemed to work. 'Seemed to work': some economists now question whether Britain's prosperity at certain points in the nineteenth century happened because of free trade or in spite of it; but at the time few people had doubts, and whether imperial gearing or the size of the Royal Navy actually masked an adverse effect on the terms of trade (even if only initially), was immaterial to people's perception.

When the orthodoxy came to be challenged, most notably by Joe Chamberlain, it was in the context of a relative, but only relative, decline in Britain's trading pre-eminence and a need, as he and others thought, to bind the empire together by preferential tariffs. When free trade was finally killed, by *Neville* Chamberlain, it was in the context of collapsing industries after the First World War which created once again a need for protection.

For almost all of the second half of the nineteenth century, then, free trade was regarded as the basis of Britain's economic success and international pre-eminence. It was more than that. It was a revelation of enlightenment that stood in contrast to the blind simplicity of the past. It was a *good* phenomenon. It was inherently implicated in British liberalism, both with an upper- and lower-case initial letter. It implied the removal of the state from economic life. Not only the state, but what would not then be called the establishment: the dominant rich classes. Cobden and Gladstone presided over the growth of new liberalism, the financial emancipation of the newly emancipated voters. This strand of Cobdenite thinking went on to morph into an Asquithian social revolution at the beginning of the twentieth century when the foundations of the welfare state was laid.

World peace was also involved. Even before 1846, Cobden had asked in a speech at Covent Garden, 'Free Trade! What is it? Why, breaking down the barriers that separate nations; those barriers, behind which nestle the feelings of pride, revenge, hatred and jealousy, which every now and then burst their bounds, and deluge whole countries with blood; those feelings which nourish the poison of war and conquest . . .'[2]

Cobden and others saw free trade as 'a great pacificator'. Lloyd George said (six years before the outbreak of the First World War) that in the last fifty years there had not been a single war with any first-class power. 'Free Trade is slowly but surely cleaving a path through the dense and dark thicket of armaments to the sunny land of brotherhood amongst nations.'[3] So free trade had a moral dimension as well as an economic one. The alternative to free trade was in no one's interests and certainly not in the interests of the advancement of a fair and just society. It thus became, truly, something close to an item of religious faith.

Free trade was then the doctrine of those people who felt themselves to be right-thinking, who wanted to be intimately implicated in Liberalism. Decent people who looked for general social progress and were prepared to vote and indeed pay for it regarded free trade as an essential vehicle for their desired direction of travel. Free trade seemed a reflection of free religion, of the right to worship in one's own way. Nonconformity and free trade were very close. To challenge free trade was to advocate rejecting all that had been done by way of moral advancement and commitment to the amelioration of the human condition in the nineteenth century. Questioning it was like questioning the assumption that cruelty to children was bad. It was something only a barbarian would suggest.

The abandonment of free trade was a Chamberlain achievement, begun by Joe but finally realised by Neville. What they did turned political economy on its head.

So when in May 1903 Joe made that call for the introduction of tariffs on goods imported into the British Empire, he was detonating a huge explosion, echoing the detonation by Robert Peel almost sixty years earlier. Repeal of the Corn Laws in 1846 and tariff reform in the following century caused huge and lasting divisions in the Conservative Party. These divisions seemed to arise every couple of generations. Two generations after tariff reform came the European Union. Just as Peel put the Conservatives out of office in 1846, so Joe Chamberlain now did, two generations later. He had achieved a double first. He had broken the Conservative Party just as he'd broken the Liberals.

Arthur Balfour, the languid, sensitive and elusive aesthete, so very different from Chamberlain, had succeeded his uncle, Lord Salisbury,* as leader of the Conservative Party. He did his best to keep the party united. His own position on tariff reform remained an enigma. Many, many years later he asked his niece, Baffy Dugdale, what his position had been on tariff reform. 'That, Uncle Arthur,' she replied, 'was exactly what we all wanted to know.'

Ultimately, Balfour resigned. Being Prime Minister had never really seemed worth the effort involved. A general election took place. The split party lost the 1906 election and did not form a majority government again until 1922.

Instances of ill health and fatigue had been manifesting themselves, but in 1903, at the age of sixty-seven, Joe Chamberlain was still fit, though frustrated by the tensions of Cabinet government. He was glad to resign office to campaign for his reforms: 'He threw his enormous efforts and the great resources of his Birmingham Duchy into his campaign. He formed a Tariff Reform League. It was well supported by manufacturers, well financed and well organised, the

---

* Robert Gascoyne-Cecil, third Marquis of Salisbury, took pains to look after his nephew's career; hence the expression, 'Bob's your uncle'.

most powerful propaganda machine that British peacetime history has seen.'⁴ Chamberlain strengthened his own personal position by increasing his control of the Liberal Unionist Party, and had unleashed a new political movement. Its aims were not achieved in his lifetime, but they were fulfilled by his son.

In 1906, as the Liberals settled in for a tenure of power which would last until 1922, a party was held in Birmingham to mark Joe's seventieth birthday and to celebrate thirty years of service as a Birmingham MP. Factories were closed, special trains brought people into the city, firework displays took place and there was a civic banquet. At Bingley Hall, Chamberlain made a moving speech – it turned out to be his last. He spoke about his connection with Birmingham, and he also spoke about Empire. He said that tariff reform would 'secure for the masses of the industrial population in this country constant employment at fair wages . . . England without an Empire would be a fifth-rate nation, existing on the sufferance of its more powerful neighbours'.⁵ He was then escorted home to his house at Highbury by a parade of torchbearers.

He went back to London. He had already blacked out once or twice but there he suffered a very serious stroke. His condition was disguised for a time and he survived for a further seven years, but he never recovered. When he took the oath in the new Parliament on 2 February 1911 he was incapable of signing his name. He simply touched a pen with which Austen signed on his behalf. He then sat on the opposition bench for a few minutes before leaving the chamber, never to return.

The change of regime after his stroke was a huge blow to this extraordinarily vigorous man who had formerly known that he was under the weather when he didn't bound up the steps of the Colonial Office two at a time. He was confined to a wheelchair, though he forced himself to attempt a daily 'walk', sweating with the effort. He told Neville one night, 'I thought the work might kill me, but I never expected this.' He often told Mary that he wished he were dead.

He did die, at his London home, on 2 July 1914. In a telling gesture of inverted romanticism, he had declined a title, choosing to die as 'Mr Chamberlain'. In the same way, his family declined burial in Westminster Abbey. Instead, he was buried in an attenuated ceremony at Birmingham. The cemetery was in his parliamentary constituency, and not far from his factories. The arrangements underlined the unique nature and base of his political power. The dominating authority which he exercised in his prime would overlay his younger son, bring him into politics and shape the nature of his own political mission. Joe's long decline towards death and the vault in which he was placed beside his first two wives also had their effect on his family. His grandchildren found his inarticulate grunts alarming. To see what *The Times* had called 'The most popular and most trusted man in England'[6] wheeled around the footpaths of Highbury in a bathchair as a helpless invalid was a poignant contrast to the image that Churchill retained of a vital titan.

When Joe had said that he wanted 'to be buried in my own grave, in the cemetery at Birmingham' he added that he hoped that his family would remember him without the need for elaborate ceremonies. After the funeral, the family made their way to Highbury. There they dined, talked about him, laughed at examples of his wit and read hymns. They continued to remember him for the rest of their lives

## Chapter 6

# The Growing Boy and the Shades of the Prison House

Although Neville remembered his mother with affection – and the emotional heart that beat behind his tightly buttoned waistcoat prompted him to write an affectionate memoir of her for his children – it was not she who brought him up.

His sister Beatrice was thirteen when Florence died, and it was increasingly she who ran the motherless family. Initially Florence's sister, Caroline ('Lina'), did what their mother had asked her to do, and looked after the children. Aunt Lina presided over a happy household and the children were successfully protected from their father's grief. There was a large, long garden in which the children had their own areas, and beyond the garden were fields and a Shetland pony, Tom Thumb. The girls, riding side-saddle, were able to control Tom, but Neville had less control and Tom developed a technique for suddenly stopping and throwing him over his head. He had also a nasty habit of scraping his rider off against the railings that ran round the field. As a result, Neville didn't much like riding.

Austen and Beatrice were sent off to boarding schools at an early date. Beatrice, who would succeed Aunt Lina as the mother figure until Mary Endicott arrived, was sent to school in Switzerland. She was a strong character and it was thought that her dominance over an influenceable Austen was a bad idea. Nothing was to interfere with grooming Austen for political leadership.

With Austen away, Neville was the oldest boy in a large circle of cousins. It was a lively, intelligent and educated circle. Joe was teasingly supposed to have read nothing except the novels of Dickens, but that was unfair, and his reading – particularly in French literature

– was extensive. The children were exposed to the world of books and were encouraged to expand their minds. From an early point, Neville was interested in entomology. Trees were coated in treacle on summer nights to catch insects which could be examined under the microscope in Austen's bedroom. There was also lots of outdoor activity: wigwams in the wood, tree climbing, tennis, swimming and rounders.

Neville was at the centre of the family circle, known for his jokes and as a mimic. The extent of the cousinly circle was so great, and its members knew each other so well, that there was no need to look outside it. For this reason, when Mary Endicott came on the scene she felt that their self-sufficiency was making them unsociable, and Neville later admitted as much. Throughout his life he regarded himself as cursed by shyness. That indeed was the case, but it was only in the outside world that he felt ill at ease, and the first signs can only be detected when he was sent away to school.

Initially, he was sent to a preparatory school at Southport where he was happy, though he missed his lively and supportive family. A letter from Southport encapsulates the stoic philosophy which he had learned from Joe and which he unfailingly followed for the rest of his life: 'I should like to go to the daffodil fields at Aunt Lina's with the others very much indeed, but as I cannot I must be content'.[1]

From Southport he moved on to a preparatory school at Rugby and it was now, says his official biographer, that 'the sparkle went out of his life'.[2] He was very unhappy there, missing the family greatly. The vivacity and fun of a large circle of children surrounded by loving adults who didn't seek to impose any unnecessary discipline contrasted with the petty conformity of a boys' school. He had enjoyed a wider existence at Southbourne, where the children were admitted to the company of some very distinguished people – Morley, John Bright, even the great Mr Gladstone (though Ida didn't like being kissed by the Grand Old Man). Young as they were, the children were encouraged to take an interest in public affairs and have their own debating society. When they debated the execution of Charles I, Neville was surprised to hear his father, listening in, say that it was quite proper for Cromwell to execute Charles for abusing his power.

In 1880, the move to Highbury took place, near to Joe's brother Arthur, who lived at Moor Green, the final home of Joe senior. The house was built to be the centre of his Midland palatinate. Here, Neville would spend the next thirty years of his life in a very substantial if gloomy building of red brick in a neo-Gothic style. Joe himself took a great deal of interest in the design of the garden and the heated glasshouses.

Highbury was an ideal place in which to entertain, a palace in which the Great Elector could rule over the Caucus. It was near enough to London for political magnates to come for the day, but it was securely in Joe Chamberlain's fiefdom. Here, at the centre of his web, he could control his empire. And here he could grow his orchids – he was by now in the grip of his orchid passion ('You must find a hobby'). Meticulous books recorded the origins of the different varieties, and he helped the Royal Botanic Gardens at Kew ('The people there should have the enjoyment of the best that a rich man could afford'). Furthermore, he cultivated original hybrids, and bought specimens for astounding sums: for a bulb of Grand Monarch he paid £25 (subject to the usual caveats, over £3,000 today).

Family life at Highbury was happy, and Aunt Clara, Joe's sister, had succeeded Harriet's sister, Caroline ('Lina'), in looking after the children. Neville and Ida had found Lina just a trifle too bossy and had hoped that she would go off and get married. To their delight, she did just that, dutifully having kept her man waiting until she felt she could leave the household. It was now that Beatrice took over. Not only were Neville and his sisters a little freer than they had been under Lina's conscientious regime, but for her part, Lina relaxed and, now that she was no longer responsible for the children, felt able to be more indulgent. When she visited in her married state they appreciated her lively sense of humour.

Neville was always aware of the contrast between the cosiness of the family circle, where he was relaxed, irrepressible, at ease, and an outside world where he had to withdraw within a carapace for self-protection. The contrast was with him all his adult life. It had started to form at the Rugby preparatory school, but he had even more to cope with when he was sent to Rugby itself in April 1882. Joe had been pleased with how Austen had done there, and he was in his last term, just about to leave for Cambridge, when Neville joined him.

Rugby, which Joe had chosen because it did not permit corporal punishment, may have worked for Austen, but it certainly didn't for

Neville. He hated it, and made a point of never visiting the school as an adult. He started off by being bullied by a boy who had been an enemy of Austen, and then a good housemaster broke down and was succeeded by a less sympathetic one. Moreover, Neville didn't like team games. He reached the Lower Sixth before he was seventeen, was head of his house and played rugby fairly well, but he wasn't happy and his father was disappointed by reports from the masters.

He wasn't a rebel, except to the extent of declining, as a non-conformist, to turn eastwards in chapel for the Creed. What he did was to *withdraw*, not to engage. Contemporaries described him as pale, quiet and shy, friendly but not extroverted, and not active in the debating society. The interests which were to sustain him and mean so much to him throughout his life – because unlike Joe, he was not a one-hobby man; he had a wealth of pursuits – were those of a solitary boy. His love of music, later to be of great importance to him, developed at Rugby. He told others that they were missing a lot in reading sensational fiction rather than authors like Dickens and Scott (a priggish position that wasn't calculated to endear him to his frivolous contemporaries). He pursued his interest in natural history – particularly entomology – and on half-holidays escaped from the cricket which he thought so overrated. He roamed the hills and woods, and continued an interest in ornithology; an uncle had already introduced him to the charms of fishing. A contemporary recalled him as 'uncompromising in his hatred of what was, and of those who were, mean and unworthy'.[3] If that is accurate he must indeed have been an outstanding prig. He left Rugby at the end of 1886.

What was to happen to him next? What was certain was that it would be something different from Austen. Joe was quite clear about what Austen's career was to be. He had been born, as Joe put it, into a red despatch box, and Joe was determined that he would be a huge political success, starting with advantages which *he* had never had, and not needing to secure his financial position. Joe succeeded in this, as he did in almost everything to which he set his hand. Austen went to Trinity College, Cambridge, in 1882 to read History. To widen his experience of the world, he then spent nine months attending the École Libre des Sciences Politiques in Paris. While he was there he was able, through his father's range of contacts, to meet men of the stature of Georges Clemenceau, Léon Gambetta and Jules Ferry. He then moved on to Germany where he stayed for a year, listening to lectures on Prussian history, which alarmed him. Few young men have been so thoroughly groomed for high political office.

Neville was every bit as much his father's conscious creation, but here Joe was forming a son for a very different career. His role was to be in the preservation – indeed promotion – of the great Chamberlain commercial empire. That was why, just as Neville was beginning to find his academic feet at Rugby, Joe transferred him to the 'modern side', not the traditional route that would provide a liberal education and a gentleman's academic background but a novel and utilitarian training entirely appropriate for the world of business. In the same spirit, he did not go on to one of the ancient universities like Austen, but rather to learn about science, metallurgy and engineering at Mason College, Birmingham.* The college had been founded by a self-made Birmingham man, Sir Josiah Mason, to serve 'useful purposes for the benefit of the community ... trusting that I, who have never been blessed with children of my own, may yet in these students leave behind me an intelligent, earnest, industrious, truth-loving and truth-seeking progeny': aims which chimed exactly with Joe's sentiments.†

Neville made his way from home to Mason College for almost two years. At the end of his second year he was bottom in metallurgy, mathematics and engineering design. The problem may have been that he had done no science at school, but it's much more likely that he simply found the subjects mundane and unchallenging: at this time he was starting to widen his reading and his interest lay in the challenging works of Darwin, Huxley and others. He and his sisters became fascinated by the implications of what they read and discussed. At no time in life was he excited by the disciplines which were taught

* Just about the same time, Stanley Baldwin was being sent to the same institution by his ironmaster father, though the two don't appear to have met there.

† The backgrounds of the half-brothers were therefore really quite different: Austen the product of Cambridge, a classical education, association with the great men of the day, Neville transferred to the 'modern side' and was injected into practical and uncongenial preparation for the world of manufacturing, trade and profit. He was far too buttoned up to reveal any sense of grievance, but later there is, just discernible, a sly sense of satisfaction that he had outperformed Austen in his world of politics, *as well* as helping him out when he was short of money in the 1920s by recommending him for paid directorships. A form of mild sibling revenge perhaps?

at Mason College, where the staff remembered him as 'modest almost to shyness'.[4]

The ideas which Neville and his sisters immersed themselves in led to a swirl of speculation in which Joe had no interest, but, living at Highbury, Neville was also immersed in what did matter to Joe. In these years between Rugby and a wider world, Neville lived in a political forcing house:

> Politics were the stuff of life. For the study at Highbury was the hub of Birmingham, and Birmingham the driving-wheel of radical movement the anti-Gladstonian war. Here were formed the immortal phrases against the Tories, who 'toil not, neither do they spin', and here in silence matured the speeches of which so filled town halls that the benches must be taken out, and thousand would stand two hours to hear the sentences which struck like a dagger.[5]

It was now that Neville began to follow his father in teaching at the Sunday School of the Church of the Messiah in Broad Street. Adjoining it were the slums of Ladywood, where the church carried out mission work. Beatrice and the other girls worked as school managers, and a proportion of the family's money was devoted to charity, a key element of Joe's vision. One of William Kenrick's daughters recorded that Neville was born a social reformer and brought up in an atmosphere of precept and example. The precept and example were not unique in the best non-conformist homes of the time, but this household was an extreme example of the acknowledged need for positive, practical and unselfish involvement in society.

After the unprofitable two years at Mason College, the next stage in Neville's structured education was an apprenticeship with chartered accountants known as Howard Smith. This was much more to his liking than the confined world of Mason College, and Neville enjoyed the work, impressing his employers who asked him to stay on, but that was not his father's plan.

Neville's experience of life was expanded by expeditions to Italy, France and Egypt, and by the age of twenty he was a well-travelled young man. He had a wide range of interests, some of them country activities like shooting, entomology and fishing. His reading was perhaps a little unstructured but expanding, and he had a real interest in painting and particularly music. He had not had the benefit of a liberal education either at school or at university, the sort of education which encourages questioning and weighing up evidence, rather than accepting what one is told, but his structured reading programme to an extent remedied the deficiencies of his formal education.

He had benefitted from or been subjected to, whichever is the more appropriate description, the influence of proximity to Joe Chamberlain, this man of wit and humour, so dynamically animated by a sense of purpose. He could see, as Joe sought to master his grief, the need to present an image of strength to the world. He told his teachers at Mason College about the family motto, '*Je tiens ferme*'. He could see that his father's highest ambitions were reserved for his older half-brother, but this did not incommode him. He knew that Joe had been disappointed by his performance at school and at college, and feeling that one had let down a father like Joe Chamberlain was not a comfortable sensation. As time passed he became close to Joe and ultimately his father recognised that it was Neville and not Austen who was possessed of true ambitious ruthlessness.[6]

That growing confidence in his younger son was behind what happened next. With the end of his accountancy training, Neville was ready to go into the family business. At the end of 1888, Joe brought home his third wife, Mary Endicott, to whom Neville would become very close; she was the last person he spoke to on his deathbed. But her first impression of him was extreme immaturity. That was to be changed very soon. In the autumn of the following year, visiting her family, Joe Chamberlain had the meeting with Sir Ambrose Shea which was to lead to the purchase of Andros. Who was to look after the family's interests in this new sphere? 'We'll send Neville.'

## Chapter 7

# A Model Statesman

In the event, Neville may have been the half-brother who inherited Joe's character, but Austen *looked* much more like him, recreating his image almost to the point of absurdity. His image was that of the most distinguished of statesmen. 'If someone had ordered a statesman from Harrods', said Roy Jenkins, 'it would have been a copy of Austen Chamberlain which would have been delivered. Indeed he lived within a few hundred yards of the emporium.'[1] He was always immaculately, if archaically, turned out. Like his father he wore a monocle and frock coat; like his father he wore an orchid on his lapel. He was one of the last MPs to continue wearing a top hat inside the Commons chamber.

He continued to aim for elegance to the last. In old age he was short of money, although not as short as he thought. He had to sell his estate in Sussex and as Sir Robert Vansittart described it, spent his last years in 'straits and a small flat' from which he emerged 'immaculate in frayed white shirt and a shiny tailcoat'.[2] The monocle was not, or not entirely, an affectation. He, like Joe, had poor sight. Muhammad Ali Jinnah, the founder of Pakistan who practised at the English Bar when Austen was at the height of his powers, and himself a flashy dresser, was mesmerised by Chamberlain and thereafter wore a monocle in imitation of this marvellously well-dressed man.*

As well as *looking* like a successful politician, Austen Chamberlain *was* one. His impact on events seems slight today, yet he held almost every important political office except that of Prime Minister – and he could have had that if he had really wanted it. In the Unionist

* At the end of his life, Jinnah owned over 300 suits.

government of 1895 (the government in which Joe Chamberlain was Colonial Secretary), at the age of just thirty-two, Austen was Civil Lord of the Admiralty. In 1902, when Balfour had succeeded Salisbury, he entered the Cabinet as Postmaster General, sitting in the same Cabinet as his father: a rare double act. In October 1903, just a few months after Joe had delivered his tariff reform speech, he became Chancellor of the Exchequer. He could well have succeeded Balfour as leader of the party when the latter stood down in 1911, but he lacked the necessary drive, just as Balfour had lost the will to lead. In May 1915 he became Secretary of State for India under Asquith and remained in that position after Asquith had been deposed by Lloyd George. In May 1918 he was given a seat in the War Cabinet and he became Chancellor of the Exchequer again in January 1919. In the following year he was offered but declined the Indian Vice-Royalty, and in March 1921 succeeded the sick Bonar Law as leader of the Conservative Party. When in the following year the Conservatives decided to leave the Lloyd George coalition, Austen as leader of the party could have become Prime Minister if he had chosen. Instead, he remained loyal to Lloyd George. Bonar Law, apparently recovered from illness, was re-elected Conservative Party leader and it was he who became Prime Minister when a Conservative government replaced the coalition.

Bonar Law's recovery was alas illusory and he resigned both as party leader and Prime Minister in 1923. Again, Austen could have had the keys of Number Ten, but again he chose still to remain loyal to Lloyd George, who would never have been loyal to him. It was Baldwin who became Prime Minister.

In 1924, after a substantial Conservative victory, Baldwin reached out to bring Austen back into government and he became Foreign Secretary.* In the course of his time as Foreign Secretary he was intimately involved in drafting the Locarno Pact, an attempt to stabilise Western Europe under the League of Nations. In its time the Pact was regarded as a huge success, an immensely hopeful sign for the future. It very swiftly proved to be very far from that, but for the moment there was an outbreak of optimism not unlike that which followed

---

* Neville was very much involved in achieving the reconciliation, and the mechanics will be explored later.

Neville's return from Munich some years later. The King, amongst many others, thought it would mean peace for many years – perhaps for ever. Austen was made a Knight of the Garter and was awarded the Nobel Peace Prize in 1925. He remained in office and on the political scene for some time, but by 1928 he was fading into ill health and elder-statesmanship.

It is slightly strange that someone who had held so many of what could then be called (without today's risk of oxymoron) the Great Offices of State, and had come so close so often to holding the highest office of all, left so little trace on the political landscape through which he moved so effortlessly. There were several reasons for this.

One was tariff reform. Austen, unlike Joe – and Neville – had no very strong views on tariff reform. After Joe made his 1903 speech and withdrew from government, his dutiful elder son found himself obliged to support his father's position as far as he could, and this false position suggested a lack of consistency. Secondly, while he was without his father's drive and passion, he was still associated with the brashness of Birmingham vulgarity. Thirdly, his political positioning was awkward – duty to his father meant that he was a Liberal Unionist and not a Conservative. Instinctively, he was 'a born Conservative',[3] whereas Neville was a radical to the end of his life. Austen's innate Conservatism strengthened after the war, when he became increasingly concerned about a threat from the Labour Party and the forces of socialism, indeed communism. As a coalitionist he should have trusted the people. This is what Lloyd George was getting at when he made his famous remark about Austen: 'He has sat on the fence so long that the iron has entered his soul.' His ambivalent position in the Commons was not assisted by his lack of the common touch, a stiffness, an aloofness. In time he came to be seen as a bore, an honourable bore but a bore nonetheless, a party hack who always got a Cabinet post but was essentially a second-rate politician, and one whose career had been at the end of his father's coat-tails.

The relationship between the brothers was frequently difficult. Neville felt that Austen, as head of the family, deserved some deference, but he didn't let that affect his career unduly. Austen would have been less than human if he had not been piqued to be overtaken by the younger brother who had never been meant to enter politics, but he rose above that. In 1931 he decided that he did not want to pursue a ministerial career and said that the decision was made in order to make it easier for Neville to become Chancellor of the Exchequer, which he did. But without office Austen fell into depression and, above all, a sense of exclusion from the political inner circle. When their father had similarly been excluded after his stroke, Austen had taken enormous efforts to keep him in the loop, writing frequent and lengthy reports and visiting him whenever possible with news of what was happening at the centre. Neville, by contrast, had now little use for his brother, and Austen noticed that. He wrote to Hilda saying how he felt out of things and how much he would appreciate a weekly letter of Cabinet news from Neville. In reality, he was lucky if he saw his brother once in six months.

Austen and his immediate family were clear thereafter that a continued political career at the highest level would impose burdens on his strength which his delicate constitution would not support. But he had his self-respect, and after Baldwin became Prime Minister he was offended by the fact that the new leader did not give proper regard to his standing and seniority. Four days after Baldwin had been preferred to Curzon in May 1923 there was a long meeting between Baldwin and Austen, but nothing came of it: Baldwin had just been picking his brains. Austen later wrote to F. E. Smith, Lord Birkenhead, that he had been 'deeply wounded' and he told Neville that 'the discourtesy shown to me down to the last detail . . . was not expected and I profoundly resent it.'[4]

He didn't have Neville's robust health, and hypochondria was never far away: 'He had a lot of ailments and he made the most of them.'[5] He worried about his weight, his teeth and his blood pressure, about the dangers of nervous collapse and above all sciatica. On a retreat to Algiers in 1906 to recuperate from that illness he met Ivy Dundas to whom he became engaged within a few days. He cabled the news to his stepmother. She hoped that marriage would be a good cure for sciatica.

Ivy was a good wife; but she was very dismissive of her sister-in-law, Mrs Neville, to employ the old-fashioned form Churchill always used of her. Annie was also of a hypochondriac disposition, so Ivy might have been kinder, but she was very disparaging about her intellectual abilities. That was unfair. Annie may or may not have been less gifted than her sister-in-law, but she was no fool. Neville never failed to say how little he would have achieved without her.

Austen Chamberlain had great advantages and considerable ability. But his disadvantage, in addition to his lack of physical resilience, was the fact that he had no burning appetite – he had been groomed for a high office he didn't really want. He wasn't a fighter like his father or his brother, and he acknowledged that Neville was more like Joe than he was. He said he would rather have been a country gentleman and acquired a sixteenth-century home in Sussex.*

But it is a mistake to write him off too easily as a two-dimensional cardboard cut-out. After he entered the Chamber of the House, between his father and his uncle Richard, he remained there for forty-five unbroken years. He attained high office. He was decent and loyal. He was at least once within a hair's breadth of positioning himself for the office of Prime Minister, and if he did not do so because he was principled and not a killer, perhaps that should be entered as a credit and not a debit in his personal balance sheet.

He attracted a disproportionate number of jokes and unkind taunts. Balfour described him as 'a bore', Leo Amery as 'a self-satisfied ass', Beatrice Webb called him 'dull and closed-minded ... intellectually dense'. Roy Jenkins again, in superior style, described him as 'glossy in dress and grooming ... failing to notice the grandest magnates were distinctly unglossy'.[6] The jibes have been remembered. 'Poor man. Austen always plays by the rules – and always loses.' His achievements have been forgotten and it requires a real physical effort to arrive at a fair judgement of this frigid individual.

Despite his remark which has been quoted already, Leo Amery made this judgement when Chamberlain died: 'He just missed greatness and the highest position, but his was a fine life of honourable public service.'[7]

That is very fair and accurate, but it will not be remembered. As well as enjoying the Twitts Ghyll joke, Roy Jenkins was fond of telling a story which has been told of others too. It is said that Austen was having dinner at Polesden Lacey as a guest of Mrs Ronald Greville when his hostess noticed that her butler was, not for the first time,

* Roy Jenkins was so amused by the name of the house, Twitts Gyll, that he mentioned the fact in two different books.

very drunk. She handed him a note: 'You are very drunk; leave the room immediately.' He struggled to focus on the handwriting, placed it on a silver salver and, with stately grace, proceeded to deliver it to the glacial and austere Austen Chamberlain.

*Chapter 8*

# Back Home and Into Harness

Bronzed from the semi-tropical sun but badly bruised in spirit by the failure of the Andros venture, Neville returned to the Midlands. He came back a very tough young man after six years of long days of working semi-naked on the edge of the Caribbean.

Maintaining that fitness mattered to him. Every morning he opened *The Culture of the Abdomen* and undertook his drill. A cardboard chart hung in his bathroom illustrating the exercises from the great work. He never lost his lean and athletic bearing, and his weight remained under ten and a half stone. Although Joe had said that *his* only exercise was a cigar, he too had taken pride in his physical fitness, and ran up the steps at the Colonial Office two at a time. Neville's regime had made him far fitter than that, and he revelled in his hardness, taking long walks on the moors and eschewing frivolous luxuries. He would not hear of having a hot water bottle in his bed and when he had a bad cold and one of his sisters surreptitiously inserted one it didn't last the night.

Neville's bedroom in his father's house was high up in the bachelor's wing, a cold room with three outside walls. Until he consented to the installation of a grate it was heated by a small gas fire. On the morning after the hot water bottle incident Neville told his family that he had leapt out of the bed in a horror at finding it inhabited by a foreign body.

Morally, as well as physically, he had changed. Mary may have thought him immature when she first knew him, but his years of exercising authority and relying on his own judgement had changed that. The chastening effect of financial failure in Andros might have blunted his confidence and desire to succeed, but on the contrary, it had created a steely determination never to fail again.

Chamberlain is primarily remembered now as a political animal, but never having been intended for Parliament he went to Westminster late in life and was there for just twenty years. He spent almost as long in Birmingham after his return from Andros. By the time he entered the House, his character was fully formed, and it was moulded by the nineteen years of commercial activity, local politics and the personal life that preceded his entry to the national stage.

Neville was well aware that his primary responsibility now was to repair the financial damage of Andros and recreate a sound basis for the two political superstars, as well as to provide for himself, to which he brought great energy to bear. His approach in 1897 was very different from the lukewarm interest he had shown in Mason College or in jaunting into the countryside to examine the books of his accountant employers' clients. He was a transformed man, and within a few years following his return to Birmingham he was a dominating figure in local business life.

The family network offered a variety of entries into commerce. The Kynoch company was one choice. It manufactured explosives on an enormous scale, and was carefully considered. But, for political reasons, Joe was not anxious to develop the existing Chamberlain connection with the firm. The armaments connection was to be an embarrassment during the South African War – radical Liberals could see the connection between manufacturing explosives and imperial aggrandisement, and they didn't like it.

A safer opening was with Elliott's Metal Company Limited, usually just 'Elliotts'. This was a substantial metalworking company, also within the clan nexus, which produced and exported brass items, particularly to India. Neville became chairman and within a few years was the largest shareholder. He also bought over another metalworking firm, Hoskins & Son, a smaller but very successful and specialised business which manufactured and fitted berths for ships all over the world. Hoskins was very much his baby. He wrote to his Andros friend, Arthur Greenwood,* that as well as becoming a director of some copperworks, he had bought another business 'which I am going to smash up all by myself . . . I shall be transformed from a Colonial to a Provincial.'[1]

---

* Not to be confused with the Labour Party politician of the same name, whom we shall encounter later.

Elliotts didn't do badly: it ultimately became part of ICI. It employed 700 men making brass, most of which was exported to Benares, now Varanasi, to be turned into devotional items. Hoskins was much smaller. It employed only seventy men but the work was much more skilled and specialised, and it sent craftsmen around Britain and further afield to fit out cabins.

Later, and despite the potential political embarrassment, he became a director also of BSA, the Birmingham Small Arms Company. BSA came to be best known for making bicycles, motor bikes and cars, but as its name suggests it started out making weapons and ammunition. The ammunition side was sold in 1897, but the company continued to make small arms, notably machine guns, and did so in quantities during the Great War.

Neville was frank about his motives for his activity. He wrote to Greenwood: 'I was intended by nature to get through a lot of money. I should never be satisfied with a cottage, and having chucked away a competence – you know where – I am going to toil and moil till I grab it back again.'[2] The reference to what had happened on Andros and to the requirement to atone for that is revealing. 'Getting through a lot of money' is a bogus flourish: just like Joe, he wanted money to allow him to do the things that mattered to him. He had no interest in money for its own sake and stopped acquiring it as soon as he had enough for his purposes. When he died his estate was valued for probate at £84,000. Comparing historic money values with present-day equivalents is difficult, but it might be helpful to know how much fellow Prime Ministers left. Stanley Baldwin, who died after Chamberlain, left £281,000, and Ramsay MacDonald, who died before him, the illegitimate son of a ploughman, left £21,000. Austen Chamberlain, whose last years were plagued with worries and economies as a result of what he thought to be his poverty, left £45,000.

Neville was very much a hands-on boss. He worked long hours and did not try to escape from trivial duties. He rushed from appointment to appointment by bicycle and did not emerge from his office until well into the evening. Looking for business involved travelling throughout the United Kingdom – often by overnight journeys on trains with no sleeping cars. He knew his men and took an interest in their welfare. He held dinner parties for employees and the Hoskins staff were invited to his home for afternoon parties every few months. He was well liked, and the staff for their part made handsome presentations to him on important events, such as the birth of his first child.

The degree of Chamberlain's personal involvement in the minutiae of the business was unusual at the time, when directors and proprietors tended to hand over the drudgery of the day-to-day running of their concerns to managers. He was capable of delegation and was ready to hand responsibility to those he trusted, but he was always aware that being in business was about making money and that the secret of that meant getting in orders, controlling the cost of production and making sure that potential income was not left to stagnate in the form of unpaid bills. He evolved a system of incentives for swift settlement of accounts.

Just as remarkable as his dynamic energy was his concern for his workers. Very unusually, he encouraged trades union membership. He set up a profit-sharing scheme at Hoskins which involved bonuses of up to 5 per cent in return for productivity: in practice that meant that in a normal year each man received approximately an extra week's wages. There was a surgery and welfare supervisors at Elliotts. At Hoskins he established a pension plan quite separate from anything the state provided. After the outbreak of the First World War there was a scheme of war benefits at Elliotts for those who had been too badly injured in the war to resume work and for the dependants of those who did not return.

During the war he had to retarget objectives. Hoskins pretty well stopped making ships' berths and were asked to build a steel mill. The government didn't waste much time in attempting to control the costs of the operation: that was left to Chamberlain's discretion. It's to his credit that when hard-faced men, as John Maynard Keynes said, were doing well out of the war, Neville continued to share profits with the workforce through the bonus scheme.

The family also made their own sacrifices. Highbury became a military hospital, so there was nothing hypocritical in what the directors said to the workforce, albeit rather floridly: it was 'a patriotic duty to see that everything shall be completed in the shortest possible time and in the best possible manner . . . The directors express their confidence that by good work and good time-keeping you will ensure that your services shall be retained so that next year you may participate in whatever funds they may then be able to distribute.'[3]

Not all employers rose to the level of events and there certainly was profiteering in Birmingham as in other industrial centres. The fault wasn't only with the bosses: there were scrambles and recriminations in a pre-conscription period, as workers tried to take advantage of elevated wages. There were strikes in 1915 – though not to any extent in the Chamberlain factories. Neville took great pride in that.[4] His reaction to the strikes elsewhere is interestingly balanced. He wrote, 'Some of our working-classes have failed to understand the situation, but their ignorance and indifference is paralleled by that of many members of the middle-class who should have enlisted and yet won't do so until they are forced.'[5]

The profit-sharing, the bonuses, the welfare provision were obviously not divorced from the profit-motive, but it would be facile to conclude that that was his only objective. There was a real concern for the welfare of his people. There was a concern also for the welfare of society in an almost abstract sense. Chamberlain wanted a neat, ordered scheme of things. To some degree this was an extension of what Joe had been after, and it was consistent with the non-conformist drive for betterment; but he put his own twist on these influences and that can be seen by putting what he did in business against the context of what he did in local government, and what he did in terms of domestic and economic reforms in Parliament.

His views about social issues developed in a pragmatic direction which had nothing to do with traditional party politics. He was ready to take control of the liquor trade out of the hands of the publicans and brewers because of the need for productivity during the war. Of the Municipal Bank, which he founded, he said, 'I have never been frightened by a name; I do not care whether it is Socialism or not, so long as it is a good thing.'[6] He thought that the extensions of state control during the war – over the railways for example – should not be reversed when peace came. He believed that there should be a minimum wage and that industrial workers should be given seats on boards of control of the enterprises in which they worked. *Representation* on consultative council was not enough: they should have real *control*. Revolutionary views indeed.

## Chapter 9

# The Domestic Cocoon

The most notable thing about Chamberlain's domestic life was its very domesticity; it was a given that national politics weren't for him. In 1901, during the South African War, Joe Chamberlain said to an acquaintance that he thought Austen had a good chance of becoming Prime Minister but that if he had been talking about Neville he would have been quite certain of it. Neville was abler; but he wasn't interested in national politics. Participation in even local politics was a matter of duty: he found public speaking difficult, although he was to do a lot of it in the Birmingham years in connection first with his extensive forays into non-political public life and latterly in local politics.

What he was interested in was his family. He became closer to Joe now than he had ever been. With him he inspected the orchids in the extensive greenhouses, maintaining a detailed record of the plants in a loose-leaf file. When Joe was at Highbury the two men talked; and he talked even more to his sisters. The closeness of his relations with his sisters is remarkable. They were far from permanently resident at Highbury, but when they were away the tradition of very long weekly letters that had started in Andros continued, as it would continue until his death. The siblings are frank, effusive and outspoken in their corre-spondence, and the nature of the relationship gives the lie to the idea that Neville was – other than publicly – an unemotional creature. When his youngest sister, Ethel, died in 1903, he was much hit by her death.

In the course of the Birmingham years he managed to travel exten-sively, often with his sisters. The scope of his travels contrasts with the notion that he was uncomfortable on foreign soil when he went to meet Hitler. In those years he was in France four times, in Italy three times and in Dalmatia, Algeria, Holland, Switzerland, Burma and India. These visits were not given over to superficial sightseeing: he took a detailed interest in the places he visited. The expedition to India and Burma, for instance, occupied four months. He already knew Egypt and the United States, and, of course, the Bahamas. Later he would visit Canada and East Africa.

When he was alone, he continued in his solitary hobbies, pursuing his studies of Darwin, ornithology, botany and entomology. But his interests were preponderantly outdoor. He fished and shot, and when his uncle, Sir George Kenrick, made shooting and fishing in Scotland available to him he seized the opportunity with delight. He tested himself. In Normandy he cycled forty miles in a day. In England he could spend a week riding on the Wiltshire Downs and when he was on a cure at Aix-les-Bains, he walked fifteen or twenty miles every other day.

Not all of his interests were pursued in solitary isolation. He went with his cousin George on expeditions into Wyre Forest and Chaddesley Woods searching for insects. He became treasurer of the Birmingham Botanical and Horticultural Society and turned its finances from a deficit into a surplus. He served as a trustee and vice-president of the Society and revived the twice-yearly shows which took place in the Botanical Gardens, giving the Society gifts of money and of plants, as he would continue to do for forty years.

If the young Neville was at heart a warm and sensitive soul, why was he still a bachelor? The answer is that he wanted a wife but simply couldn't find one. He wrote to his friend Arthur Greenwood in the Bahamas in 1901 saying that he was 'growing into a regular old bach-elor – faddy and fussy, you know.* I feel a bit restless sometimes at the idea but haven't come across the lady yet and begin to think there isn't one!'[1] There were, though, opportunities of meeting women. At Highbury, a dance floor was laid out in the great hall. The extended family danced and partied regularly, though Neville wasn't much of a dancer. He inflicted his waltzing on the extensive and available cous-ins. Hilda said, however, that he was a popular party partner because he could talk even if he couldn't dance, but his conversational style was too forensic for the local girls.

---

* He was in fact just thirty-two.

The difficulty in meeting kindred spirits was compounded by the amount of time he devoted to work and local public life, but he was on the lookout for love and he thought he had found it in the form of Rosalind Craig Sellar, a professional singer and a friend of Hilda whom he met in 1903. She performed at the Birmingham Triennial Festival in 1900 and 1903, and was much discussed in the course of a visit Neville made to Italy in the autumn of 1903 with Hilda and Ida. His diary contains repeated suspicious deletions and excisions. He wrote to Mary:

> the girls are very nice about it and Hilda in particular gives me much sympathy. I have cross questioned her closely about possible rivals but she doesn't think that there is anyone established. If only he isn't establishing himself now ... I can't help returning to the subject which fills so much of my thoughts ... This is the most egotistical letter I ever wrote, all I – I – I –, but I hope you will pardon it. Of course it is not to be answered. I have written it for the pleasure of writing to one who understands and sympathises and to whom I am very grateful for her help of every kind.[2]

In his diary and the correspondence there is a slight sense of hope-lessness. It may proceed from hindsight, because on his return to England, and despite an idyllic half hour when he was able to speak to Rosalind alone – there *were* rivals – he had to admit defeat. He felt the despair of a rejected suitor. He feared that full happiness and the serenity of reciprocated love would be denied to him forever. His admission to his stepmother reveals the man's stoicism and self-disci-pline: 'I have all the family instinct and cannot bear to let my agony be seen, so you will all help me best by never speaking to me of this again.'

This attitude of mind reflects something Neville had said to his Andros friend Father Matthews when the latter was burdened by debt: '[Y]ou have deliberately chosen a difficult path and are fighting your way through like a man, and though I cannot pretend to be a religious man yet I do honour above all anyone who does what he conceives to be right without flinching.'[3]

The correspondence between Neville and, in particular, Hilda at this stage is particularly touching. Hilda took on Ethel's little daughter,

Hilda Mary, and Hilda and Neville corresponded about the implications of this, particularly in relation to Hilda's possible marriage. He wrote to her very sensitively and perceptively, aware that both of them wanted to marry but could see no immediate prospect of doing so. She was equally delicate in her letters, aware that he was bracing himself to a life without love. On his fortieth birthday she wrote to him:

> You've got a fine position in the town by the work (hard enough but not outwardly conspicuous) which you have put into it, and it is a wonderful tribute to the way in which character and ability tell. Besides, in spite of your forty years, you impress everyone with your promise as well as your performance. You will be like Papa in that you will go on growing and developing every year, instead of standing still or sinking back into the ruck of middle age as so many men do. You are the prop of the family financially, but you are a great deal more than that to all of us, and you are life and spirit itself to me.[4]

What is particularly interesting is that he is no longer talking about rejection by Rosalind – and there had never really been a grand passion there anyway. What he was suffering from wasn't unreciprocated love for a woman he adored. He was suffering not from love, but from a lack of love. It is unusual for an abstract absence to matter so much – and to be so frankly referred to.

But his life was not to be without love, and that, as in the case of so much else in Chamberlain's personal life, was due to a sister (or half-sister), Beatrice. Indeed, the wide resources of the Chamberlain clan were involved because Annie de Vere Cole, in a complicated and not particularly interesting way, was part of the family.*

When Annie visited her aunt at Cannes in April 1910, she met Joseph and his wife and Beatrice. Beatrice sensed the possibilities and invited Annie to meet Neville at a dinner and theatre party in London. They were engaged just a few weeks later – Neville was a hot-blooded suitor – and married shortly afterwards, on 5 January 1911. Although Annie initially had some difficulty in making up her mind, Neville was *very* determined: Annie said that he gave her no choice and Aunt

---

* Her uncle Alfred married Lillian, the widow of Joe Chamberlain's younger brother, Herbert.

Lillian, who very much approved of the match, said that her nephew's methods took her breath away. Annie came from a military family. She was a woman possessed of great charm and sympathy, but determined too, and ambitious in her way. She had travelled purposefully in her youth, visiting a different European country every year.

Neville sent a telegram to Beatrice, who was in America: JUST ENGAGED TO ANNIE COLE. ALL YOUR FAULT. He cut his moustache shorter as Annie wanted, and his letters to her during the engagement are ecstatic: 'My own darling Annie', 'My dearest, best and sweetest girl'. Her love 'is the most precious thing on earth to me and to know from you that I have it makes me happier than I can say'. 'I love and want you more than ever, indeed I can't do without you. I can't be too glad that we fixed our wedding reasonably soon, for it would be intolerable to have to wait a moment longer.'[5] All of this is a little cloying in cold print, but it corroborates what Hilda Chamberlain said: that her brother was a domestic man and that only family life brought him true happiness.

Annie was twenty-nine when she married (a little older than average as a bride in those days) and her bridegroom forty-one. Despite his worries about bachelorhood, Neville, at forty-one, was not unusually old for a man of his class and of his time to be getting married; Austen had been a year older.

Annie's brother Horace was a famous practical joker. At Cambridge he dressed up as the uncle of the Sultan of Zanzibar and made a formal visit to the city and university. He was received by the Mayor and shown over a number of colleges. On another occasion he and his friends dressed as workmen and dug up a part of Piccadilly Circus which remained in that state for some six weeks. Most famously he appeared as the Emperor of Abyssinia, and with his suite arrived to inspect HMS *Dreadnought*. One of his entourage was Virginia Woolf, wearing a moustache, beard, gold chain and turban. The Emperor and his interpreter, Adrian Stephen (Woolf's brother), spoke in a mixture of Latin and Greek – 'A rum lingo they speak', said one of the junior officers. There was great embarrassment about the episode, in the course of which the Royal Abyssinian Order had been conferred on the Admiral, appropriate flags had been hoisted and a special train ordered.

Annie asked Neville at their first meeting what he thought about this. Tact did not get in the way of honesty and he admitted that he deprecated the incident. Fortunately she was of the same view, as was the case in most matters. They may not have been facetious, but they shared a love of music and the arts, and also of outdoor pursuits and the countryside. In Birmingham she cycled around his ward and constituency, talking to everyone she met. In time she encouraged Neville to look beyond Birmingham and sustained him when he bore the burdens of Prime Minister. He claimed that he would never have reached that position without her and that she had inspired a devotion amongst those on whom he relied. She lived until February 1967, having helped Keith Feiling when he was compiling the official biography.

One historian has said that Annie was in need of a husband, 'as even the dimmest observer would have recognised'.[6] It is true that at twenty-nine she was no doubt aware that she risked missing the matrimonial bus. He also says that she was not rich, nor intelligent. The former is true, but it's not clear that the second is the case. She was lively, unpredictable and undisciplined, but that is not to say that she was dim. The idea that she wasn't particularly bright seems to have originated from Austen's wife, Ivy, who never greatly liked her. Neville's sisters, however, did. And despite her illnesses – just like Austen she was a hypochondriac prone to depression and nervous exhaustion – she was a devoted and loving wife who supported and indeed encouraged her husband's ambitions.

Joe Chamberlain's wedding present cost £1,000 and consisted partly in jewels for Annie. Hoskins gave a generous present, as did the various family employees. The young couple set up home, refurbishing a house built in the classical style in 1824, Westbourne, conveniently next to the botanical gardens in Edgbaston. Neville settled into domestic life. He was interested in the gardens and he himself concentrated on a large rockery. The gardener, Mr Cat, was to work for Chamberlain for thirty years – Cat was slow of speech with quaint vocabulary, and Chamberlain did a perfect imitation of him. One of the garden boys, Ernie Darlow, was asked by Chamberlain, 'Are you doing gardening just to fill in, or do you want to get on and learn a trade properly?' When the boy said he wanted to learn a trade seriously, Chamberlain said that he should go to evening classes and that he would inspect the boy's homework. Chamberlain opened a garden diary, which he maintained from 1911 to 1939. He also opened 'the Gentleman's Cellar Book' and recorded his stocks of wine, annotated with the comments of a connoisseur. He was particularly fond of port but it was consumed with moderation and is unlikely to have had anything to do with the excruciating gout he suffered from.

Annie was pregnant quite soon after the marriage and Chamberlain thought it was the crowning joy: '[T]hough it comes very late to me I am so thankful that it should come at all that I have no room for regret. I want *lots*! And only wish I could get them all at once.'[7] Dorothy was born on Christmas Day 1911, 'A splendid baby with no resemblance to her father that I can see but like her mother, which is lucky for her.' Hoskins presented an ornament in silver and the poor office boy, Charlie Bridges, had to make a speech. Chamberlain insisted that Charlie have a drink which was a mistake – Charlie changed colour and had to sit down.

Poor incapacitated Joe had already been besotted by Austen's two sons, and he now doted on Dorothy. Alas, when he tried to attract the attention of the children, his inarticulate grunts sometimes distressed them. Neville and Annie visited him whenever they could and to his delight Dorothy was sent to stay with him on one occasion. Annie had become like a favourite daughter to him.

When Joe died on 2 July 1914, Austen left Birmingham for good. Neville didn't. Like his father, he saw Birmingham as his essential base. Neville suggested that his father's library should be preserved, but the government had no interest in the suggestion, and so while Highbury itself was used as a military hospital, the contents, from oriental china to state papers, were sold in their entirety. Neville paid just under £20 for a few pieces for himself.

Dorothy's brother, Frank, was born on 22 January 1914. Neville Chamberlain's relationship with his young children was surprising. Children born in the first decade or two of the twentieth century to a man who had lived through three decades of the previous one mostly got a fairly standard Victorian paterfamilias. Neville Chamberlain, by contrast, treated his children in a very modern way, acting and reacting with them in terms of affectionate equality, ready to make himself a figure of fun. He said that he thought Frank would never have Dorothy's brains: when Neville deliberately gave the wrong names to animals in a scrapbook Frank immediately said 'Yes', whereas Dorothy caught him out at once. 'But when he comes up in the morning and seizes my hands, shouting "Come 'long Papa, p'ay toys", he is irresistible.'[8] A letter to the sisters had to be broken off every couple of minutes because Dorothy came running up to talk to him. She had been given a sandbox and twice in the course of the morning had dragged Neville out to build a castle and to play the part of a visitor, a policeman, a butler and finally the king. The castle was ornamented with a piece of holly. This isn't the dried-up Chamberlain of popular imagination. One of his biographers says that it is not easy for those who imagine Chamberlain as a dry, conventional figure 'to imagine his zest and sense of fun'.[9] In the course of an early summer holiday in 1916 the Chamberlains went to Abersoch, a seaside resort on the Welsh coast, and walked miles barefoot along the beach and lay basking in the sun: Neville was at the heart of a surprisingly relaxed and modern household.

Austen and his wife, Ivy, gradually drifted out of the tight family nexus, but Neville and his sisters remained as close after his marriage as they had been before; indeed Annie was like a sister herself to the sisters. Although by now Chamberlain was a captain of industry, Lord Mayor of Birmingham and a well-known figure even at a national level, he and his family remained very close, unpretentious, delighting in the little things of life.

These Birmingham years marked the emergence of Neville Chamberlain as a significant and successful businessman finally surrounded by the reassuring cocoon of family life. Hand in hand with his increasing security and confidence he was to develop an astonishing range of activities in the local community, first in apolitical public affairs and then in municipal politics.

*Chapter 10*

# Earnest Engagements

The range of bodies in which the youngish Chamberlain was involved – and he was very much *involved*, no mere member – is formidable. They included the Institute of Mechanical Engineers, the Birmingham and District Clerks' Provident Association, the Territorial Army, the Birmingham General Hospital, the University, the London School of Tropical Medicine, the Birmingham Jewellers' and Silversmiths' Association, and the Navy League.[1]

It's worth noting that in many of these allegiances, he was following in Joe's footsteps. The importance to Neville of continuing the great work of a great father cannot be overestimated, and I make no apology for emphasising it. The creation of the University of Birmingham had been one of Joe's pole projects: he had worked hard for its establishment and was its first Chancellor in 1900. Neville had a remarkable ability to raise funds for any of the charities or organisations which he favoured, and the University was an important beneficiary of his efforts. For example, in a period of trade depression in 1908–09, the University was particularly short of cash. Neville raised £250,000, and joined the University council. There was a pleasing circularity here, as the University was, in part, a new incarnation of Mason College. He was aware that his own education had been patchy and he wanted young people to have the opportunity of a more rigorous approach.[2]

The most important focus for his activities was healthcare. He was a member of Birmingham General Hospital's Board of Management and became its chairman. Before his more formal involvement with the hospital, he had been an official visitor, a role which, unlike most of the other visitors, he took very seriously. On one occasion when he arrived at a casualty department to see for himself what was happening he was assumed to be a patient and asked to remove his cap. He insisted on getting behind the scenes, examining the kitchens, looking at details like the laborious way in which cream was being removed from milk and making practical improvements. He was also Treasurer of the Birmingham General Dispensary. The Provident Dispensaries Scheme involved providing medical help as a matter of right, a foreshadowing of William Beveridge and his report that would form the basis of the post-Second World War welfare state.

His vision was remarkably modern. An efficient system of medical relief was one that allowed a working man to go to a doctor – and a doctor who had time to give him proper attention and who, if possible, should have some previous knowledge of his constitution. It should also be a system which would permit the person who was too ill to go to a doctor to be visited by a medical man, and in which patients should not have to go too far to the doctor's surgery in hours when they could be earning wages. Finally, it should be a system which would enable a patient to obtain, if necessary, the assistance of a consultant or specialist at a fee in some measure adapted to his means; and, if the case could only be properly treated at the hospital, the patient should be able to go there with a recommendation from his doctor, and not be badgered for the production of a ticket to justify his treatment.[3]

His programme involved persuading the best medical practitioners to work on the dispensary scheme for half their normal fee. Left to himself, Chamberlain would have gone further. He wanted municipal or state control of the larger hospitals. He instituted a triage system, so that patients who had formerly clogged up the outpatient departments of the hospital were routed direct to local surgeries. In this he created a system that was widely applied later when Lloyd George passed the 1911 National Insurance Act. This was all very revolutionary and was certainly not part of the Tory creed. Instead, it smacked of socialism.

His various initiatives added up to a complicated programme which involved upsetting an array of established practices' vested interests. His immersion in the detail of the issues and his involvement in the consequent negotiations were typical of the approach which he brought to technical problems both in Birmingham and later at Westminster. He was also a magistrate, active in the Chamber of Commerce and was Honorary Secretary of the local Liberal Unionist Association. There was pretty well nothing that he didn't take on if he felt he could be of any value – and all this was in addition to working hard and long to build up his businesses.

In addition to these more formal appointments he continued to teach at Sunday School, although he had by now given up his belief in formal religion. He shared his enthusiasm for Darwinism with his pupils in the Sunday School – a risky business – as he did in the Birmingham and Edgbaston Debating Society of which he became president (*nota bene*: as Joe had been). When he retired as president in September 1910, his valedictory address was on human development as an aspect of natural selection. Again ahead of his time, his address highlighted the injurious effect of human activity upon natural selection. Species were being extinguished and if 'stringency of selection' was interfered with then 'some day, when the race has forgotten the existence of consumption or measles or smallpox, one of these diseases may reappear and, falling on a people which has laid aside its armoury of immunity, bring about a catastrophe more hideous than any yet recorded.'[4]

Apart from his secretaryship of the Liberal Unionist Association, these activities were not political, and in those days in any case local politics were not necessarily conducted in an explicitly partisan way. Particularly in rural areas, there were many independent representatives on the County Councils. Local politics and the sort of participation in local affairs in which Chamberlain had engaged from his early days in Birmingham were part of the same phenomenon.

He continued to make it clear that he had no wish at all to be involved in national politics – indeed he doubted his qualifications for the life. He would turn down several suggestions in the coming years that he should stand for Westminster, but equally it was inevitable that he would move into *local* politics. After all, he was not allergic to political life. He had been deputising for Joe, whose medical condition was kept very quiet, and spoke for him frequently. He already talked of tariff reform with enthusiasm (when Austen only pretended to do so). He spoke at Liberal Unionist meetings and at meetings of various tariff reform associations. He said that he had been in favour of tariff reform for years, and was optimistic about its adoption, even after the Liberal landslide in 1906.

In all this he was supported by Annie. She had complete confidence in Neville, and it was she, rather than Neville, who already foresaw a role for him in national politics, and would encourage him to think of going to London. She was clear – and she was far from alone – that he had the qualities that were needed. It is significant that his entry into local politics followed very shortly on his marriage.

He first had an approach from the City Council asking if he would consent to become an Alderman. The role of Alderman – now extinct except in an honorific form – was a strange one. It was an office dating from Anglo-Saxon times (the word is a corruption of the Old English *ealdorman*) and it involved election to the council not by the electorate but by councillors. In terms of status, an Alderman ranked immediately after the Mayor. Until the practice was proscribed, an Alderman could be elected by outgoing council members, so that the control of the council would often remain in the hands of a defeated political party.

For that reason, and as the Alderman's tenure was six years as opposed to three years for an ordinary council member, Aldermen were not synonymous with a vibrant modern democracy. Chamberlain declined the offer and instead sought the approval of the electorate as a Liberal Unionist candidate for an ordinary councillorship in November 1911. His manifesto, typically, emphasised town planning, development of canals and inland waterways, and the importance of improved technical education. These were exactly the practical if unexciting issues that absorbed him throughout his life. If he had been asked he would have said that politics weren't meant to be exciting or dramatic: politics were about practical improvement. For him the attraction of the council was in these strands: town planning, education and health. For the moment, they fused into the creation of Greater Birmingham, but later they were what animated his great reforming period at Westminster. *They* were what he was about; and yet he's remembered for involvement in areas of policy that were alien to him.

He joined the council of a vibrant city at a pivotal moment. The Greater Birmingham Act had received the Royal Assent just five months earlier, on 3 June 1911. The act greatly expanded the area of the city, taking in parts of Warwickshire, Staffordshire and Worcestershire. Birmingham now became the largest local authority outside London, overtaking Glasgow, which had been much the larger city in 1900.* Joe Chamberlain had extravagantly claimed the title of 'Second City of the Empire' for Birmingham some years before. Now, it was a reality.

Neville Chamberlain's abilities were recognised as soon as he joined the council. He was immediately appointed chairman of the Town Planning Committee of this new vast conurbation as well as of the Health Committee. He enacted the first two town planning schemes in Britain in the course of the next two years, and in 1913 he was appointed chairman of the Special Committee to address the housing conditions of the poor. This was work which he regarded as crucially important. Two years later he spoke about moving 'the working classes from their hideous and depressing surroundings to cleaner, brighter and more wholesome dwellings in the still uncontaminated country which lay within [Birmingham's] boundaries'.⁵ He was utterly sincere, and his ambition was not an ignoble one. It was an ambition in which he was substantially successful.

These preoccupations were not those of the ordinary Tory or even the ordinary Liberal Unionist, and his anomalous concern about the conditions of ordinary people was recognised at the time. It was said that 'he should have been a Labour Man'.⁶

Chamberlain was an outstanding administrator. There was little doubt that he would become Lord Mayor and that he did in 1915, following – of course – in his father's footsteps, as well as those of ten other relatives. He wrote to his stepmother, 'At the moment of putting on my armour, I feel how far I am short of what Father's son should be, but it is a great encouragement to know that I shall have your good will and good wishes. I have often thought lately how pleased and interested he would have been in my new office and it will be my endeavour not to disgrace him.'⁷

Initially he consciously copied his father's way of speaking – people frequently said they were reminded of him. The imitation became progressively less marked, but Chamberlain remained conscious that

---

* Boundary changes made a big difference of course, but between 1900 and 1910 Birmingham's population increased by 245 per cent.

he looked at things in the way his father had done; although, with characteristic humility (in public, anyway) he maintained that his powers of imagination, his grasp and his originality were not those of his father. In truth they were not; but in his diligence he was superior. By now he had been re-elected to the council, this time as an Alderman: he had won his spurs and didn't need to prove his popularity. He was subsequently re-elected for a second term as Lord Mayor although supervening events meant that he did not serve out the whole of that second term. Lloyd George is said to have described Chamberlain as a good Mayor of Birmingham in a bad year. It wasn't Lloyd George's wittiest remark, and it could not have been less truthful. Greater Birmingham was a new concept, almost an ideal. Birmingham was akin to a medieval city-state, and Chamberlain ruled his fiefdom like a Renaissance prince, unshackled by the central government controls which were to develop later in the century. The city was to a large extent autonomous and it was also an autarky: at that time local government expenditure was not underwritten by central government. The city was responsible for everything that went on within its boundaries; and beyond those boundaries it had farms and reservoirs in Wales and sanatoria in the Cotswolds. It was an immense enterprise, and could only be ruled by a powerful, able and confident leader.

Chamberlain had the right qualities and he enjoyed himself and impressed himself favourably on the council. At that stage in his life, he reached out to Labour as he would not do later. He got on well with his Labour colleagues on the council and it is interesting that when he welcomed the TUC to its annual meeting in Birmingham in September 1916 he explained his essentially non-partisan, and perhaps more accurately socialist, plans for the city and asked for cooperation between capital and labour. His vision then was an infinitely generous one. Later, his political spirit was outstandingly cribbed and mean.

Despite or because of the scale of Chamberlain's mayoral vision, a history of his mayoralty would be infinitely tedious since it would reflect the essence of his purpose, which was to seek practical solutions by investigation, discussion and negotiation to the multiplicity of small problems which needed to be resolved in sum, to enhance the quality of life. Happily this is not a history of his mayoralty and I wish simply to touch on one or two of the strands of his time in office, in order to explore the man.

First of all, as in business, he was hands-on. He never had an easy and relaxed style, although he was now rather more accessible to the ordinary man and woman than he would be later. A response to an informal, even amusing, address he gave to one audience was 'Ain't 'e awful!', which suggests the music hall cheeky chappy. He was free from pomposity, and there was no sense of talking down. Annie, too, certainly didn't stand on her dignity, and as she carried out many engagements on his behalf, she related easily to ordinary people.

When the war broke out Neville raised money to send every Birmingham man at the front a tin containing a Christmas pudding and biscuits. The men were to know they were being remembered, because 'they are perpetually afraid that they have passed out of mind'.[8] He and Annie devised a message of sympathy for the families of those who died: 'We feel sure it will ever be a source of pride to you to know that in giving up his life in the noblest of all causes he has won the undying gratitude of his Country.' Neville and Annie signed each one of these cards themselves, and Annie and fellow workers visited the bereaved wives and mothers. Similarly, Neville and Annie toured the hospitals on Christmas Day, visiting every ward in the course of no less than six hours, all the while, as Chamberlain unexpectedly described it, 'doing the affable' – not the expression of a humourless man. Presents between the adults in the Chamberlain family were banned as being inappropriate in a time of war, but the children weren't affected by the ban. After the stint in the hospital, Chamberlain went to the far end of his garden, dressed up as Father Christmas, and arrived at the house with his sack of presents.

The war had a huge impact on Birmingham. For a start, in response to the need for economy, Chamberlain waived half the mayoral salary. He would have had difficulty in getting by on the reduced figure of £500 a year but for the generosity of his uncle George Kenrick, who turned what would have been a legacy into an immediate gift.

Chamberlain's agenda for his mayoralty was tripartite. Housing and health have been mentioned; his third objective was the transformation of Birmingham in other ways: 'I should like to get my three Lord Mayoral ideas carried through – bank, orchestra and civic recreation; if only I live, I fancy I shall do it.'[9]

At the start of the war, Birmingham had no Trustee Savings Bank or anything of the sort, and the city, like others throughout Britain, was asked to establish a savings committee to help fund the war. Chamberlain had seen the need for a local bank before he became Lord Mayor, but as soon as he had the mayoral powers he was able to do something about it. As ever, he didn't behave as Conservative politicians and businessmen elsewhere in the country tended to: he thought the bank would better be run by the city than by private enterprise. He got ahead with this in the face of considerable hostility. There was resistance from the existing joint-stock banks, and from trades union members. Bosses were to be responsible for transferring sums on behalf of their employees to the bank, but the unions didn't want employers to know about the private circumstances of their employees. Finally, the Treasury in London saw the project as encroaching on its role and undermining projects such as war loans. The government preferred that Birmingham should do like other towns and work through the National Savings Movement. Chamberlain, on the other hand, was looking beyond the war, towards what he saw as, although he did not use the term, a property-owning democracy, in which people would save for their own houses. Chamberlain very speedily became frustrated by the Treasury's blinkered approach and by its slow pace of working, so different from his own drive and vigour.

He lobbied the government through Austen, who was discouraging and unhelpful. After a few months Austen confirmed that the government was not likely to do anything. Neville got involved personally, and after a great deal of negotiation, done in a very short space of time, the bank was established. Birmingham guaranteed a high rate of interest and deposits were made from workers' salaries. The confidentiality issue was addressed by allowing a committee in each factory to have access to the books. An additional encouragement to savings were prizes, drawn by lot – an early form of premium bond.

The experience of dealing with the government and the Treasury was instructive for Chamberlain. He reflected that if he had been an MP he couldn't possibly have promoted such a scheme, but as Lord Mayor 'Hey Presto, it goes through in a twinkling!' This disillusionment with London and its ways was reflected in other matters. German air raids had begun, and Neville discovered that instituting air-raid precautions, even of the most basic kind, seemed to be beyond the wit of government. He immediately went off to the Home Office. He had formulated a plan which involved dividing the Midlands into districts, and a series of warnings of different characters would be issued as airships (a bigger threat than aeroplanes at this stage), crossed the coast. Further warnings would be given as other observation lines were crossed. All very like the system which operated in the Second World War. He liaised with the mayors of all the Midlands towns, along with Lord French for the military, and with Lloyd George, Minister of Munitions at this stage. The detail of what he was doing, the micromanagement and the consequent control over civilian lives is remarkable, as was the drive with which he pushed his proposals through. An office bearer from another city told him that when he had been at the War Office he had mentioned Chamberlain's name. 'Don't send *him* here again', was the anguished response.

In the course of all this, Chamberlain was becoming known and respected, if not necessarily liked, at a national level. In 1915 Lloyd George asked him to serve on the Liquor Control Board, which was designed to reduce the effect of the consumption of alcohol on the war effort. He impressed his colleagues, but decided fairly soon that he couldn't combine attendance at the Control Board with the discharge of his duties as Lord Mayor.

Lloyd George was in some ways a little like Neville Chamberlain. He was a practical man who was ready to break with tradition to get things done, but the similarity doesn't go much further than that. Lloyd George was devious, little trammelled by principle and ultimately unreliable, whereas Chamberlain's principles were undeviating. All the same, Chamberlain was glad when Lloyd George replaced Asquith as Prime Minister in December 1916. Whatever Neville thought of Lloyd George's personal qualities, he could see nothing but good in his replacing the vacillating Asquith. His experience as a dynamic Lord Mayor had developed his allergy to inertia and stasis.

What Chamberlain wanted was a streamlined and efficient direction of the war. He had supported the Territorial Army from the time that Richard Haldane established it, and he was strongly in favour of an assertive defence policy, which the traditional wing of the Liberal Party certainly was not. Given the easy assumption that he was not wholehearted in his resistance to Hitler and shrank from the more muscular approach expressed by Churchill, it is worth recording his views well before the outbreak of the First World War. He wrote to his friend Arthur Greenwood in 1908, 'Although Asquith has declared his intention to maintain the two-power standard in the Navy, I have no confidence that he will hold out against the fanatics and demagogues who clamour for economy at any price ... [T]he real enemy is Germany.'[10] At this time, incidentally, Churchill was resisting pressure for increases in the naval estimates. Neville demanded eight new battleships, and criticised this 'accursed mischievous, cowardly govern-ment'.[11] Just as in the case of the navy, he was vocally critical about reductions in the size of the army.

Chamberlain's mayoralty wasn't just drains and planning. He was a deeply sensitive and artistic man. Music was of all the arts the one which meant most to him, but painting and literature, and aesthetic appreciation in its widest sense, were also important. Just as he was sustained – as he remained throughout his life – by an artistic hinter-land, he wanted the lives of the people of Birmingham to be enriched by exposure to the arts. They were as important to Chamberlain's city-state as they were to Lorenzo the Magnificent in his.

Birmingham had had a Museum and Art Gallery since 1885, but unlike some great cities in Europe and America, it had no resident orchestra. In Manchester the Hallé Orchestra had played in the Free Trade Hall since 1858 (why does Birmingham not have a Tariff Reform Hall?) and it was after a visit by the Hallé to Birmingham in 1916 that Chamberlain became seized by the idea of an opera or orchestra for Birmingham, partly funded by the city. Again, he was not averse to spending public money for a project that was partially social engineering: cheap seats were to be available to attract newcomers to music. Nothing was uncontentious in local government, and opposi-tion to the establishment of an orchestra threatened to crystallise on a party basis. Chamberlain, as in other matters, got his results by nego-tiation and persuasiveness. The City of Birmingham Symphony Orchestra was established, with the city subsidising it and with Sir Thomas Beecham acting as musical adviser. In the long term, Beecham's relationship with the city was fractious, but by then Chamberlain was absent. In the short term, Beecham's enthusiasm was an asset.

Chamberlain remained committed to the Liberal Unionist cause. He improved the party's organisation throughout the Midlands and worked diplomatically for a union of the Conservative Midland Union and the Midland Liberal Unionist Association. It was a sensitive issue because the Liberal Unionists didn't want to lose their identity within the larger Conservative fold; but the marriage was accomplished in April 1914 after two years of courtship. A subsequent Secretary of the Midland Conservative and Unionist Associations said that, 'Under the suave, almost perfect chairmanship of Lord Dartmouth [the chairman of the Conservative Association], and the virile, tactful and business-like guidance of Mr Chamberlain, the negotiations were proceeded with ... [E]ven at the last moment, it was only the persuasive elements of Mr Chamberlain that caused a unanimous vote to be recorded.'[12]

But if Chamberlain was Liberal Unionist, he was not *too* Liberal Unionist, not tribal. He was interested more in results than in means and dogged party loyalties. He wrote to Beatrice in March 1916 saying that although he still cared about what the party had been about, he had 'really ceased to think of myself as a Party man'.[13]

By now Chamberlain was a national figure, and was frequently in London on behalf of Birmingham. His negotiations with the Treasury over the Birmingham Savings Bank, was only one of many contacts with central government.[14] Neville was privy to and interested in what was going on at the centre of politics, thanks to some quite indiscreet information which Austen passed on to him. As Minister of Munitions, Lloyd George had considered him for a job, and although he didn't make the appointment, he did of course ask Chamberlain to serve on the Liquor Commission.

With hindsight, Chamberlain's move to Westminster may seem to have been inevitable, but it's a mistake to think that there was anything hypocritical about his repeated denials of ambitions in that direction. He continued to be critical about his speaking abilities and he envied Austen's aptitude for making important speeches with little apparent effort. Neville agonised over the composition of speeches, spending days shaping them and making his notes. Austen said he just jotted down a few points and then lay back and 'wombled', using a description of how Gladstone was supposed to compose his speeches. Furthermore, Neville had realised how much more power he had as

Lord Mayor than he would have as a backbencher, and had been unimpressed by the negativism of the Whitehall departments.

But there was an irresistible momentum. When Joe Chamberlain finally had to abandon his seat in the Commons, he wanted Austen to succeed him in West Birmingham. West Birmingham embarrassingly said that they would prefer Neville, a hurtful preference which Neville kept from his brother. When one of the constituency committee learned that Neville wouldn't be available, he said that he didn't know much about Mr Austen but that he would do all right if he was anything like Mr Neville. This was in 1914, but it wasn't the first approach he had had. In 1911, South Birmingham had wanted him; he emphatically declined and recommended instead Leo Amery. Even that was not the first approach. As early as 1900 there was a suggestion that he should stand for South Wolverhampton. In that year, however, there had been no Annie. By 1911 there was, and she very strongly encouraged him to move to what was then often called the Imperial Parliament. He still resisted, but by 1916 the move had become inevitable. He was too well known as a man who could get things done to resist the pressure, and perhaps his desire to resist it diminished as he grew in self-esteem and in a realistic appreciation of his own abilities which had not yet hardened into arrogance. The shame of Andros had been wiped out by twenty years of hard work and success.

And yet before he could step onto the national stage he had to face two blows, one of which, a second Andros, would dent that self-esteem. The pain of the other left a mark on his sensitive psyche and would inform his attitude when he faced the dictators.

*Chapter 11*

# An Extraordinary Display of Discourtesy

On 19 December 1916, Chamberlain was returning from a meeting in London in connection with the Local Government Board when he was intercepted at Paddington Station by a messenger from Austen asking him to go straight to the India Office to meet Lloyd George. His meeting with the new Prime Minister lasted no more than ten minutes. Lloyd George wanted him in London on the national stage and at the centre of events as the Director General of National Service. It proved to be a disastrous move.

He was appointed at the end of December 1916 and well within the month, by 21 January 1917, he was expecting to be dismissed. Just less than seven months later he did indeed resign. He could very well have been facing the end of any kind of political career: he had resigned office as Lord Mayor on his appointment as Director General and the bridge back to local government was burnt.

His appointment was quintessential Lloyd George. Lloyd George had succeeded Asquith as Prime Minister on 6 December 1916. His unique selling point, the reason he had displaced Asquith, the charming but faded 'Squiffy', was that he would replace amateurish lethargy and an absence of joined-up government by bringing purpose, energy and direction to the conduct of the war. The defects of the previous regime were particularly evident in relation to use of manpower. Kitchener's appeal, 'Your Country Needs You', brought a million men into the armed forces by January 1915, but when the flow of volunteers slowed it became evident that a degree of compulsion was required.

Conscription was foreign to British tradition and there was much hostility to it in Parliament. In the autumn of 1915 Lord Derby, the Director General of Recruiting, devised a scheme, named after him, which involved a requirement that eligible men should 'attest' whether or not they would join the forces. Some 38 per cent of single men and 54 per cent of married men declined to attest positively. Conscription was finally introduced in January 1916 and extended by further legislation in May of the same year.

But that wasn't enough to solve all the manpower issues involved by total war. The military were not the only interest group that required men: there were competing demands from, for example, the mines, the docks, the munitions factories and the Merchant Navy. Chamberlain's appointment was designed to reconcile these conflicting demands.

The need for someone to adjudicate had been evident before Lloyd George's appointment as Prime Minister. In September 1916 a Manpower Board, under Austen's chairmanship, had recommended steps towards a sort of industrial conscription. Something needed to be done and Lloyd George lost no time in doing it. He set up two new departments, one of Labour and one of National Service. Neville's appointment to lead the latter was made within a couple of weeks of Lloyd George's becoming Prime Minister. Lloyd George liked parachuting in 'men of push and go', industrialists and others from outside the political mainstream, to energise the war effort. Neville was just such a man. Moreover, he had been vocal about the need for some form of national service. It was Austen who innocently pressed for the appointment which almost cost his brother his political life, but he didn't have to press hard – Neville was a fairly obvious choice.

In the face of the new Prime Minister's whirlwind approach, Neville had no time to reflect on the proffered appointment. Lloyd George told him that the Cabinet unanimously wished him to take on a critical task. The support of Labour was essential and – interestingly – the Labour leaders had been enthusiastic. When Chamberlain said he should have to consult with his colleagues in Birmingham he was reminded that this was war time. Lloyd George wanted to announce the appointment to Parliament that very day. Chamberlain allowed himself only two minutes' reflection and the appointment was indeed announced that afternoon.[1]

At the end of the brief meeting, Chamberlain had no clear idea what his duties were to be. He did not know whether he would have a salary. He had no information about his powers: would he have any degree of compulsion in the direction of national service? What would his staff consist of? What was his official rank in government? He was informally assured that he would *rank* as a minister, whatever that meant. His department, whatever it consisted of, would be a few rooms in St Ermin's Hotel.

Despite these meagre realities, when he addressed the Commons, Lloyd George sought to invest Chamberlain's appointment with immense significance. Chamberlain would immediately organise 'this great new system of enrolment for industrial purposes', and so started off under the burden of huge and unrealistic expectations. It was hoped that 'before Parliament resumes its duties in another few weeks we shall be able to report that we have secured a sufficiently large industrial army in order to mobilise the whole of the labour strength of this country for war purposes'.[2]

The job specification remained hopelessly vague. Even after three meetings with Lloyd George, Neville knew not whether he was responsible for Scotland and Ireland, or whether he had authority over munitions. All he was told was that he had to recruit volunteers. In the course of these three meetings with Lloyd George that was all he learned, except that he would not have the authority that came from a seat in Parliament. One observer in the Commons said, 'If Mr Chamberlain were an archangel, or if he were Hindenburg and Bismarck, and all the great men of the world rolled into one, his task would be wholly beyond his powers.'[3]

Of course, it was absurd to suggest that there could be any question of a report in just a few weeks' time on an enterprise of such a scale. Lloyd George was annoyed that the impossible wasn't possible and relations between the two men deteriorated very badly and very quickly, and were never thereafter repaired. Apart from a shared hyper-activity, the two men were of radically different temperament. Lloyd George was mercurial, reactive, instinctual, inconsistent. He was an amateur phrenologist and at an early stage decided that Chamberlain should never have been appointed because his forehead was too narrow, calling him a 'pinheaded incompetent'.[4] Chamberlain didn't think much of Lloyd George either ('that mean little skunk', a 'dirty little Welsh attorney'). Lloyd George regarded detail as obstructive, but Chamberlain worked by considering, analysing and mastering detail.

By 8 January Chamberlain was already being warned that his performance was beginning to disappoint. Shortly afterwards, Lloyd George asked Chamberlain to set out his programme for a special meeting of the War Cabinet. At that meeting, on 12 January, the new Cabinet Secretary, Maurice Hankey, recorded that Chamberlain had made a bad impression. Lloyd George told Hankey that Chamberlain didn't seem to have made any progress in working out his scheme. By 14 January Hankey was recording that the Prime Minister was 'very angry with Neville Chamberlain ... who, he considers, is not getting ahead'.[5] This just a week or two after his appointment.

Chamberlain did ultimately produce a plan which would be implemented largely on a voluntary basis, and which would suspend certain existing exemptions from military service, in order to direct recruits into 'the industrial army'. Volunteers would be routed to the type of service for which they were best qualified. Use would be made of Local Authorities and the employment exchanges, with the exchanges coming under the control of the National Service Department for the duration of the war. In the event, the system worked to a limited extent. By the end of the first week in March, 110,000 men had volunteered for direction into essential civilian occupations, and by a few months later the figure had increased to 350,000. The intention had been that these men would liberate others for military service, but in practice the army was not yet ready to take the latter aboard.

This was the essence of the problem: there was no co-ordination amongst the different interested bodies: the Board of Trade, the Home Office, the Local Government Board, the Board of Agriculture, the Ministries for Shipping, Labour and Food, and the military and naval authorities. In particular, there was very distinct hostility between Chamberlain's Department and the Ministry of Labour, which was responsible for the labour exchanges. At the time the most vicious attacks on Chamberlain came from the Minister of Munitions, Christopher Addison, but it is interesting that Addison conceded in his memoirs that Chamberlain had been propelled with an inadequate staff 'into a job that, I think, was impossible for attainment at any time by a State Department in a complex community like ours ... He never really had a fair chance.'[6] This was very different from the vitriolic attacks that he made on his colleague at the time.

Addison's reference to a lack of adequate staff is a very real point. Chamberlain particularly wanted James Stevenson.* Stevenson worked for the Ministry of Munitions and Addison was most reluctant to let him go. Equally unhelpfully, Lloyd George *did* give Chamberlain an assistant, Kennedy Jones, a journalist from Lord Northcliffe's empire, but he did this without telling Chamberlain, who regarded this as an underhand trick. Years later he referred to 'that beastly Saturday when Ll G tried to hoist KJ onto me'. Kennedy Jones admitted to Chamberlain that he had made it a condition that he would only come if he were to run the show. Bonar Law, the Conservative leader, sought to console Chamberlain, and Lloyd George made an unconvincing apology which didn't cut much ice.

Relations with Lloyd George did not improve, and the Prime Minister wrote on 20 February saying that he had anticipated that a hundred meetings would already have been arranged. He wanted a good deal more life put into the enrolment of the volunteer army. Next, he appointed Stephen Walsh to act as Parliamentary Secretary for Chamberlain's Department, again without consulting or even advising the Director General. To compound matters, just a few months later, Chamberlain read in his newspaper that Walsh had been moved to the Local Government Board and that Cecil Beck would take his place at the National Service Department. Chamberlain had heard nothing of this. He wrote to Lloyd George in terms 'which Annie thinks will paralyse him with fury. I only hope it does.' He accused Lloyd George of what 'seems to me an exhibition of discourtesy so extraordinary that I have difficulty in believing it to be unintentional. I accepted office at your urgent request with great reluctance. I have done my best in very difficult circumstances, with very little support. If your disregard of me yesterday signifies your want of confidence in me, the sooner I know it the better.'[7]

Lloyd George convinced no one by saying that it was an inadvertent mistake for which he apologised. Chamberlain never forgot these incidents; nor did Lloyd George. His *War Memoirs*, published in 1934,

---

* A man of push-and-go from the Johnnie Walker whisky company, later Sir James Stevenson and later still Lord Stevenson, and a post-war novelist under the pseudonym Roland Dunster. He is believed to have devised the Johnnie Walker slogan, 'Born in 1820 – still going strong'.

are far from reliable and gave him a chance to have the last word about many of his enemies. He recalled the task which he had given Chamberlain, calling as it did for 'a great breadth and boldness of conception, a remorseless energy and thoroughness of execution, and for the exercise of supreme tact ... [A] man of exceptional gifts', but 'Mr Neville Chamberlain is a man of rigid competency ... lost in an emergency or in creative tasks at any time [with a] vein of self-sufficient obstinacy. The Ministry only worked smoothly and efficiently after he had gone.'

Even if Chamberlain had had a proper department and proper support from the Prime Minister, he was being asked to do an impossible job. He was being asked to do by voluntary means what could only be done by compulsion. When Lloyd George announced Chamberlain's appointment he had told the house that the government would not hesitate to use compulsory powers, despite undertakings to the contrary already given. In the event, such powers were never taken. Not only had Lloyd George said that; Austen had assured his brother that *he* would make sure he was given whatever powers he needed. Chamberlain was misled. What Lloyd George envisaged was some metaphysical expression of immediate, frenzied activity and improvisation, but he was not yet ready to embrace the total controls that were required by total war and for which the Northcliffe press was already agitating. Although Lloyd George was frequently referred to as a dictator (a description which did not yet have the pejorative sense that the 1930s would bring), the reach of the government was much less extensive even by 1918 than it was in 1940. Churchill observed the stalemate between the Director General of National Service and the other agencies, in the same way as he watched Lloyd George struggling with the service chiefs. He addressed both problems in 1940 and created a new office, the Ministry for Defence, for himself, so that he had overall direction of the military effort. He also appointed Ernest Bevin as Minister for Labour *and* National Service, giving him enormous powers, and injected him into Parliament and the Cabinet.

This last factor, the lack of a parliamentary seat, was an important one. Chamberlain himself had repeatedly told Annie that no one could be a minister without serving an apprenticeship in the House of Commons. Should he have strayed from his own advice? Probably not. Not being in the Commons to answer questions drew criticism. He had, to be sure, been told by Austen that the lack of a seat would not cause him any difficulties and Lloyd George had been equally reassuring. And his remarks to Annie related to normal, peacetime conditions, and conditions in December 1916 were instead very special. The offensive on the Somme had ended without the promised breakthrough, attacks on Allied shipping were introducing Britain to the prospects of starvation, and losses on the Western Front continued to mount. In such a situation for a man as patriotic as Chamberlain, a man who believed that nothing was worth doing unless it was difficult, declining to serve his country was unthinkable.

More significant than the lack of a seat was the fact that he didn't have the experience of government or Whitehall which would have enabled him to deal with departmental disputes. Stronger civil service backup would have helped him, but experience in local government, where everyone was pulling in more or less the same direction, was no preparation for the obstructiveness he met in London. Arthur Henderson, a Labour member of Lloyd George's War Cabinet, concluded that it was 'impossible to have a Central Department controlling the allocation of manpower against the determined opposition of the Ministries of Munitions and Labour'.[8] And Chamberlain's attempts to make the impossible possible not only alienated his colleagues but won little applause from the general public or the press. There were many examples of small businesses forced to close down and of men who had given up their old jobs but found no new employment.

By 22 June 1917 Chamberlain's patience was close to breaking. He submitted his tenth report to the War Cabinet, complaining about restrictions that had been imposed on his department, clashes with other departments and the fact that the War Cabinet had failed to cancel military exemptions for men in certain age groups. On 13 July he told Lloyd George that unless his grievances were addressed he would not remain in office. The War Cabinet's response was to say that his department should be reorganised and that military recruiting should be its main activity. That pretty much amounted to dismissal and Chamberlain resigned.

Lloyd George said that Chamberlain's problems rose from his not having followed his advice in taking a chief of staff, of whom he said he had offered three, including Auckland Geddes.* Geddes was one of Lloyd George's favourite men of push-and-go. He had been a doctor who made a meteoric ascent to reach the rank of Brigadier General by 1916 despite having very poor sight and having been injured in a fall from his horse. Before Chamberlain had even resigned, backstage machinations were taking place to tee Geddes up to replace him, and on Chamberlain's resignation Geddes became Minister of National Service with responsibility for military recruiting *and* the retention of skilled men in vital war industries. The downgrading of the department that would have taken place if Chamberlain had remained was no longer necessary. Geddes not only had the rank of general, but Lloyd George now made him a Privy Councillor and he was awarded a CBE. Unlike Chamberlain, he was parachuted into the House of Commons via an unopposed election. In office he displayed cyclonic energy. He was better in improvisation than in deliberation, the reverse of Chamberlain. He had exactly the right qualities for his office in a time of war and exactly the wrong qualities in time of peace, the obverse of Chamberlain's situation. Interestingly, Chamberlain was vindicated to a large extent by the fact that Geddes insisted on and was given the power to withdraw age exemptions.

How did Chamberlain react to this expensive exploration of a cul-de-sac? He was certainly embittered. He peremptorily declined a knighthood from Lloyd George, whom he continued to regard as personally responsible for what he described as his misfortunes. He was filled with a sense of failure, and the episode in his life to which his thoughts returned is revealing. He wrote in his diary that he was reminded of the Bahamas 'when the plants didn't grow'. After twenty years, success in business and local politics, marriage and children, the wound of Andros was still unhealed. Failure then still caused him pain, and so did failure now. But there were differences. Most importantly,

---

* Geddes's family was a remarkable one. Among his siblings were Dr Mona Chalmers-Watson, the first woman awarded a Doctorate of Medicine by Edinburgh University, a suffragette and the first Chief Controller of the Woman's Army Auxiliary Corps; Irvine Geddes, chairman of the Orient Steam Navigation Company and a Scottish Rugby Cap; and Eric Geddes, railwayman, Minister of Transport and at one time a civilian First Lord of the Admiralty who had the rank of Vice Admiral. It was said that no men were more ignorant of naval affairs than Geddes and Lloyd George. He was, however, highly successful.

he now had the support of Annie and his family. Annie had had her difficulties at this time too. There was a miscarriage and an unpleasant operation; but she was able to join Neville in London, first staying with Beatrice and then renting rooms nearby. Neville got back to the children at Westbourne whenever he could. Frank recalled his father bounding up the stairs two at a time. 'I would climb up his legs and sit on his shoulder and out of his pockets he would pull out the most wonderful camels and kangaroos ... They would appear from the most strange parts of his clothes and this would always happen whenever he went to London.' Neville helped Dorothy and Frank to build wooden brick castles. He told them stories, read his own letters from Andros, and over a period of two years delivered a fresh instalment of a long narrative tale every Sunday.

As well as the love of his family, he was reassured by the support and loyalty of his staff in the department at St Ermin's once they had got past his initial restraint. When he left, he gave a dinner for thirty of his senior staff and was surprised to be presented with a silver cigar box. Later, when he and Annie went to St Ermin's, 400 of the staff gathered to present them with more silver – this time an inscribed dish. Annie was close to tears and Neville himself was moved and heartened.

So he accepted his reverse more philosophically than he could have done earlier. He learned some practical lessons from it: he concluded that to administer effectively in Whitehall one had to be in Parliament. The twenty years of success and experience since Andros had greatly strengthened his self-regard and confidence. In April 1918, when he saw Churchill, the Minster of Munitions, congratulating himself on the increase in output in spite of the release of men, he allowed himself a moment of self-satisfaction: 'Precisely! That is what I always said would happen, whereas Addison said that it wouldn't and Ll G would not take the risk.' But while this time he was absolutely certain that the failure was not of his making, that is not to say that he did not feel the failure very bitterly. He said so to his stepmother. 'After twenty years of success and with an enhanced self-confidence, though not yet arrogance, failure was not something that I welcomed or wished to meet again.'[9]

Having turned his back on local politics, even as the dust was still rising from the ruins of his brief career in the Department of National

Service, Chamberlain felt he had no choice but to continue in public life. But he did so in despair and as a result of a tortured sense of duty, without any hopes of success. He had no hopes and no pleasure in the prospect of continued public life:

> Every now and then a feeling of almost irresistible nausea and revulsion comes over me at the thought of all the drudgery, the humiliation, the meanness and pettiness of that life, and of the hopeless impossibility of getting things done. And then I grind my teeth and think if it hadn't been for my d——d well-meaning brother I might still have been Lord Mayor of Birmingham, practically in control of the town and about to enter upon my third year of office.[10]

And again, just a couple of months later:

> My career is broken. How can a man of nearly 50, entering the House with this stigma upon him, hope to achieve anything? The fate I foresee is that after mooning about for a year or two I shall find myself making no progress ... I shall perhaps be defeated in an election, or else shall retire, and that will be the end. I would not attempt to re-enter public life if it were not wartime. But I can't be satisfied with a purely selfish attention to business for the rest of my life.[11]

*Chapter 12*

# The Most Intimate Friend I Had

Nineteen days after Chamberlain resigned as Director General of National Service he wrote, 'I could not settle down to make money, much as I should like to be rich. When I think of Johnnie and Norman, I feel I could not back out of public work of some kind.'

Johnnie and Norman were two of his cousins, both killed in action during the First World War. The example and influence of Norman on Neville was immense. Neville was the older of the two, but Neville regarded his young cousin as immeasurably his moral superior. Norman's death on 1 December 1917 was another, perhaps the last single, incident that formed the character of the mature man.

It was Norman's sacrifice in the cause of duty which meant that however much Neville would have preferred to resist and however pessimistic he was about his chances of success, he had no alternative but to persevere in public life, to do his own duty. Norman's death not only informed this commitment, but also dictated that part of that duty was to try to ensure that the lives of future generations of young men were not wasted in the futility of war as Norman's had been. Chamberlain's determination to avoid another war cannot be fully understood without remembering his reaction to Norman's death.

Norman was the son of Joseph Chamberlain's brother Herbert. We know little about him apart from what Neville told us. He was the subject of the only book that Chamberlain wrote, a memoir published in 1923 for private circulation within the family so that they would realise 'how greatly Norman had contributed to the family fame'. He was educated at Eton and Oxford, and did voluntary work at Toynbee Hall. He was one of those young men who died on the Western Front who seem to have had radiated a golden glow. It may be no more than an illusion, an idealisation arising from a sense of loss, but there may, on the other hand, have been something very special about a genera- tion in whom a sense of duty was inculcated, who were informed by late-Victorian religious zeal and by a profound belief in the concept of progress and the opportunity for improving the life of one's fellow men.

The experience of the war, which gave the lie to so much of Western Europe's hopes, left little room for those who survived to retain this faith, but perhaps Norman Chamberlain and men like him maintained what survivors might think of as an ideal innocence, and their memories seemed all the brighter in a darker world. At any rate, Norman, fifteen years younger than Neville, seemed to his older cousin to be 'one of the very few people who roused in me all the sensations of a willing and enthusiastic *follower*'. [The emphasis is mine.] He was 'the most intimate friend I had'.

Although he was his cousin's junior, Norman was already a member of Birmingham Council when Neville joined it. He contributed vigorously to the council's work. He saw the city as bound to work for the wellbeing of its citizens. He was chairman of the Parks Committee and pressed for the acquisition of more playing fields. He was particularly concerned for young people and campaigned for the raising of the school leaving age despite the unpopularity of such a policy with employers. He was pained to see young boys hanging around the city unemployed or doing nothing more fulfilling than selling papers. He was seized by what he described as 'a burning sort of enthusiasm and indignation which nothing seems able to put out'.[1] He responded not only in his municipal work but at his private cost, trying to find work for the boys, opening a club for them and paying for the passage of some of them to Canada and lending them money with which to make a start in their new lives. Like Joe, Norman was a passionate believer in tariff reform.

What particularly chimed with Neville's own views was Norman's *practical* sense of purpose. The two men liked to get things done. Norman admired his cousin's 'real constructive power – ... [H]ow clear and consistent had been his purpose', and how Neville was 'redeemed from priggishness by a keen sense of humour, which caused him to recoil from anything approaching sloppy sentimentality or cant with positive horror'. Norman, who was much less reserved

than Neville, seems to have appreciated his cousin's qualities. On 24
April 1916 he wrote to him:

> My Dear Neville,
> I don't want to be effusive, or make you blush, but I can't put into
> reasonable words the pleasure and pride your letter gave me. It
> made me happy, somehow, for days and the mere thought of it
> cheers me up. I believe it's because I am so awfully proud of you
> and the way you get things done – and have your own schemes all
> ready to be done – and also because you think me worthwhile [of]
> such a letter when I know how busy you are. You're like a breath of
> fresh air and hope, after all the sloppy inefficiency one sees on all
> sides out here and in the papers.[2]

When Chamberlain resigned from the Department of National
Service, Norman wrote from France, aware of his cousin's reticence,
his tendency to stifle his emotions and concerned that he would
descend into depression under the burden of his unexpressed frustra-
tion: 'I am so afraid you won't say anything.'[3]

Norman was right to be worried. Neville did become depressed
and surrounding circumstances did nothing to help. Annie was seriously ill in the spring of the year and Neville was physically below par.
Stress took its toll: he suffered from headaches, sciatica and a loss of
weight. He was still a member of the council and a member of the
Planning Committee, but he turned down a suggestion that he might
resume office as mayor: the mayorship was not a plaything to be put
down and picked up again. He worked again at Hoskins and Elliotts,
and the Birmingham Small Arms Company, but his main efforts were
directed to welfare and the alleviation of social conditions. This culminated in a proposal for university extension teaching for the working
man, but none of this provided fulfilment, particularly when he
thought of his cousins at the front.

Johnnie was the first to die, and that increased Neville's concern for
Norman, who was much dearer to him. He saw Norman for the last
time in October 1917. He was killed in France in December that year,
although his body was not found until February 1918. On 1 December
his battalion of the Grenadier Guards made an advance of 1,000 yards.
Norman's company gained the crest of a ridge and were caught by

machine-gun fire. No one returned, and when a search was made at dusk no one was found. It was nine days before the battalion discovered what had happened. Every man in Norman's party had been killed. Around their bodies lay the corpses of twenty Germans.

Even at the front, Norman, as committed to progress as Neville, had been absorbed by ways of bettering society. When his body was found in no-man's-land he was carrying papers, now soiled by rain and mud, setting out his views on education. He had left a letter for the boys in his Boys' Club in Birmingham in case he should not return, which still brings tears to the eyes. He told the boys not to

> forget that nothing worth doing is done without failures for the time being, without misunderstandings, and without a damned lot of unpleasantness.
>
> We have all been able to help one another a lot; go on doing that amongst the club and amongst your own families. And I think somehow you will feel that I can still sympathise with your bad luck and all the unfairness and difficulties that surround one when one is trying to make good – even if I am not there to tell you and keep you at it.
>
> Anyway, keep pegging on, don't be downhearted and don't forget
>
> Your old pal,
>
> Norman Chamberlain[4]

Neville channelled his grief into starting work at once on the memoir. He looked, in vain, for Norman's grave in France, and to perpetuate what he had started Neville began work with the Street Boys' Union in Birmingham.

On 27 February he wrote in his diary: 'Returned from W. Woodhay, where attended Memorial Service for my dear friend Norman. Strange that we do not fully realise men's characters while they are alive. Only now do I begin to see the extraordinary beauty of his. His life was devoted to others, and I feel a despicable thing beside him.'[5] Remember how very difficult, almost impossible, Neville Chamberlain found it to unburden himself and reflect how strong his feelings must have been. How far he was from the idea that we have preserved of him, when he wrote these intensely personal words: '*I feel a despicable thing beside him*'.

Although he started assembling materials at once for his memoir of Norman, Neville did not complete it until 1922. He found the exercise difficult. Of all the books which Neville Chamberlain might have written, there is none for which he could have been less suited than this. He was disappointed with what he had done and felt that he had not done justice to the man he said he had regarded as a brother. He does, however, bring out *why* he so regarded him:

> Naturally reserved, shy and sensitive ... it was only to his intimates that he showed all that was in him. It was easier to him to write than to speak about the things on which he felt most deeply ... He was intensely affectionate ... He had little facility for what is called small-talk, but to anyone who shared his interest in his fellows, or who himself was taking part in public work of any kind, his conversation was always stimulating and attractive.[6]

Neville Chamberlain's letters and diaries throughout the war show very clearly that he felt the tragedy of the slaughter, but if anything had been needed to bring home the human hurt and waste behind the statistics, the deaths of Johnnie and Norman did that. Their deaths, particularly Norman's, reinforced elements in Chamberlain's psychology which had already been present: the need for practical purpose and for discernibly improving the lot of the ordinary man and woman. They also *hardened* his commitment to these ends: to do justice to Norman, to so many Normans, and to atone for failures on Andros and at the Department of National Service, the frivolous and trivial had to be put aside. And a new element was injected into the psychological mixture: a determination to work for peace.

In one of his letters home, Norman had said that what he and so many others were going through could only be justified if it never, ever happened again. As we have seen, Neville Chamberlain, like his father, had been for a forward foreign policy, supported by a powerful army and navy. He had been active in the Territorial Association and had opposed naval and military cutbacks. That remained the broad thrust of his views. He was never remotely a pacifist. He always took a realistic view of how his country's interests must be defended; but if anyone is inclined to think that he was merely supine or credulous when he was dealing with Hitler, they should read again these moving entries in his diary when he thought of the *waste* of the talents, the energy and the promise for the future that were encapsulated in the death of Norman Chamberlain.

## Chapter 13

# An Interim Assessment

Chamberlain was now at a turning point in his life, moving inexorably towards the public stage, a mature man in his forty-ninth year. He had very substantial achievements behind him in business and as leader of the 'Second City of the Empire', had come through the formative experience of an upbringing by a dynamic father, a man of huge energies and ambitions, and had suffered what – to him – were the hugely chastening reverses in Andros and at the Department of National Service. Furthermore, the loss of Norman had wounded him grievously.

At this stage in his life Neville is a thoroughly decent man, perhaps a trifle priggish, earnest and humourless, but concerned for the generality of his fellow-men and prepared to work himself to the bone for their good. He wasn't clubbable, not a jolly companion for the evening, but his interests were rounded and his endeavours were honourable. A good and admirable citizen. But this characterisation shouldn't be retained as his final image. The last third of his life shaped the man at least as much as the first two-thirds. The sensitive reader will have noted some of Chamberlain's less attractive foibles – a certain tetchiness, self-confidence that bordered on arrogance. The years ahead accentuated the unappealing features of his character and they ought to be recognised.

By the end of his life he was not an appealing personality. Possibly he was the most unlikeable Prime Minister of the twentieth century – even less appealing than Edward Heath. Whether or not it's necessary to *like* Chamberlain in order to consider him a successful politician is debatable, although exploring that question is full of fascination. Some have argued that Chamberlain must have been likeable, because his sisters liked him. This they certainly did, but his absorption in his family could easily be seen as self-absorption, his letters to his sisters really addressed to himself, and while the 'diary letters' indubitably do reveal much of the inner Chamberlain, what they really reveal is far from entirely favourable, unless everything is taken at face value in a totally uncritical and unanalytical way.

Nick Smart explored Chamberlain's character in the light of the access we now have to the whole of the 'diary letters', the huge weekly outpouring of his innermost thoughts to his sisters and which they preserved in the confidence that in the fullness of time they would rehabilitate their brother.* Smart found his exploration of Chamberlain's character 'interesting', despite concluding that Chamberlain was 'an unpleasant man, a nasty piece of work'.[1] For Smart, a full reading of the diary letters led to the realisation ' – and it is in many ways a dreadful one – that Neville Chamberlain was unobservant, bumptious and utterly self-absorbed'.[2]

My only reservation would be in relation to the word 'utterly'. I wouldn't disagree with Smart's judgement of Chamberlain, taking his life as a whole. He wasn't as bad at the age of forty-nine as he would be at sixty-nine. But he was corrupted by his time in Parliament. 'All power tends to corrupt', said Lord Acton, 'and absolute power corrupts absolutely,' and he was probably right, though the 'tends' is important: some resist corruption. Chamberlain did not. Sir David Cannadine, himself from Birmingham, noting that there is no monument to Chamberlain in his home town other than a blue plaque on his Edgbaston home, described him as he was as early as 1929 in terms of an uninspired simile, 'in a rut of self-righteous narrow-mindedness which hardly equipped him to cope at ever higher level with the tumultuous decade that was to come. As a person and a politician, he was just like his umbrella, stiff and rolled up tight.'[3]

Chamberlain was corrupted by his own abilities. He was more intelligent, more articulate and much more energetic than almost all of his political contemporaries. He overbore his colleagues and his enemies by the clarity of his views and the force with which he deployed them. He saw issues very clearly. He came to despise those

* See Nick Smart, *Neville Chamberlain*, in the Routledge Historical Biographies Series, 2010.

who opposed him and he made no attempt to conceal his contempt. He was often right – though very certainly not always – and he came to feel that since his ends were to him so evidently good ones, some very dirty tricks could reasonably be employed as means.

But in 1917 all this was in the future, an incremental process that would do him no good at all. The personal tragedy of Neville Chamberlain was what his abilities did to a fundamentally decent individual. Chamberlain's doctor, Lord Horder, said, 'I was very fond of him. I like all unlovable men.' Iain Macleod said, 'Horder was wrong. It is impossible to read Neville Chamberlain's diaries or his letters to his family and theirs to him, without knowing that he could not have been unlovable, for he was dearly loved.'[4]

And he had endearing qualities. His sense of humour was unreliable, and Lord Dunglass, as his parliamentary private secretary, extracted 'terrible' jokes from his draft speeches.* On the other hand, he and Annie could laugh at Charlie Chaplin until they ached. For all his confidence in his abilities, he could be self-critical. He saw himself on a newsreel film in 1937:'I suppose it is a good thing to see oneself as others see us, but it is a very painful process . . . If I had not previously seen the person who addressed us from the screen, I should call him pompous, insufferably slow in diction and unspeakably repellent in person!' He had occasional moments of humility. Shortly before he resigned from public life he was offered a peerage. He declined.When he did resign he was offered the Garter.Again he declined, preferring 'to die plain "Mr Chamberlain" like my father before me'. (But was that a form of arrogance?) When he stayed with the Londonderrys, fishing a stretch of the River Brora, he left by the train which used to run between Inverness and Golspie. Unusually, he did so standing in the cab beside the engine driver.

He was, like Margaret Thatcher, highly intelligent but not an intellectual. He was directed to the causes in which he believed – like social reform or protective tariffs – by practical observation rather than by abstract argument. But despite his arrogant confidence in his own abilities and apparent self-assurance, he was an emotional man.

---

* It has to be said that Lord Dunglass, later the Earl of Home, then Sir Alec Douglas-Home, finally Baron Home of the Hirsel, is scarcely remembered as a master of mirth.

Emotion, and not just a desire for administrative consistency drove him in his determination to improve the ordinary life of working people. Even as a Cabinet minister, when he approved the purchase of boots for children who were going to school barefoot in winter and of disinfectant for teachers who had to pluck lice from the hair of children he could hardly bring himself to speak about it 'for the fear of breaking down'.[5]

That reticence disguised what drove him – for he was driven, driven to work hard and for long hours when he could have indulged his love of art or the outdoors, driven to a political life which truly held no great attraction for him, driven to speak in public when he hated doing so. What drove him was a restless passion, an irresistible sense of a duty to improve the practical circumstance of his fellow-men.

It has been said that he was not particularly close to his children when they had grown up. I have not found any evidence of that. Certainly, as we have seen, the children, and the home life of which they were part, were an essential piece of the world into which he retreated. He enjoyed rough and tumble with them and their cousins. When his children caught scarlet fever he disobeyed the instructions which Annie followed. She quarantined them and communicated with them by standing on the lawn and shouting toward their room at the top of her voice. *He* went into the sickroom and played with the children as if nothing were amiss. The children adored him and valued their time with him. As adults, after his death, they spoke of him with real affection.

Equally, his affection for Annie was unbounded. Almost to her embarrassment she was repeatedly reminded by him of how lucky he felt himself to be married to a beautiful, devoted and loving wife. There was no reserve between them and he paid her the compliment of genuine love when he gently teased her. He undoubtedly meant it when he said, as he did, that he could never have become Prime Minister without her. He was saying no more than the truth: she not only provided the essential hinterland of domestic contentment, but also encouraged him to extend his political horizons. The only criticism that can be made of her is that this complete confidence in his abilities served to reinforce his self-confidence, to his ultimate damage.

He was more than usually interested in art and to the end of his life continued to explore the work of new artists. As Chancellor of the

Exchequer he fought with Kenneth Clark, the Director of the National Gallery, to ensure that Eleven Downing Street was furnished with the work of painters – some of distinctly minority tastes – whom he admired. That is not to say that his tastes were hugely advanced. In art, literature and music, his tastes were very fixed. He regarded George Bernard Shaw's plays as 'dreadful piffle' and thought that Keynes was 'a crank', some of whose ideas showed 'mental aberration of a dangerous kind'.[6] He went to see paintings by Stanley Spencer having read an enthusiastic review in *The Times*, but 'I was not prepared for the hideous, sordid, grotesque productions which I saw at Burlington House. It rouses me to fury to think that imposters should have the impudence to fob off such stuff as "art".'[7] It was typical of him that he reacted against this modernist, as he did against many others, in such violent terms and not simply by saying that it was a question of taste.

He very regularly attended concerts and piano recitals. Here he was not as averse to modernity as might be expected. His interest in theatre was patchy: he was devoted to Shakespeare and to Shakespeare scholarship. When he read Dover Wilson's book, *What Happens in Hamlet*, he got so excited that he immediately read it all over again.

Despite his cantankerous rejection of what he did not like in the arts, the fact is that the arts probably mattered to him more than to any other twentieth-century Prime Minister. Balfour and Macmillan would be in the running, but their interest was less catholic and less important to them.

He took his reading very seriously, listing what he read. As well as reading the canonical novels of the eighteenth and nineteenth centuries, he educated himself by reading *about* their authors. In 1939 he read the important study of Jane Austen by Mary Lascelles, history, like Temperley's *Foreign Policy of Canning*, biographies of Napoleon, Pitt and Chatham, as well as books on animal and bird painting, and fishing.[8]

It is a considerable understatement to say that he was not clubbable. The only club of which he was a member was the Carlton Club, the trades union of the Conservative Party of which membership was effectively obligatory. In this he was very untypical of his time and circle. Most Conservative Members of Parliament would be members of a variety of clubs. He was not, however, a hermit. He avoided dinner parties, because they interrupted the long evenings and early mornings which he devoted to work, but he was not averse to going out for lunch. When he was there he didn't say a great deal and could seem austere and withdrawn.

Although he enjoyed country house weekends and shooting parties, he preferred the more solitary sport of angling, which he took very seriously indeed. Nature mattered to him a great deal. He was a Fellow of the Royal Horticultural Society and loved the natural world, perhaps particularly birds. As Chancellor he put up a nesting box and bird table in the garden of Eleven Downing Street.

All in all, not 'nasty', as Smart described him. Arthur Neville Chamberlain, our Neville, is far from the only Neville Chamberlain. One of several, to none of whom he was related, was Colonel Neville Francis Fitzgerald Chamberlain. If he is remembered at all it's because he invented the game of snooker. It's difficult to imagine Arthur Neville doing anything so frivolous, but the qualities we can identify in him as he approached his fifties, together with his burning passion for the practical assistance of his fellow-men, hardly characterise 'a nasty piece of work'.

# Chapter 14

# Inescapable Destiny: Westminster

'It was still the case,' said Roy Jenkins in a wonderfully incongruous simile, 'that for a Chamberlain to feel a desire for Parliament was for him to command its fulfilment. With seven seats (to be made twelve in 1918) at the disposal of the Birmingham Unionists Association it was almost like a Sultan entering his harem, inappropriate although such a self-indulgence seemingly sounds in relation to Neville Chamberlain.'[1] It was more a sense of acquiescence rather than a lust for Parliament that carried Neville to Westminster in 1918, but there was certainly no difficulty in getting there.

The Representation of the People Act 1918 hugely extended the franchise. The vote was given to men of twenty-one and over, and women over thirty. Birmingham was divided into twelve constituencies instead of the former seven, and the Birmingham electorate increased from 95,000 to 427,000. In Chamberlain's view his party was disastrously unprepared for the new circumstances. In the summer of 1918 negotiations about the union of the Birmingham Conservatives and the Birmingham Liberal Unionists were resumed. Neville was in the chair. In due course a joint management committee was set up, and again he was chairman. He wrote to Hilda that his position placed the direction of Unionist politics in his hands: 'I am not sure whether all those present perceived this. I didn't mention it.'[2]

He accelerated the fusion and imposed a tight control over the united entity. His intention was to continue the work his father had done in basing a large and spreading political network on Birmingham. He aimed not just to increase the efficiency of the machine, but to use it to train increasing numbers of professional agents and extend its reach. As chairman of the joint association, his personal position was enhanced by the organisational changes and he was well aware that the direction of Unionist politics in Birmingham was in his hands.[3]

His move onto the national stage, the move from being a puppet master to player, seems to have *emerged* as a given, rather than being an outcome of an isolated decision. There was not an identifiable moment at which he stopped turning down offers of constituencies and decided to accept one. The constituency for which he finally stood was one of the new constituencies, Ladywood, and here he prepared for the seismic election of 1918. This is known as the Coupon Election because of the letter of endorsement which was given to those candidates who supported the Lloyd George–Bonar Law coalition, the coalition that had just won the war. The candidates who carried the coupon were swept to a victory which marked the end of Victorian politics.

There were unusual features in the way Chamberlain approached the 1918 general election. He was careful to select a constituency in which there were no significant works in which he had a financial interest. As a matter of principle, too, he took no advantage of the 'coupon'. He received one, but far from making use of it he was at pains to stress that coalition candidates were not Lloyd George's creatures and that he would vote for or against government measures according to his own judgement.

He was explicit in seeing himself as a non-partisan candidate, even though he wore a Unionist badge. He felt himself to be a representative of those with whom he had worked in common cause now for many years. His programme, in a working-class constituency which contained a lot of slum housing, was not a typical Conservative one: he wanted a minimum wage, employment protection, shorter hours, a larger share of the profits of industry going to workers, trades unions given their place, schemes for national housing, and maternity and infant welfare. It was a manifesto that involved a great deal of spending and that spending was not to be at the expense of the ordinary man. Preferential tariffs – note the nod to Joe – were to encourage the use of Empire products; cheap imports from third-party countries were to be discouraged.

But as always with Chamberlain, fastidiousness and principle was matched by disdain. At an intellectual level he cared about the condition of the poor, but at a personal level he was too prissy to enjoy close contact and he unappealingly described canvassing his working-class electorate as 'slumming'. He did not have an easy relationship with people whose background was so different from his own. Austen told his sisters on one occasion that 'Neville's manner freezes people'.[4] As he responded to the imperatives of political life it becomes increasingly difficult to reconcile Chamberlain's image with the young man who had sweated, half-naked, alongside his labourers in Andros or was so affected by Norman's death as to consider himself contemptible by comparison. He won the seat with a majority of almost 7,000 votes and, at just short of his fiftieth birthday he entered the House of Commons.

In the middle of the campaign, to add to the loss of Norman, his sister Beatrice died, a victim of the influenza pandemic of the time, her resistance probably already weakened by her commitment to war work over the preceding years. He suffered from her loss, and the lack of her sympathy and support. But in a letter to his friend Richard Redmayne, he said something very revealing about how he coped with his losses. 'This election', he said, 'has been a good thing for me for it has forced me to put a sort of crust over my emotions.' Putting a crust over his emotions was for him a good thing that needed no justification. He had indeed been developing a truly impermeable crust for very many years now. That tendency may have helped him with the constructive work which he wished to do, but it did an enormous amount of damage to the image which his contemporaries saw and which history has remembered. If he had allowed himself to break down when he talked about social problems, instead of fighting not to, his image would have been a much more human one.

The Coupon Election changed the face of politics. The great Liberal Party as represented by the independent Asquithians was reduced to thirty-four seats. The Labour Party, perhaps surprisingly, had only sixty seats. The Lloyd George Liberals had 137 and the Conservatives, with whom they were in coalition, a massive 374. The coalition, with a total representation of 511 seats, had absolute power, and Lloyd George at the head of it was regarded as a virtual dictator. His personal popularity insulated him from any concern that he relied on a party which had historically distrusted him.

Neville Chamberlain was now in the Commons. Here he would spend the rest of his life and here, it might have been thought, was his natural habitat; though in fact only setback and tragedy had brought him to Westminster.

He spent just twenty-two years there: most of his adult life was not concerned with Parliament. The two men he would ultimately succeed as Prime Minister were Ramsay MacDonald and Stanley Baldwin. MacDonald was thirty-five when he became an MP and remained an MP for thirty-six years. Baldwin entered the House at the age of forty-one and remained there for twenty-nine years. Chamberlain's successor, Winston Churchill, was of course exceptional. He entered the House at the age of twenty-six and remained a Member (with the odd break) for sixty-four years. Churchill's successor was Clement Attlee. His arrival at Westminster was delayed by service in the First World War, but was thirty-nine when he was first elected MP and he remained an MP for thirty-three years. Chamberlain's twenty-two years were only two-thirds of Attlee's time on the green benches and not much more than a third of Churchill's; but they were busy, important and productive years.

Neville Chamberlain's political career falls into two reasonably distinct chunks. The first sees him continue with the great causes that had seized him in Birmingham: dealing with poverty, housing and health. The second and final phase of his parliamentary career sees him move increasingly into the area of foreign affairs and the threat of the dictators – the passage which absorbed his final years and has distorted his memory. In that part of his history, he becomes much more identified with the Conservative Party at a black time in its own history; whereas in domestic affairs he is much more apolitical, indeed very far from traditional conservatism.

I shall start by looking at the matrix, the main political scaffolding. While the minutiae will be avoided, it will be helpful to have an overall outline of the way in which Chamberlain's political career developed so that he came to dominate his party almost as much as Lloyd George had dominated his coalition in 1918. This chapter, then, will deal with the nature of post-war politics, at the national level where Chamberlain found himself. The following chapter will look in just a little more detail at the years in which he climbed the ministerial ladder, and in subsequent chapters, I shall examine the themes of the domestic policies which so interested Chamberlain and which reveal the essence of the man.

The House of Commons which Chamberlain entered had a character of its own, and not a pleasant one. It was dominated by the Conservative Party, and that Party was in a particularly conservative mood. The economist John Maynard Keynes looked at the benches filled with the 1918 intake, and this was when he made the remark, hinted at above, about lots of hard-faced men who had done well out of the war. While the war might have been financially good for many profiteers, there was a widespread feeling amongst the Conservatives – and perhaps amongst some Liberals too – that at a social and economic level a lot of undesirable things had happened under the stress of the struggle for national survival and that the clock needed to be put back.

As in 1900, so too in 1918 the rich were a lot richer than the poor, but there had been some compressions in the middle, as necessities of war production and of feeding the nation impinged on traditional patterns of supply and demand. The hard-faced industrialist profiteers were themselves not typical of the nineteenth-century Conservative Party.

There had been other changes too. Women had emerged as an important element in the economy. The trades unions had, of necessity, been admitted to a degree at least to the body politic. Appeals had been made during the war to the nation to pull together, implying a commonalty of purpose which had eroded some of the sense of hierarchy that had pervaded Victorian and Edwardian society. Ordinary working-class men in uniform had examined their social betters at close quarters and had not always been impressed by what they saw. Widespread promotion from the ranks into the officer class, immensely rare in earlier times, had become common. All this threatened barriers that had formerly been impassable.

All these changes could, for those who were nervous about the structure of society, appear to be reflections of much more dramatic moves on mainland Europe, where the great and grandiose empires of Russia, Austria-Hungary and Germany had fallen. Arrogant dynasties that had ruled these age-old polities were expelled and subsisted with difficulty as exiles, sometimes in fairly seedy surroundings. Republics occupied what had been left of the Holy Roman Empire, and international communism, established in the capital of the Tsar, threatened to spread worldwide. George V, the Tsar's cousin, reflected the nervous mood of the British establishment when he declined to offer his cousin succour in Britain in case *his* throne too were to come under attack.

When we look at the history of the interwar years, we must remember that the British Establishment, and its political expression, chiefly the Conservative Party, was informed by this sense of threat and insecurity. There were idealistic and radical members of the Conservative Party. The young Harold Macmillan ('I would probably have been a socialist if I hadn't been rich') was one, and the not so young Neville Chamberlain was another. Macmillan, like Chamberlain, came from a background in which wealth had only been a feature for a few generations. Although he was an Anglican, his recent forebears had been Presbyterians. What particularly fed his radicalism was the experience of living alongside his men on the Western Front, reinforced by what he saw of unemployment and poverty in the North East during the depression. We have seen what the formative influences on Chamberlain had been and how he wished to see society better ordered for the benefit of the ordinary man. He was very different from Macmillan, but both men were animated by a supressed romanticism, and both were very untypical of the party to which they belonged. Both were ready to admit that they were different from their colleagues.

The second thing which needs to be remembered about the political world in the interwar years is the economic situation. Britain had entered the First World War as the major creditor nation in the world. It emerged as a debtor, and post-war recovery had no sooner got under way than it was brought to a halt by the Great Depression. In those pre-Keynesian days, the reflex, the response to recession, was to curtail expenditure. The savage imposition of cuts and retrenchment was collectively described as the Geddes Axe.* Using the unsophisticated model of domestic economics that Mrs Thatcher would relish some generations later, it seemed wildly irresponsible, when the national income fell, to do anything other than reduce national expenditure. The result was huge unemployment, industrial stagnation and ultimately deflation. The combination of deflation and

---

* Because it was the recommendation of a Committee of National Expenditure chaired by Sir Eric Geddes, brother of Auckland Geddes, Chamberlain's successor at the Department of National Service.

stagnation is particularly socially divisive. Those who were out of work suffered greatly, while those who were in a safe employment found that their disposable income increased as prices fell. Even the vocally socialist academic A. J. P. Taylor admitted that for someone in secure employment in these years, life could be very good.

For a lot of people life was *not* very good. More than three million were unemployed, with unemployment unevenly spread across the country. In some industrial areas the level of unemployment was as high as 70 per cent. In Glasgow, even across the city as a whole and not just in the worst areas, it was 30 per cent. There were parts of the country which were in effect subcultures of extreme deprivation where housing, nutrition and health had broken down. There were negligible unemployment benefits and reliance was on an archaic system of poor relief. Chamberlain would have a crucial role to play in addressing these financial and social evils.

But while addressing these problems would show Chamberlain at his considerable best in domestic politics, as Minister for Health, in relation to housing and as Chancellor of the Exchequer, I want particularly to stress the influence of the Depression on policy makers and politicians in general. The young Labour Party, which started with pretty minimal representation in 1918 but grew fast between the wars, taking office first as a minority government and then as a rather shame-faced element of the National Government, drew its own lessons, which informed policy when Labour formed a majority government in 1945. The Conservative Party (and, for that matter, most of the crumbling Liberal Party) reacted in another way. They felt threatened by economic developments in the same way as they were by social developments. They laagered their wagons, hunkered down and sought to weather the storm. This desire to resist change and preserve an archaic set of values was what W. H. Auden had in mind when he wrote of the 1930s as being 'a low dishonest decade'. His conclusion in 'September 1, 1939' was, 'we must love one another or die'. That was not the conclusion of the British Establishment or its political representatives, the Conservative and Unionist Party.

In a later chapter I shall look at the black arts which it practised to defend the status quo. It is enough here to recognise the extent to which it felt threatened. In the meantime, having tried to examine the mood of the times, the background music against which politics played out, I shall now sketch briefly the political framework of Chamberlain's political career.

Not many newly elected Members of Parliament are received with the immediate offer of a government job; but Chamberlain was no ordinary backbencher. In fact, the offer was actually rather half-hearted. Bonar Law asked him if he would be prepared to take an under-secretaryship, and was sorry that he couldn't offer more but felt that his hands were tied by the fact that Austen was now in the Cabinet as Chancellor of the Exchequer. Chamberlain said he wasn't worried about the lowly rank (and he probably wasn't), but that he wouldn't want to work with or under Lloyd George – whom he frequently failed to dignify with his full name (the Prime Minister was simply 'George' or, quite often, 'the Goat').

His distaste for Lloyd George had by now developed into contempt and disgust. Everything he saw of the Prime Minister and his methods reinforced the view he had developed when he had been Director General of National Service – and underlying that was his recollection of how Lloyd George had criticised Joe in the course of the South African war. His filial piety was total and uncritical. Not only had he declined a knighthood after the Department of National Service episode, but subsequently he congratulated himself on the fact that his name was not in what he thought to be a discreditable list of names in the New Year Honours. He underlined his independent stance in his maiden speech, when he proposed a motion against the government, a departure from the convention that a maiden speech should be uncontroversial. But he made a good impression on the House.

Austen was less fastidious, and had been out of office for a time. He had been Secretary of State for India under Asquith, and in that office he was technically responsible for the defeat of an Indian Army force under General Townsend which retreated to Kut on the Persian Gulf and finally surrendered on 16 April 1916 when 6,000 Indian troops and 3,000 British were taken prisoner. The resulting commission reported unfavourably and Austen's perhaps over-delicate sense of honour required him to resign: he played the game and always lost. His resignation was given to Lloyd George who had replaced Asquith in December 1916. Lloyd George saw no need for the resignation and pressed him to stay on. When Austen insisted on going he was offered the Paris Embassy, but that too he felt he should not accept.

After he felt that he had served his time he returned to government and joined the War Cabinet in April 1918 as a Minister without Portfolio. At that point Austen had no strong sense of attachment for Lloyd George. Indeed, he tended to regard him as untrustworthy, even crooked; but in a matter of months he was succumbing to the Welshman's charm – which so many found difficult to resist – and felt obliged to support him and save him from his weaknesses. His loyalty to Lloyd George soon became as strong as his earlier aversion had been and in January 1919 he became Chancellor of the Exchequer for the second time. There was a slight and brief estrangement between the brothers.

Lloyd George's unprincipled pragmatism was the antithesis of Neville's approach, but that didn't mean he thought much of conservatism, 'reactionary Toryism'. That in itself put a strain on his relationship with Austen, who was now leader of the Conservative Party and thus the embodiment of that reactionary Toryism. In his election address Neville had said that the best monument to those who had died in the war was social improvement. This reshaping of society would be achieved through pensions, minimum wages, shorter hours and state housing. These views made Neville 'wild' in his stepbrother's eyes; and Neville thought Austen blinkered and unimaginative, 'unprogressive and prejudiced'. The two brothers, very different in outlook, each told their sisters what he thought of the other.

Neville continued to be slightly detached from his Westminster career. He would rather have been walking on the moors, listening to the birds or fishing for trout or salmon in Scotland. In the Alps he skied, skated and tobogganed. What had taken him to Westminster was not the appeal of political life there but the sense of duty that would not allow him to do nothing. As he had said to his sister in August 1917, when he thought of Johnnie and Norman he felt he couldn't face the reproach that perhaps he could have done something if he had tried.

And so, in these early months and years in Parliament, he maintained his outside interests. He was gratified to see his garden restored after the war years. The azaleas, Japanese cherries and orchids meant much to him, as also did the arrival of a greater spotted woodpecker. He was improving his technique as a fisherman, buying paintings and regretting that he had lost touch with music – 'life is really not long enough to follow up more than five or six interests properly'.[5]

In Parliament, he took interest on those issues that mattered to him. One of them was the Bastardy Bill which he brought to a second reading against the government in May 1920. Anyone who persists in thinking of Chamberlain as unemotional and desiccated should note that he was moved to be involved in infant welfare. Over 40,000 illegitimate children were born every year and they died at twice the rate of legitimate children: 'the punishment of innocent children for the faults of their parents is revolting to humanity, and is contrary to the best interests of the state'. More predictably he was making his mark in relation to matters such as the future of canals and clearing slums, and was chairman of Departmental Committees on both these issues. Throughout all this he made no attempt to hide his radicalism. He declared his readiness to limit profits, to publish trading accounts and to promote state ownership of minerals.

In his determination to distance himself from the reactionary Tories, Neville delayed joining the Carlton Club, the home of the Tory Party, until February 1922, eight months before the historic meeting of the Club in October 1922 when the Tory Party resolved to break with Lloyd George and his wing of the Liberal Party.

Conservative reservations about the coalition government had been building up long before the meeting. In February 1922 a backbencher, Colonel John Gretton,[*] accompanied by thirty-five other MPs told Austen Chamberlain that it was time that the alliance was ended. Austen would have none of this, but only days later Lord Salisbury launched an appeal for funds to establish a pure Conservative Party. A fighting fund of £22,000 was raised.

Although Neville had joined the Carlton Club in time to attend the crucial meeting, he didn't do so. He was abroad. He and Annie were in Canada, visiting the Endicotts, which was as well for the sake

---

[*] Chairman of Bass, the brewers, arch-reactionary, eminent opposer of the India Bill, who snored so loudly in the House that he threatened to interrupt debates. Lord Balneil described him thus: 'One of the best-hearted fellows one has ever met, kind, generous, self-effacing: ugly as possible, blinking at one through gold-rimmed spectacles: inarticulate, for it is almost impossible to hear a word he says, and his handwriting is simply deplorable. He has all the noble qualities of the mole.' (J. Vincent, *The Crawford Papers*, p. 169.)

of his relationship with Austen, delicate enough at this time. Each was aware of the loyalty they owed to the other and to overarching family solidarity. Even more than Austen, Neville was always ready to acknowledge his respect and regard for his half-sibling. He accepted that Austen was head of the family and thus de facto successor to Joe, even if it was Neville who was the true heir to Radical Joe's policies.

Austen, playing the game, considered that his duty as leader of the Conservative Party was to be unwaveringly loyal to the Goat. If he had opposed Lloyd George he would have walked into Number Ten, but he risked his own career to save Lloyd George's. In any event his essentially conservative disposition led him to see a Liberal/Conservative Alliance as an essential bulwark against the forces of socialism.

In Canada, Neville was taken aback to receive a perplexing telegram from Austen: 'ARTHUR', whoever Arthur was, 'BETTER. HOPES TO START EARLIEST POSSIBLE DAY BUT PLEASE SAY NOTHING ABOUT HIS PLANS AS HE MAY BE DELAYED BY BUSINESS.' The telegram was in code and had arrived before a letter from Austen providing the key: 'Arthur better' would mean that Parliament was to be dissolved. Just before Neville and Annie started off they received a further telegram saying that Arthur had given up all idea of his trip. That in turn was superseded by a third one saying that Arthur had recovered again.

When Neville and Annie got back they returned to a political world turned upside down. In 1918 Bonar Law had said that Lloyd George could if he wished be Prime Minister for the rest of his life. Now, just four years later, Lloyd George was not Prime Minister and indeed would never return to office.* Instead, Bonar Law, thinking that he had recovered from his cancer of 1921, became Prime Minister. He was now able to offer something more substantial to Neville than the under-secretaryship which was all he could offer when in coalition, the Postmaster Generalship. Neville found himself in a difficult position. Bonar Law had feared that the job on offer was too lowly. That wasn't the problem – Chamberlain's first instinct was to look for something

---

* But we shouldn't blind ourselves with hindsight. Throughout the twenties and thirties Lloyd George remained a colossus on the opposition benches. He remained full of devious vigour and enthusiasm. By methods that were unethical and illegal, and would not be tolerated today, he had built up a large personal war chest. No government could allow themselves to assume that he would not leap from the back benches to dominate politics as he had done so pre-eminently and for so long.

less than the head of a major department. What worried him – and worried him very greatly – was how Austen would be affected. He knew that the leapfrog would be hurtful. He went off to see Austen in Birmingham. He told him – I wonder if he meant it – that he would give up politics if his brother didn't want him to take Bonar Law's shilling. Austen was very unhappy and Neville left the meeting concluding that he would have to decline the offer. Later that same day he returned for dinner. He argued that accepting the offer wouldn't amount to a breach between the two brothers, but on the contrary (a pretty specious argument) that it would provide a link between them, so that if Bonar Law fell after the oncoming general election, or retired sick, Austen could take over as the head of a new coalition.

When Austen resisted these hypothetical convolutions, Neville said that he would decline the offer; but that would mean the end of his political career. He could not expect to continue if he had declined offers from first the coalition and now from Bonar Law. Austen gave way. He said to Neville and later to his sisters that he couldn't be responsible for such a sacrifice. The interview had been a painful one. Many years later Neville said that this had been 'the only time in our lives when we nearly quarrelled'.[6]

Austen found his climbdown for the sake of his brother's career all the more poignant because, for some reason, he believed that if Neville hadn't joined the government he, Austen, would have been able to turn Bonar Law out in six months' time. For all the Chamberlains, the family was paramount, an ideal concept of solidity and loyalty. This was truest of Neville, in his unquestioning reverence for Joe and all his policies. Relations between the half-brothers had always been affectionate if formal: they were never quite the same again.

But Austen's own loyalty to Lloyd George continued resolute. He maintained that loyalty in the face of attractive offers from Bonar Law, anxious to strengthen his administration by bringing Austen and the other Tory Lloyd Georgians aboard. In 1923 Bonar Law told Austen that if he would join the Cabinet he, Bonar Law, would resign six months later in his favour. Austen refused to come back – certainly without his colleagues, such as Churchill and F. E. Smith, Lord Birkenhead. But when Bonar Law died in October 1923 Austen acted as one of his pallbearers. He was a man of stubborn principle, but there was nothing petty about him.

*Chapter 15*

# At the Centre

Thus Neville Chamberlain entered government and was sworn of the Privy Council at the age of fifty-three. Just four months later he entered the Cabinet. The Bonar Law government in contrast to its meretricious predecessor was described by Lord Birkenhead, himself as meretricious as can be imagined, as an assembly of second-class brains. Lord Robert Cecil's response was, 'Better second-class brains than second-class character.' Its leader, Bonar Law, was described by his predecessor, Lloyd George, as 'honest to the verge of simplicity', a description which says quite a lot about Lloyd George.

Neville's duties included responsibility for wireless communications across the Empire. There was a debate about whether the system should be run as a government monopoly or as a private enterprise. As so often, Chamberlain preferred the collective approach to free enterprise. At the end of January 1923 he was asked to take on the additional post of Paymaster General. This was not in itself a hugely demanding job, its responsibility consisting of acting as banker for the spending departments, paying pensions and other administrative financial tasks. All the same, so soon after coming into government, Chamberlain was already discharging responsibilities on a much larger scale than most of his colleagues. This would be the pattern for the rest of his political career. Work was attracted to him and it was discharged speedily, efficiently and uncomplainingly. Bonar Law had told him at the outset that he could see him at any time if he had any suggestions to make, and he did immediately become involved in the kind of topics which had interested him already and with which he would come to be intimately involved: housing subsidies, slum clearance and rent restriction.

Chamberlain described himself and Sam Hoare as being 'the only socialists' in the 1922 Conservative government.* He believed in a big, directing government, 'the supervisory state' as he called it. But, perhaps even more, he valued efficient government at a local level. This he considered indispensable for the efficient running of the country. He was more interested in how efficient the local machine was than whether it was controlled by a Conservative or a Labour majority.

There was a general election in November 1922. The Minister of Health, Sir Arthur Griffith-Boscawen, lost his seat and because of his various interests Chamberlain seemed an obvious replacement. Bonar Law said as much, though there were more senior candidates in the queue. In the event, because of a by-election defeat and a refusal by one of the others, Chamberlain *was* offered the job in March 1923. With remarkable confidence and composure he asked not only for time to think but for an assurance that if he took the position he would have full responsibility for rent control and housing policy in addition to his mainstream responsibilities in regard to health.† He got what he wanted and made his first speech as a minister on 8 March 1923. He allowed himself one of his increasingly frequent moments of self-congratulation, reckoning that for the first time he had been in command of both himself and the House. Note this confidence in a man who had been forty-two before he left his father's house and fifty-three before he achieved his first junior ministerial office, and who was without any significant political following.

In May 1923 Bonar Law's health finally gave out and he was succeeded as Prime Minister by Stanley Baldwin. Bonar Law had been so impressed by what Neville had done in his few months at Health that he thought that with rather more parliamentary

---

* Hoare was at this time Secretary of State for Air. He went on to be Secretary of State for India, Foreign Secretary, First Lord of the Admiralty and Home Secretary. Ultra-loyal to Chamberlain and fiercely critical of those who deserted him, after a pause which followed the fall of Chamberlain's government, he was appointed Ambassador to Spain. He gave great service to his country in that role, securing the return of thousands of escaped servicemen to the United Kingdom, and, critically, keeping Franco from joining the Axis. He had gained valuable and relevant skills in his shadowy Intelligence work in Russia during the First World War. An outstanding figure-skater, but lacking bonhomie; R. A. Butler described him as 'the coldest fish with whom I ever had to deal'.

† And the responsibilities at Health were vastly extensive.

experience he might have been his successor. Maybe, but he did have far too little experience. Baldwin was another product of the Midlands and of industry – and indeed of Mason College. 'I shall be interested to see how I get on with Stanley Baldwin, but I fancy he will be all right. After all he is a businessman himself.'[1] Indeed, they both were or had been businessmen, Chamberlain in *quite* a big way and Baldwin in a *very* big way, but it was odd that he regarded that as their defining characteristic. Baldwin by now had been involved in politics at a fairly high level for quite a long time and Neville himself, had he been careless enough to walk under a bus in 1923, would have been remembered much more as a very successful local politician than as a manufacturer of nuts and bolts.

From now on, Baldwin and Chamberlain worked closely together, and long before Baldwin resigned in 1937 Chamberlain effectively ran the government of which the other was the head. They were very different men, but their qualities were complementary. Baldwin was genial, relaxed and contemplative, with an instinctive understanding of the mood of the House and the inarticulate feelings of the nation at large. His policy, like Walpole's, was to let sleeping dogs lie, to take the long view, to expect temporary passions to play themselves out. Sometimes it was difficult to know where constructive delay ended and indolence began, but he got on with people and people liked him as they did not like Chamberlain – so evidently if not an old man in a hurry, then a middle-aged man with an awfully earnest sense of purpose. He was decisive and restlessly active, though without the easy manner which prevented these qualities from being abrasive.

Baldwin did not feel threatened by Chamberlain, who was just two years his junior and not the thrusting representative of a younger generation. Baldwin, as Neville acknowledged, had an 'acute intuitive political sensitivity' but it was Chamberlain who supplied rigour and determination to the government.[2] Baldwin used to reflect that he and Chamberlain made a good team: *he* understood the mood of the times and Chamberlain supplied the constructive work. Their relationship was fairly cordial for the most part, and as a team they shaped the nature of Conservative politics for the next fourteen years, until Chamberlain himself became Prime Minister.

Chamberlain hoped that the change in Prime Minister might be an opportunity to bring back Austen and the other Georgians to the mainstream of Tory politics. Baldwin, the great conciliator, thought unity was essential and he was supported by the sick Bonar Law and by the King.* In the event, Baldwin made the mistake of offering Austen the Washington Embassy, which the latter resented as an end of representing his people in Birmingham and indeed of his political career.† In truth, Austen had too much self-esteem to have been tempted back by anything other than a return to the Exchequer, and that Baldwin wanted to give to Reginald McKenna. Austen was encouraged by the arrogant Birkenhead, another unreconciled Georgian although a high Tory, who was convinced that the mediocrities as he saw them of the present administration would soon be replaced by a more brilliant cast.

There was a meeting at Cherkley, Lord Beaverbrook's fairy-tale palace in Surrey, on 12 November 1923 when Baldwin offered jobs to both Birkenhead and Austen. The two coalitionists were ready to accept this so that they could work against Baldwin from within. But Baldwin was much wilier than Birkenhead allowed. A. J. P. Taylor said that Austen had been taken in by Baldwin and 'in his simple-minded way could not understand the difference between Empire Free Trade and Protection'.‡ ³ Baldwin's government was far too solid (at this stage; things would be different a few years later) to be subverted, and Austen and Birkenhead would have been Baldwin's prisoners. The scheme failed for the most trivial of causes. For some reason, the playwright Arnold Bennett had been at the meeting, and he revealed the plan to a *Daily News* reporter, after which Baldwin felt obliged to withdraw the offer. Reconciliation was, however, only delayed.

None of this fevered scheming for Neville. In August 1923, when he was in Argyll, fishing on the Oykell, he was astonished to receive a letter from Baldwin. McKenna had been judged unsuitable for the

---

* George V took a remarkable interest in the mechanics and personalities of politics, the last monarch to do so.
† Which indeed it would have been. At that time no one went to Washington without being ennobled. Washington was a convenient place for getting rid of troublesome rivals. Churchill dangled the office, unsuccessfully, in front of Lloyd George in 1940 (Mrs Thatcher did no better with Edward Heath in 1979) and successfully in front of Lord Halifax in the following year.
‡ Empire Free Trade meant free trade within the Empire. Protection meant penal tariffs on non-Empire imports.

Exchequer and the job was offered to him: 'What a day! Two salmon this morning, and the offer of the Exchequer the afternoon.' His intellectual confidence – indeed arrogance – would grow quite speedily as the years passed, but his immediate reaction was to decline the offer saying that he felt he had no gifts for finance. An odd reaction for an astute businessman who had trained as an accountant. Baldwin pressed, saying that he wanted a reliable colleague at his side.

Neville would probably have responded to this plea in any event, but Baldwin was starting to think about tariff reform and such thoughts were seductive to Joe's son. Baldwin doubted that free trade could continue in the context of a worldwide slump. The prospect of being Chancellor and having the opportunity to toy with protectionism was irresistible.

He reflected to his sisters that it would have pleased their father to think that a second son had succeeded to this, the most important office after that of Prime Minister: Austen had become Chancellor exactly twenty years earlier. When Austen congratulated Neville he told him that he could find no other case where two brothers had held the Treasury and only one other case (Chatham and his sons) where his father and two sons had sat in Cabinet.

When Baldwin succeeded Bonar Law he had a substantial parliamentary majority and had no need to go to the country. He accordingly surprised the political world by declaring on 25 October 1923 that he could only effectively fight unemployment if he had a mandate for tariff reform. Bonar Law had given a pledge that there wouldn't be change to free trade, so Baldwin needed a mandate.

Austen was sceptical about Baldwin's precipitate conversion to protectionism. He thought he hadn't done his homework. But blood was blood and tariff reform was in that blood, so Austen was ready to campaign for the new policy. Neville was against an early election on an issue he thought the electorate wasn't ready for. He wanted some 'education' to prepare people for abandoning the sacred doctrine. He thought that eighteen months would be needed for this educative process. He himself needed no education, but he was aware of what he called the 'hair-trigger consciences' of some of his free trade colleagues. He didn't push the point. Indeed he almost came to admire the Prime Minister's bravura: 'He is not so simple as he makes out . . . Here he has sprung a protectionist policy on the country almost at a moment's notice, with a Cabinet a substantial portion of which consists of free traders. Not one of them has resigned . . .'[4]

But his first instinct had been right. The country was vulnerable to fears about food taxes and the end of free trade. The general election of December 1923 left the Conservatives the largest party, but they had lost 86 seats and could only form a minority government. On 21 January 1924 Labour and the Liberals combined to bring the government down.

In the debate on the Labour motion of no confidence, Asquith, still leader of the tiny band of uncorrupted Liberals, made it clear that he would support the socialists. It was a speech of great principle which Neville described in his diary as 'the speech of his life', but for Austen Chamberlain it was a divisive move that would ultimately allow his own return to the Unionist Front Bench. He saw what Asquith had done:

He has taken his choice, and he has by that choice constituted his own immortality. He will go down to history as the last Prime Minister of a Liberal Administration. He has sung the swan song of the Liberal Party. When next the country is called upon for a decision, if it wants a Socialist government it will vote for a Socialist; if it does not want a Socialist government it will vote for a Unionist. It will not vote again for those who denatured its mandate and betrayed its trust.[5]

So Neville's first period as Chancellor had been a brief one, but he would be back, and in the meantime he had one little private victory. He persuaded his colleagues that they must bring Austen on board and that if they were to do so they would have to hold their noses and embrace Birkenhead as well. He invited Baldwin and Austen to dine with him on 5 February 1924. Austen said he would return to the party if he were allowed to bring his friends with him. Baldwin agreed. 'Austen was a bit stiff at first but gradually thawed . . . After that all went like clockwork and very soon it was "My dear Stanley" and "My dear Austen" as if they had ne'er been parted . . . so reunion has come at last, thanks, I think I may say, to me.'[6]

On the fall of Baldwin's government in January 1924 Ramsay MacDonald formed a first, brief minority Labour administration,* but a further general election in October 1924, with tariff reform *off* the manifesto, brought the Conservatives back. The party which came back to power was a united party. Austen and Birkenhead weren't the only Conservatives who had remained true to the coalition since 1922. During the short period of opposition, between January and October 1924, Neville Chamberlain applied his organisational talents to wooing them, and back they came, Churchill among them, first into the Shadow Cabinet and then into the Cabinet itself. Austen and Neville were both members of Baldwin's cabinet between 1924 and 1929, just as Austen had served in Cabinet along with Joe. A direct continuing link now ran from Joe to Neville.

Neville's personal election experience at Birmingham, Ladywood, was, however, not satisfactory. His opponent was Oswald Mosely, the future Fascist leader. Mosely had started as a Conservative, become an independent and was currently a Labour Party candidate. He was an outstandingly effective speaker and Neville compared poorly with him. The count was so close that at one point Mosely left the town hall to announce that he had won. Finally, after many recounts Neville was declared the winner at 4.30 a.m., his margin only seventy-seven votes.† Mosely didn't think much of the Chamberlains, Austen or Neville. He called them plaster effigies, and they were certainly not like him. It rained heavily on the day of the poll. Mosely said that the downpour had 'washed the lifeless body of the last of the Chamberlains back to Westminster'. For the 1929 general election, Chamberlain moved from Birmingham, Ladywood, to Birmingham, Edgbaston. Ladywood had been precarious, but Edgbaston was not, and it provided a safe basis for the rest of his parliamentary life.

The fact that Mosely with his populist appeal had made such powerful contact with disaffected voters reinforced Neville in his view that the country needed fundamental social reorganisation. As early as 28 November 1924 he wrote in *The Times* that the

---

* George V took it well for a very conservative monarch. He did, however, confide in his diary: 'Today twenty-three years ago dear Grandmama died. I wonder what she would have thought of a Labour government.'
† Rumours persisted that a bundle of voting papers was flushed down a lavatory.

government must use its powers to improve the condition of the people. Mosely may only have been nominally Labour, but Neville was not even nominally Conservative. He didn't *think* of himself as a Conservative, didn't call himself a Conservative and had not been elected as a Conservative. He was a member of the Birmingham Unionist Party and he remained a Liberal Unionist to the end.

Neville disapproved of the paternalistic 'One Nation' approach, the Disraelian tradition. He was sometimes called a socialist, which at that time didn't imply *quasi*-communist Clause Four doctrines, but rather the use of the power of the state to effect change. He did not reject the description. Although he was dirigiste, he was practical, and not theoretical. This essential practicality directed him towards a non-party consensual approach, not far away from non-dogmatic socialism. Parties got in the way of consensus, and the narrow outlook of traditional Conservatism, which he regarded as divisive, had no appeal for him. He wanted to 'discard the odious title of Conservative'.[7] The National Government when it came in 1931 was not – for him – an illusion designed to consolidate Conservative hegemony under a flag of convenience, but a means to create a 'fused party under a National Name'.[8]

A week after the election, on 5 December 1924, there was a huge celebration of the Conservative victory at the Royal Albert Hall. The building was adorned with a large poster of Baldwin. Banners proclaimed 'confidence, contentment, comradeship' and 'ordered progress, not revolution'. The audience received the Prime Minister on its feet, waving Union Jacks. All of this, managed mass meetings, the concept of a government operating above the level of party politics for the good of the nation as a whole, is full of hints of the approach that would be made over the next decade in Germany and Italy. Indeed Mosely, while still in the Labour Party, and John Strachey, who never left it, used techniques of mass management of the type which the Fascists would use. In the course of the thirties, the National Government under Chamberlain would, as we shall see, succumb to the conviction that it knew best and was accordingly entitled to resort to discipline and bullying to stifle dissent within the party that threatened to rock the boat. Fortunately, no one was tempted to take this tendency too far.

## Chapter 16

# A Radical at the Heart of the Tory Party

Chamberlain's choice of role in the new government is interesting. He could have remained at the Exchequer. It was assumed that he would, but he preferred instead to return to the Ministry of Health. The man who *did* go to Number Eleven was Winston Churchill. His most recent parliamentary years had been in the Liberal Party, but when the kaleidoscope was shaken and the coalition broke up he found little to keep him there. He stood at the election not as Liberal or Conservative but as a 'Constitutionalist'. His famous story was that when Baldwin asked if he would be prepared to be Chancellor he replied that he would indeed be happy to be Chancellor of the Duchy of Lancaster. A good story, but he knew that Baldwin was prepared to pay a high price to repair the split in the party.

The Chancellorship of course ranks above Health, and if Chamberlain's interest had been purely political advancement he would not have wanted to leave the Exchequer. But he was concerned about the apparently inexorable rise of socialism and the Labour movement. He knew already a very great deal about the social and economic conditions on which he believed that rise depended. He had unfinished business from Birmingham and from his first stint at Health and was very happy to remain in the department. He was very active there until 1929, a long stint.

Chamberlain's departmental responsibilities did not involve him directly in the 1926 General Strike, although he was active behind the scenes. His position was a moderate one, and was aware of the problems of the working classes and opposed anti-trades union legislation in the aftermath of the strike. Despite an increasing contempt for Labour politicians, he had a good deal of time for trades union leaders like Ernest Bevin, Secretary of the Transport and General Workers' Union, and Arthur Pugh, the chairman of the General Council of the TUC. On the other hand, of the mine owners he said, 'They are *not* a prepossessing crowd and once more I am compelled to say that they are about the stupidest and most narrow-minded employers I know, though I must say some of the ship builders run them pretty hard. I believe it is not without significance that in both trades the leaders are Scotsmen and Welshmen.'[1]

Chamberlain's attitude to the strike reflected the fact that he was never, except in the heat of partisan debate, a reactionary. He broadcast, saying that he was 'a man of peace'. The Managing Director of Elliotts and Hoskins who had enjoyed such good relations with his labour force that there had never been a day's strike, declared as soon as the General Strike had ended that it was 'the time to show generosity'.

His main involvement in the strike was as a member of a Supply and Transport Committee of the Cabinet. He told his sisters, 'The fact is that constitutional govt. is fighting for its life; if we failed it would be the Revolution, for the nominal leaders would be whirled away in an instant.'[2] Before the strike had actually been declared, the Cabinet considered whether to introduce a bill making a secret ballot obligatory before such a strike and whether or not to remove the immunity of trades union funds in the case of a national strike. Douglas Hogg, the Attorney General,* drafted a Bill which Chamberlain was prepared to support on the basis of legal advice given by Sir John Simon, deputy leader of the Liberal Party. In the event the legislation was not enacted and in retrospect Baldwin thought that Chamberlain had been unduly influenced by Hogg, an aggressive and partisan politician.

The next general election had to be held by October 1929. By the time that date approached, Chamberlain, a member of the House for

---

* In his last years of practice, years of very expensive litigation, he had a huge income as a KC. Like Chamberlain he began his adult life in the West Indies (and British Guiana) where he worked for eight years in the family firm of sugar merchants. Bonar Law appointed him Attorney General before he had a seat in Parliament. In an extraordinarily short time he was one of the party's stars. According to Harold Macmillan, Lord Derby told the Duke of Devonshire that 'They have found a wonderful little man. One of those attorney fellows, you know. He will do all the work.' In what Macmillan called 'a truly Trollopian scene', Derby said that the little man's name was 'Pig'. (Macmillan, *Winds of Change, 1914–1939*, p.129.)

such a very short time, was a man of significance. In September 1927, looking ahead to a retirement which in the event he postponed for quite a long time, Baldwin judged that he himself would be succeeded either by Douglas Hogg or by Chamberlain, probably the former. In March 1929 he had to find a new Lord Chancellor. When he told Chamberlain that he was thinking of Hogg, Chamberlain was surprised. He thought it was important to keep Hogg in the Commons as a future party leader – a self-denying position for him to take: if Hogg sat on the Woolsack he would be a Member of the House of Lords and not eligible to be Prime Minister. Chamberlain recommended Birkenhead, a former Lord Chancellor, largely to get him out of the India Office. The job was offered to Birkenhead, but rather to Baldwin's relief he turned it down. Hogg was in a quandary: he quite liked the idea of becoming Lord Chancellor but didn't want to bow 'out of political life if there were any danger of Churchill becoming Prime Minister.

Hogg and Chamberlain discussed the matter frankly, and Chamberlain said that he was aware that the two of them were talked of as Baldwin's successors. He knew from Austen that Birkenhead and Churchill would serve under Hogg. He didn't know whether they would serve under him. In any event, he didn't want to be Prime Minister. He did his best to hold Baldwin back, but for some reason the prince of indolence moved fast. By now he was clear that he didn't want Birkenhead, an unpredictable alcoholic, to return to the Woolsack on which he had sat with distinction in more temperate days. Hogg became Lord Chancellor. Churchill would probably not have been an acceptable choice as leader in 1929, but his conduct over the India Bill made sure that he was unacceptable by the time Baldwin did resign. Chamberlain thus became Baldwin's inevitable successor.

In the run-up to the general election which would take place in May 1929, Baldwin asked Chamberlain if he wanted to be Colonial Secretary in the next government. Neville wanted that job, Joe's job, more than anything else and said so. When Baldwin, who enjoyed his life as a gentleman farmer, murmured that maybe the Ministry of Agriculture would be more fun, Chamberlain politely disagreed. Amazingly, Baldwin then wondered if Churchill would be interested in looking after the nation's farms. Churchill assured him that he would not. Baldwin continued to mull things over. He wondered if

Churchill might be a good candidate for the India Office: an appalling prospect, but perhaps not as bad as the later thought that he might be a good Viceroy. He then asked Chamberlain if he couldn't be persuaded to take the Exchequer rather than the Colonial Office. Chamberlain reiterated his preference for filial continuity but did say he would consider being Chancellor if Baldwin really wanted him to take the job.

This was the situation as the Conservatives approached the general election. The government of 1924–9 had taken a lot of important practical measures, many of them at Chamberlain's instigation; and in days when opinion polls were in their infancy and enjoyed little credibility a further period of Conservative rule seemed likely. These were, however, grim years. Unemployment had been high for a long time, morale was low, conditions in the depressed areas, particularly South Wales and Durham, were deplorable, and prolonged unemployment and poverty affected the nation's health. Chamberlain knew from his medical officers of the extent of anaemia amongst women, poor recovery from the effects of childbirth and an increase in the cases of rickets amongst children. A memorandum of the Chief General Inspector at the Ministry of Health recorded that a typical diet consisted of 'bread, margarine, tea and sugar, an infinitesimal quantity of milk, usually skimmed and condensed, with some meat only on Sunday ... In the poorest houses the Sunday meat is often as little as a shilling's worth ... It is a deplorable diet and except in the face of facts it would be incredible that a family can exist in health on it week after week for prolonged periods.'[3] Chamberlain proposed that the government should give £155,000 to a relief fund operated by the Lord Mayor of London.

The Conservatives lost the general election. They had expected to have a majority of fifty or sixty over the other parties combined. In the event Labour became the largest party in the Commons for the first time, with 288 seats against the Conservatives' 260 and the Liberals' 59. Chamberlain was very disappointed. He expected that Labour would form a minority government for about two years after which it would win a majority and remain in office for a further four or five years. Thinking of his personal prospects he said, 'Gladstone and Disraeli were both Prime Ministers in their old age – but they didn't altogether make a success of it!'[4]

Between 1929 and 1931 Chamberlain and the Conservative Party was in opposition. It was a time of crisis for the party and in particular for Baldwin's leadership. For Chamberlain it was a period in which he consolidated his authority, for the most part being eminently support-ive and loyal to his leader. He spent some months during this period in East Africa, preparing for the Colonial brief. He also turned, as he had so often done before, to the *management* of politics, something in which Baldwin had little interest, and founded a Conservative Party Research Department which he headed for the rest of his life.

The East African visit took place in the winter of 1929–30. When the ship entered the Indian Ocean there was a fancy-dress party at which Neville was dressed as the Grand Inquisitor – an arresting image. In Kenya he asked to have the chance of inspecting a sisal plan-tation – Andros was not forgotten.

On his return to England and in charge of the Research Department, he used the opposition years, as Rab Butler, Iain MacLeod and Enoch Powell did between 1945 and 1951, to modernise the Conservative Party. In truth, Butler and his subordinates were reorganising a party structure which, however imperfect, already existed. Chamberlain was in many respects constructing from scratch. In 1930 he also began to manage an inner Shadow Cabinet business committee. This was detailed technical work which was exactly what he enjoyed and excelled at. In his diary he frankly said that he would now have his finger on the springs of policy.[5]

The chairman of the party was J. C. C. Davidson. Davidson had had to ensure that the party's finances were untainted by the scandalous sale of honours by its former Liberal allies under Lloyd George and Maundy Gregory. He had also started on the process of modernisa-tion. *He* may truly have been the man behind the Research Department. Lord Blake, the historian of the Tory Party, maintained that some of the innovations credited to Chamberlain were truly Davidson's achievements. All the same, after the 1929 defeat Davidson and Central Office were under attack, and Chamberlain took it upon himself to tell Davidson that he must go – without even consulting Baldwin.

In Nick Smart's view, Chamberlain was engaged in devious personal advancement when he deposed Davidson from chairmanship of the party and took the job himself 'after much manoeuvre and studied reluctance',[6] but the evidence of neat-footed positioning is far from strong. If Neville was manoeuvring for the succession, he made a pretty invisible job of it. It is the case, however, that Baldwin was currently skating on very thin ice, very vulnerable after the election defeat, and a successor might be needed very soon. In these middle years, Baldwin's lackadaisical approach was much criticised and Chamberlain was indeed commendably loyal. He moaned to his sisters about his chief's indecisiveness. He complained about the weight of the burdens he carried, but he refrained from striking. In any event, in June 1930 Chamberlain became chairman of the party, an appointment which acknowledged his dominating role.

Baldwin, quiescent, ruminative, conciliatory, not to say temperamentally indolent, was not a forceful opposition leader. He neither had the will nor the character, and his ineffectiveness was criticised by the great press lords, Beaverbrook and Rothermere. Chamberlain's position was invidious. Everyone knew – and he certainly did – that if Baldwin went, he would succeed him. If he had passively stood by, Baldwin might well have been ditched, but at the risk of offending his leader, he alerted Baldwin to the discontent of the back benches.

What was particularly piquant was that the newspaper proprietors, Beaverbrook in particular, chose to attack Baldwin on an issue with which Chamberlain's personal views put him hugely in sympathy: Empire free trade, with consequent tariffs and imperial preference. As his diary for 27 July 1929 confirms, Chamberlain saw tariffs and customs as very much part of a larger imperial trade policy. Although Baldwin had flirted with tariff reform on the view that the increasingly weak economy required protection, he wasn't prepared to countenance tax on food imports, an essential part of Empire preference. Beaverbrook, a Canadian by birth, was engaged on an imperial campaign of his own: his vision wasn't far from Joe's. His newspapers carried the image of a crusader in chains and 'crusader' candidates stood for the policy of a referendum on food taxes. It reflects the peculiar status of free trade as almost an element of the constitution that it was thought that a referendum was needed to address it.

A referendum then, as now, was an anomalous, dangerous and illogical innovation that cuts across the British system of representative democracy in order to address some great issue of principle which is conceived to transcend party politics, but finally Baldwin, despite his innate political common sense, went so far as to agree to a referendum (though it was never held).

Despite Chamberlain's efforts at conciliation ('The Beaver, whom I now call Max ... I confess I am getting to like the creature'),[7] the press lords were not satisfied. They were hugely disruptive. Rothermere enjoyed the exercise of power with almost as much gusto as his brother, Northcliffe, whose 'diseased vanity', as Lloyd George described it, bordered on clinical insanity. To the vanity was added the fact that he supported Nazism, Oswald Mosely and the British Union of Fascists. He himself wrote an editorial under the headline 'Hurrah for the Blackshirts'.

The influence of the popular press in the years between the wars – and during the wars themselves – is now difficult to comprehend, and the power of the proprietors was far greater than that of more modern newspapermen like Rupert Murdoch and Conrad Black. The owners were of course influenced by commercial considerations, and there was fierce competition in the newspaper wars of these years. But even more important was the scale of the egos involved. No ego was greater than that of Max Aitken, Lord Beaverbrook. He had been a Member of Parliament before the First World War and was a Minister in Lloyd George's government and under Churchill in the Second World War. He exercised more political power from the shadows than he did in government and he relished it. He possibly exaggerated how influential he had been in his 1928 book, *Politicians and The War*, but he certainly believed, as did the Harmsworth Brothers, Northcliffe and Rothermere, that he could make and break any ministerial career. Just as Rothermere believed in Fascism, Beaverbrook claimed to believe in close imperial ties founded on Empire free trade. He probably genuinely did so believe, but there was a good deal of personal dislike in his treatment of Baldwin, whose plain, down-to-earth approach was very different from the flamboyance which Beaverbrook preferred. It would be a mistake also to minimise the extent of his purely unconstructive malicious mischievousness.*

* After the Second World War he would often phone the editor of 'Londoner's Diary' in the *Evening Standard*, which he owned, simply to sing 'Stir the Pot of Discord' to the tune of 'Polly Put the Kettle On'.

Chamberlain's loyalty was tested. The press lords made it clear that if he became Prime Minister, that if he took Baldwin's place, he would have their total support. He dismissed the idea out of hand: 'The commonest loyalty makes it impossible to listen to such a suggestion.'[8]

When he planted out heaths and dwarf azaleas at Christmas 1930 he claimed to find politics 'very nauseating'. But by now he truly *was* a politician – not simply a man with a public duty who found himself there. He was part of politics whether he liked it or not, and he *did* now like it. There was no suggestion of turning his back on Westminster.

The Baldwin crisis continued in the new year. As chairman of the Conservative Party, Chamberlain received letters of complaint and criticism on an almost daily basis. He appreciated the exquisite poignancy of the situation. He was the one person who could get rid of Baldwin at any moment, but as he would be the beneficiary of such a move, it was one which he could not make.[9] It was that consideration – and a his genuine sense of loyalty – that ensured his reticence. He had said that he would not play Lloyd George to Baldwin's Asquith, and he stayed true to that position. In terms of political or practical principles there was nothing he particularly admired in Baldwin. His laissez-faire lethargy was very far from Neville's constructive, organised energy, but he didn't think it right for Baldwin or for the party that he should be pushed out in a moment of weakness.

The main political issue about which Baldwin had distinct views at this time was nothing to do with imperial preference or tariff reform. He did feel strongly about the future of the Indian subcontinent and he did want, before he left the stage, to do something about it. This was a divisive issue in the party. A hint of the division was given when Churchill resigned from the Shadow Cabinet in part over India at the beginning of 1931. Most of the Tory Party was uninterested in tariff reform and didn't really understand it, but there were many diehards in Westminster and in the country who were fiercely opposed to letting go of the jewel in the crown.

There were now three elements to the opposition to Baldwin: an incoherent view that he wasn't up to the job, a desire for full-blooded imperial preference which would make Britain great again, and a reactionary opposition to weakening the connection with India which, as Churchill said, would reduce Britain to the status of a mere European weakling like Belgium. This last item was critical. Baldwin faced the party at a meeting at Caxton Hall in June 1930. At his best he was a magnificent speaker: he obtained a resounding vote of confidence. The Conservative Party prefers to depose its leaders in private, not in public. The assaults continued. Chamberlain attempted to clarify policy and unite the Cabinet by not excluding the possibility of food taxes. The Cabinet failed to gather behind the policy but Chamberlain continued to promote it, claiming that nineteenth-century free trade doctrines were out of place in a world of mass unemployment and that Britain could only remain a great power as the leader of her Dominions.

Baldwin's standing continued to fall. In February 1931 the party's chief agent, Robert Topping, drew up a memorandum, stressing how critical matters had become. Chamberlain's position was difficult. He was told on all hands that he would make a better leader than Baldwin. He knew that if Baldwin went 'the whole party would heave a sigh of relief'.[10] But Chamberlain's loyalty was pretty well total. I say 'pretty well' because Chamberlain's behaviour with the Topping memorandum was suspect. He showed it to senior colleagues, claiming he only did so to see what their views were on showing it to Baldwin himself. They almost all said that Baldwin would have to resign. Neville decided that it was his duty to put the letter to Baldwin. Roy Jenkins wrote, 'This document, which was rich in wounding phrases, was by no means unwelcome to Chamberlain, particularly as it ended with a fairly clear hint that he ought to be the new leader. He then behaved somewhat unctuously, showing it to half the Shadow Cabinet in order to get their advice on whether or not he ought to worry Baldwin with it.' Well, perhaps. But could he have done otherwise?

On 1 March 1931 he sent the memorandum to Baldwin, going so far as to say that Topping had accurately represented the views of his colleagues. Baldwin prepared to fall on his sword. He summoned Chamberlain and told him that he would resign. Chamberlain passed the news on to his sister. Geoffrey Dawson, the editor of *The Times*, prepared a leading article under the heading 'Mr Baldwin Withdraws'. It is not known who passed the news to him, but he and Chamberlain were very friendly.

Within twenty-four hours Baldwin changed his mind – he didn't lack courage. He told Chamberlain on 2 March that he would not resign. He would give up his seat at Bewdley and stand as the official candidate at the upcoming by-election in the Westminster St George's constituency: 'he would go down fighting'. It was an extraordinary position to take, and a very brave one. But Chamberlain didn't like it. He said that Baldwin couldn't do this because of the effect on his successor. Baldwin's response was blunt and straight: 'I don't give a damn about my successor, Neville.'

The Westminster by-election was required following the death of the sitting member, Sir Laming Worthington-Evans. The official Tory candidate, John Moore-Brabazon,* had withdrawn precisely because he could not support the party leader, and Sir Ernest Petter had announced that he would stand as an anti-Baldwinite. One Shadow Cabinet member who dissented from the view that Baldwin should go was William Bridgeman. Bridgeman now changed the history of the Conservative Party. While Dawson was writing his editorial, it was Bridgeman who put steel into Baldwin and persuaded him to sit tight and to fight the St George's by-election.

In the event, Baldwin didn't have to fight. Alfred Duff Cooper came to the rescue and fought the seat as an official Conservative candidate. Chamberlain and the rest of the Shadow Cabinet accepted that Baldwin's final decision should be delayed until the outcome of the by-election was known. Duff Cooper was supported by Chamberlain and all the resources of the party and of course by Baldwin himself. Baldwin made a famous speech at the Queen's Hall on 17 March in which he flayed the press lords with his famous reference to 'power without responsibility, the prerogative of the harlot throughout the ages'. The quotation is so familiar that it's easy to overlook just how bold and devastating the attack was.† Duff Cooper was elected with a majority of 5,000. Baldwin's authority had been

---

* Later enobled with the magnificent title of Lord Brabazon of Tara. He had a distinguished First World War career but was passionately against fighting Hitler. He made common cause with Mosely to that end but was brought into Churchill's war administration. He was the first person in Britain to qualify as a pilot. In 1909 he won a £1,000 prize from the *Daily Mail* by proving that pigs could fly: he placed one in a waste-paper basket which he tied to the wing-strut of his aeroplane. In 1955, at the age of seventy-one, he won the Cresta Run Coronation Cup at an average speed of 44 mph.

† Some Tory wit remarked that the jibe (which had been supplied by Baldwin's cousin, Rudyard Kipling) would cost the party 'the tarts' vote'.

reasserted and he was clear that he would go when he wanted to and not when Chamberlain, or anyone else, told him to go.

So Baldwin did not resign in 1930 as everyone from the editor of *The Times* down expected him to do. He was to go on until 1937 when he resigned very much at a time of his own choosing. Chamberlain's relationship with Baldwin briefly suffered. At Austen's instigation Neville gave up the chairmanship of the party which he told Baldwin had put strains on their friendship. There was a reconciliation at a meeting on 25 March. Neville said that he had been hurt by some apparent slights on Baldwin's part. Baldwin apologised and said that the fault lay in his own shyness and reserve. Thereafter the two of them settled back into their old partnership. Chamberlain persuaded Baldwin to take up an aggressive stance as leader of the opposition and carry the attack against the Labour Party.

Chamberlain made peace with Beaverbrook. He caught four salmon in a day on the River Dee, had time to fish too on the Avon, Piddle and Char. Moreover his garden had never been more beautiful: the delphiniums and roses were particularly good; and he congratulated himself that he had seen off his main competitors for the succession, Churchill, Hailsham and Robert Horne.*

But however well things went on the Piddle, the country's economy could not be ignored. The second Labour minority administration, which Ramsay MacDonald had led since the 1929 general election, faced increasingly grave problems. By now, 1930–1, the economic crisis was bearing hard on politics. Unemployment was at 2.5 million and confidence in the pound was declining so fast that in July 1931 £66 million was withdrawn from the city: the Bank was losing gold at a rate of £2.5 million a day. Chamberlain told the Labour Chancellor, Snowdon, that he must balance the Budget.

Then he went to fish the Tummel, noting how good it was to smell the bog plants and birches. In the continuing crisis he did not have

---

* Horne had been Chancellor in 1921, like Austen declined to join Bonar Law's administration, declined a return to the Chancellorship under Baldwin in 1923, but came back to the front bench in a now united Tory Party in 1924. He was briefly vice-chairman of Baldwin & Co: ultimately he was more interested in money and directorships than in political service and Baldwin wrote him off as 'that rare thing, a Scotch cad'.

time to stay in the Tummel valley for long. He was called to London on 11 August 1931 to confer with MacDonald, Snowdon, Baldwin and the Bank. Baldwin did not allow the collapse of his country's economy to interfere with his holidays and returned to his cure at Aix. By 24 August MacDonald had managed to secure international credits to balance the books, but at the cost of cuts which lost him eight ministers.

Chamberlain was in tune with most other economic thinkers of the time in adhering to the traditional view that the government was simply spending more than it could afford. Ramsay MacDonald was of the same mind: that desperate remedies were required for which the Labour Party was not prepared. A coalition government was mooted. The Conservatives initially rejected the idea; but by early August Chamberlain in particular was persuaded of the need for a cross-party approach. In the summer months, Baldwin was almost impossible to winkle out from the spas of Europe, where he delighted to aestivate. It has been computed that he travelled to and from the spas (even at the height of the abdication crisis in 1936) more slowly than he would have done in the days of stagecoaches. It was largely therefore left to Chamberlain to conduct the negotiations with Labour which led to the formation of a National Government on 24 August 1931.

There had been vague talk of a National Government from the early summer of 1931. In July, MacDonald approached the Conservative Party chairman, Lord Stonehaven, with a proposal of that sort. Baldwin rejected the idea altogether. He had no wish to join in another disastrous coalition. He spoke publicly about the idea on 6 July in Hull and reiterated his position to the Cabinet Secretary, Maurice Hankey. Even as the demand for a National Government became stronger and the deteriorating economic position underscored the need, Baldwin kept repeating that he had destroyed one coalition and did not want to enter another.

His change of heart was to an extent precipitated by the King, who persuaded him to agree to serve in a National Government under MacDonald. A few hours after Baldwin left the King, Ramsay MacDonald arrived at the palace to say that eleven members of the Cabinet had voted in favour of necessary economies, including a 10 per cent cut in the dole, but eight had voted against. MacDonald said that he had no alternative but to tender his resignation. The King liked

MacDonald and told him that he was the only man to lead the country through the crisis. He said that he expected him to remain as his Prime Minister and that it was the duty of the Liberals and Conservatives to support him in restoring confidence in the financial stability of the country and that he should therefore reconsider his decision.

MacDonald, like the King, took a high, patriotic line. It was clear enough that a National Government could be formed, and he would do his best to get the economy proposals through even though that would be his political death warrant. He would not continue thereafter in office. Stanley Baldwin, present at this meeting, maintained an unhelpful silence: it was Chamberlain who sought to persuade MacDonald that he had many supporters in the country and indeed admirers beyond the country and that he would be failing them if he did not continue as Prime Minister. He asked him also to consider the effect on foreign opinion.[11]

Baldwin had told the King that if the government fell he would be ready to form a government. He thought that the likeliest and best outcome of these delicate negotiations would be his taking over as Prime Minister. He said so in a letter to his wife on 24 August. The fact that he did not become Prime Minister was due to the King's vision, MacDonald's sense of duty and Neville Chamberlain's advocacy. The importance of the first of these and the extent of the King's personal involvement is very different from modern constitutional theory and practice.*

MacDonald *had* intended to resign, even when the King pressed him to stay on. Chamberlain's intervention, pressing him to do what the King wanted, rather than simply support the new government from the back benches had been important. Keith Feiling argued that Chamberlain's role was critical in keeping MacDonald at Number Ten and Baldwin out of it.[12] It now seems more likely that Chamberlain was neither disloyal to his own chief nor Machiavellian, and that the more important elements in what happened were Baldwin's frequent absences on holiday together with the very active role of the King.[13]

The King went back to Balmoral. He wrote to Ramsay MacDonald on 27 August, 'I wish you and your colleagues every success in the

---

* But remember that this was not a modern monarch. In his naval days he had sailed the world in a wooden man-of-war.

difficult task imposed upon you. I am happy to feel that I have been able to return to my Highland home without changing my Prime Minister, in whom I have full confidence.'[14]

Thus the National Government was formed. There were four Labour men in the Cabinet, four Conservatives (Baldwin, Chamberlain, Hoare, Cunliffe-Lister) and two Liberals. Chamberlain returned to the Ministry of Health. The Budget was balanced, but at the cost of substantial increases in taxation and almost equal cuts in expenditure, including reductions in unemployment benefit. There were repercussions too, demonstrations and clashes with the police.

The National Government, intended to have a very limited life, went to the country on 27 October and returned to power to live on until it fell under the stresses of a world war in 1940. The government's manifesto in October was more a demand than a promise, a demand for 'a doctor's mandate'. What did that bland expression mean? It's doubtful whether anyone knew or even wondered. In practice the euphemism meant that the government could do pretty well anything it wanted. It reflected the fact that the electorate seemed to have abandoned any confidence in the traditional party-political set-up and blindly surrendered effective democratic control to an extreme and reactionary coalition.

Feiling in his life of Chamberlain says that 'On 27 October, by something rather over two to one, or by fourteen and a half million votes against six and a half, democracy declared its will.'[15] It would be truer to say that democracy abdicated. The National Government had 558 MPs of which 471 were Conservatives, 35 National Liberals and 32 official Liberals, and the Reading–Samuel Liberal group which accepted tariffs only as a temporary expedient in opposition to Lloyd George's policy.* The tiny group of Lloyd George Liberals – just four – were in opposition. There were just fifty-two Labour Members. Of the Labour front bench who had not followed MacDonald, only Lansbury survived. A parliamentary revolution had taken place of an unprecedented scale and character. The National Government, and particularly its Conservative

* The Liberal Party was now divided as Gaul had been. Lloyd George presided over the Independent Liberals, who were opposed to the National Government. John Simon led the Liberal National Party. Herbert Samuel was the head of the official party, which progressively dissented over tariff reform and finally went into opposition.

element, had been invested with vast powers and an authority which it would abuse for the rest of the decade.

In a way, the National Government was a failure: there was no real sense of national unity. Austerity and stable government was attacked by a naval mutiny at Invergordon, by hunger marches, demonstrations and later by violence on the streets as fascists and communists clashed. Less than a month after the National Government was formed to maintain the parity of the pound, the gold standard was abandoned and parity with it.* On the other hand the National Government, unkind, repressive and reactionary, reflected what some wanted in this unhappy decade.

MacDonald continued to occupy the figurehead role of Prime Minister until 1935, and indeed remained in the Cabinet thereafter. He made speeches in a beautiful voice. It was said that before he spoke no one knew what he was going to say and after he had spoken no one know what he had said. He was increasingly and seriously ill, but he told reporters that all he was suffering from was 'loss of memory'. It was a sad end for a courageous and idealistic leader who always considered himself to be a loyal Labour man and not the leader who had betrayed the party. That he did remain as Prime Minister in a government that was controlled by the Conservatives was to a considerable extent the result of Chamberlain's cross-party views. It was again a reflection of Chamberlain's outlook that the Labour Member Phillip Snowdon was allowed to remain Chancellor of the Exchequer until the October general election, while Chamberlain himself returned to the Ministry of Health.

Baldwin was perfectly content to be the titular leader of his party. Idle, genial and reassuring, he was neither jealous of MacDonald's apparent power, nor of the real power exerted by Neville Chamberlain. Chamberlain's industry, ability and sheer competence made him the

---

* Before the First World War the pound and the dollar (and other currencies) were tied to the value of different weights of gold and their values were thus fixed, one against the other. Britain suspended the convertibility of the pound during the war, but, as Chancellor, Churchill returned to the gold standard on the advice of Treasury officials in 1925. The return never worked. It overvalued the pound, and the whole system was now flawed because of the policy of various countries, notably France, which had devalued before returning to gold, and the US, which had moved away from strict convertibility in 1913 when the States adopted the Federal Reserve System.

dominating figure in the Cabinet. After the October general election, at which Snowdon did not stand, he took over as Chancellor and remained at the Exchequer from 1931 to 1937. He looked far beyond his own brief, which was indeed remarkably extensive in itself. He dealt thus not only with the fiscal and tariff and economic issues that inevitably fell to his own department, but also with the social issues which always preoccupied him. Even in relation to foreign affairs and the need to address Hitler's growing military strength, which were areas far beyond any construction of the borders of his departmental authority, he was increasingly the dominant voice in the Cabinet.*

By 1935 he was certainly feeling restless: 'I am more and more carrying this government on my back. The PM is ill and tired, S[tanley] B[aldwin] is tired and won't apply his mind to problems. It is certainly time there was a change.'[16] A couple of weeks after he made that diary entry he wrote to Hilda: 'As you will see I have become a sort of acting PM – only without the actual power of the PM. I have to say, "Have you thought", or "What would you say" when it would be quicker to say, "This is what you must do".'

But when MacDonald retired on 7 June 1935 it was inevitably Baldwin who succeeded him, and in the general election of 14 November 1935, the last to be held until July 1945, his reassuring presence gave the National Government – a Conservative government in all but name – a comfortable majority of 242. All the same, Baldwin was, as Chamberlain had said in his diary, far from well, and the pressure he came under in 1936 as a result both of international politics and the abdication crisis at home, took their toll on him.

Baldwin announced that he would retire in May 1937, and Chamberlain succeeded him as Prime Minister on the 28th day of that month. At the age of sixty-eight years and seventy-one days he took office, older than any subsequent Prime Minister of Great Britain. Henry Campbell-Bannerman was slightly older when he took office in 1905 and before C-B only Palmerston beat him, back in February 1855. Chamberlain's age did not tell on him – he remained very much on the ball to the end of his life. What caused him more

---

* As Prime Minister, when Cabinet discussion turned to foreign affairs, Baldwin would ostentatiously close his eyes and say, 'Wake me up when you've finished with that.' Thus he addressed himself to the threats of the dictators. Charming or disgraceful?

difficulty and impaired his capacity to manage the House was rather the age when he became an MP and his consequent lack of political experience and flair coupled with his unfortunate manner.

So now we have Chamberlain in office as Prime Minister, where he would remain for almost exactly three years until he was toppled by the famous debate on the conduct of the Norway Campaign, implicitly on his role as a wartime Prime Minister. These three years saw him more and more embroiled in the world of foreign affairs and rearmament in which he had already been dabbling, and it is largely from this brief part of his whole political life that he acquired, wrongly, the reputation for that combination of gullibility and lack of backbone which is implied by the 'appeasement' label.

That period will be examined later. In the meantime, I want to look at his time in those offices which so closely reflected his true political interests: Health in 1923, from 1924 to 1929 and briefly again in 1931; and the Exchequer in 1923 and again from 1931 to 1937.

*Chapter 17*

# The Health of the Nation

'As you walk through the industrial towns you lose yourself in laby-rinths of little brick houses blackened by smoke, festering in planless chaos round miry alleys and little cindered yards where there are stinking dust-bins and lines of grimy washing and half-ruinous W.C.s.' In *The Road to Wigan Pier*, George Orwell started by describing the housing in the mining towns in the north of England, houses that were 'poky and ugly, and insanitary and comfortless . . . , distributed in incredibly filthy slums round belching foundries and stinking canals and slag-heaps that deluge them with sulphurous smoke', houses that were simply not fit for human habitation. He goes on to describe the kind of lives that were lived in such houses. His argument is that a steady, independent, distinctly bolshie working class that had lived in more prosperous conditions before the First World War had been ground down by poverty and increased unemployment to accept conditions that *he* would not live in for a week if he were paid to, but which their inhabitants hung on to because there was nothing better to go to.

The harsh squalor of the lives of millions of Britons in these bleak, interwar years and the physical surroundings in which they were lived is so far from our experience that it takes a conscious mental effort to envisage them. Chamberlain knew what life for the poor and excluded was like. He had seen that life as he walked to work through Birmingham. Now, as Minister for Health, it was his duty and his opportunity to do something about it.

An assessment of Neville Chamberlain must rest on his several stints at the Ministry of Health as much as on any other part of his career. What emerges here is, above all, his zest, his drive, his *passion* for the work he did at the ministry. He was at Health in 1923 quite briefly, before he became Chancellor for the first time. When the Conservatives returned to office in 1924 he came back to Health, rather than remaining at the Exchequer. In 1931 he returned again to Health but only for a short period before moving back to being Chancellor.

It is very revealing that in 1924 he chose Health rather than the Exchequer. Whatever it was in theory, the move was not in reality demotion, but an essential part of Chamberlain's political strategy. He, like Baldwin, wanted to reunite the party and bring back the Georgians. Putting Churchill at the Exchequer, despite the fact that he had no background in finance or business, achieved that objective.

An important role for Churchill at the centre of government was crucial, much more significant than anything that happened to Austen, whom nobody but Neville much cared about, or to Birkenhead, amoral, alcoholic, a burnt-out comet whose former brilliance was now forgotten. Churchill had been about as close as anyone to Lloyd George: detaching him from allegiance to the king over the water was much to be desired. The problem was his commitment to free trade, of which he had always been a very prominent supporter. Indeed, his opposition to Joe Chamberlain's imperial protectionism was what had taken him out of the Conservative Party in the first place. Now that the party wanted, when the electorate was prepared to allow it, to implement the policies that Joe had advocated, it was better to have Churchill inside the tent, than outside protesting. Austen had said something similar. When Baldwin had been wondering whether to bring Churchill into the government at all, Austen told them that if he left Churchill out he would be leading a Tory rump within six months.[1]

Neville wasn't quite so sure. He thought, wrongly as it turned out, that Churchill was so hostile to protection that he would divide the party. He described Churchill and the President of the Board of Trade, Sir Philip Cunliffe-Lister, as 'a pair of economic prudes ... always drawing up their skirts lest the purity of their Free Trade Principles should be injured by giving a helping hand to anyone who is in need'.[2]

He was, however, quite clear that *he* didn't want to go back to the Exchequer. He had said before that he liked spending money far better than saving it and he hadn't enjoyed his own stay at the Treasury. Health

*Above left*. NC, recognisable even in a smock, apparently already preoccupied by big ideas.

*Above right*. An even more recognisable Neville, with Ida.

*Left*. In his time at Rugby.

(By permission of Cadbury Research Library: Special Collections, University of Birmingham, The Chamberlain Family Collection, C/9/1 (album pp. 20–21)

On the unpromising sisal plantation, Andros. Lennox Forbes, left, a neighbour who became a close friend, and Michael Knowles, NC's manager. In the background, just discernible, the schooner *Pride of Andros*.

Joe, left, and Austen, captioned in NC's handwriting, 'on my west Piazza 1893', informally dressed.

NC's surprisingly comfortable sitting room on Andros.

(Images copyright Francis Chamberlain)

The Chamberlain family at Highbury, c. 1900. Back row from left: a dour Neville, a dapper Austen and an elegant Joe. Front: Beatrice and Mary Chamberlain, Joe's third wife. (Mirrorpix / Alamy Stock Photo)

An illustration from F.A. Hornibrook's *The Culture of the Abdomen.* Chamberlain pinned up illustrations of the exercises and performed them every day. Of this, Exercise VII, 'Hip Roll', Hornibrook says, 'The movement is not particularly elegant; neither is a loose and pendulous abdomen.' (Author's collection)

The outdoor Chamberlain, relaxed and perhaps truer to himself. Here with Arthur Wood and Wood's friend Miss Robinson at Cairnton on the Aberdeenshire Dee. Wood was a passionate salmon fisherman who is credited with developing the greased or floating line technique. (Francis Chamberlain)

One image of the 1930s. To the left, Lady Edwina Mountbatten, with, as the original caption narrated, 'her lady friends Mrs Baillie Hamilton and Emily Ashley. The gowns and jewels are presented by the three women prior to the Jewels of the Empire Ball to be held at the Park Lane Hotel in London.' (Classic Picture Library / Alamy Stock Photo)

An image of the 1930s that mattered more to Chamberlain. The housing conditions he worked so hard to improve. (Classic Image / Alamy Stock Photo)

*Above*. The Jarrow March, 1936. (Granger, NYC / Alamy Stock Photo)

*Left*. Hopelessness: An unemployed miner in Wigan. (Granger, NYC / Alamy Stock Photo)

*Above*. Austen Chamberlain, Stanley Baldwin and Winston Churchill: Three of the politicians whose careers frequently touch on Neville Chamberlain's. The photograph was taken in 1924, marking the return of Austen and Winston to the Tory fold, and the appointment of the latter as Chancellor of the Exchequer. (Fremantle / Alamy Stock Photo)

*Right*. Chamberlain, purposeful and vigorous. The Hornibrook exercises were working. (Scherl/Süddeutsche Zeitung Photo / Alamy Stock Photo)

We, the German Führer and Chancellor and the
British Prime Minister, have had a further
meeting today and are agreed in recognising that
the question of Anglo-German relations is of the
first importance for the two countries and for
Europe.

We regard the agreement signed last night
and the Anglo-German Naval Agreement as symbolic
of the desire of our two peoples never to go to
war with one another again.

We are resolved that the method of
consultation shall be the method adopted to deal
with any other questions that may concern our two
countries, and we are determined to continue our
efforts to remove possible sources of difference
and thus to contribute to assure the peace of
Europe.

*[signatures: Adolf Hitler and Neville Chamberlain]*

*September 30, 1938.*

The 'piece of paper' that Chamberlain and Hitler signed at Munich. It meant nothing to Hitler, as his scrawled signature suggests. Chamberlain took more trouble with his, but in private he too doubted if the agreement would amount to much. (INTERFOTO / History / Alamy Stock Photo)

The *Daily Mirror* reports on Chamberlain's return from Munich. Public opinion knew what it wanted Munich to mean, but people would speedily come to be ashamed of their reaction. (Mirrorpix / Alamy Stock Photo)

was a different matter: 'I remain convinced that I might be a great Minister of Health but am not likely to be more than a second rate Chancellor.'[3] Churchill said much the same of the respective importance of their two offices. '*You* are in the van,' he told Chamberlain. '*You* can raise a monument. *You* can have a name in history.' He continued, 'You and I can command everything if we work together.'[4]

Churchill was lucky with his bosses. Asquith had regarded him with tolerant amusement and studiously ignored criticism of him from, for instance, the Palace. Baldwin, like very many others, thought that Churchill had no judgement, and used to tell a story about Churchill's birth. Fairies surrounded his crib and showered gifts on the baby: eloquence, charm, courage and energy. But one fairy, looking on, thought it was wrong that any child should have so many advantages and took away the quality of judgement.

But overall Baldwin rather respected and indeed liked Churchill. We have seen that in a few years he would seriously consider Churchill as Secretary of State for India and then indeed as Viceroy, notions which were wildly bizarre even at the time. Even after Churchill was in his wilderness years, Baldwin allowed him unusual access to secret documents on national defence and security, despite the fact that Churchill seized on any ammunition he could find in these documents to attack the government. After Baldwin was out of office and Churchill was in power, he did not return Baldwin's kindness.

Finding a place for Churchill was not Chamberlain's principal reason for wanting Health rather than the Exchequer. At the Ministry of Health he could get on with the great work of improving the lives of the people. The first thing to understand is the importance of the Ministry of Health. Its remit was enormous, and tonsils and adenoids were a very minor part of Neville Chamberlain's concerns. The ministry was responsible for almost every aspect of the human condition of the British people, particularly after Chamberlain assumed responsibility for the functions of the Local Government Board. In those days there was, for instance, no Ministry of Housing. Chamberlain was now doing for the nation exactly what he had done for Birmingham. He could continue the radical social engineering that mattered to him. The Exchequer offered less scope for creativity and has generally remained so with the exception of Gordon Brown's time as Chancellor.

Chamberlain's period as Minister of Health from 1924 to 1929 was the most productive period of his life, a period of passionate social reform. He returned to his work at the Ministry of Health with what one historian has described as 'a zeal amounting almost to fanaticism'.[5]

This wasn't glamorous work. There was none of the exposure to the wider world that Austen enjoyed as Foreign Secretary, attending the series of international conferences that were held in the watering-places of Europe as the Great Powers tried to put the world together after the Great War. There was nothing sexy about what Neville immersed himself in. But it was unquestionably *useful* work, good work. Would any but a good man have undertaken it?

He worked very hard, for long hours, and he mastered detail. He believed he could only handle big issues if he had total mastery of all the little ones. David Dilks lists some of the matters with which he had to be simultaneously involved:

> The presence in the port of London of vermin infected with Bubonic Plague; the alleged risk of death from the black widow spider and the poisoning from cheap lipstick; investigations show-ing that the citizens of Manchester had to spend 7.5d. more each week than an inhabitant of Halifax if he or she wished to be clean; compensation to farmers for the discovery of tuberculosis in their cows; the smell from a sewage farm on Mitcham Common; the alarming incidence of diphtheria in West Bromwich; an estimate by an honourable Member that at least 1m bushels of soot fell over London in two days in December 1925; apprenticeships in the Building Trade; the importation of bricks; embezzlement by a rent collector in Stoke Newington.[6]

I do not propose to go through the minutiae of his time at Health. Neither I nor perhaps my readers have Chamberlain's capacity for focussing on such detail. What I want to do is to highlight the essence of what he did and draw the strands together.

He approached his new office with an enormous sense of purpose. He had a pre-planned programme which involved enacting twenty-five bills over four years. The ambition was pretty well achieved:

twenty-one of these bills had indeed been enacted by the general election of 1929 and the others were enacted subsequently.

His relationship with his civil servants was of a military nature. In 1929, at the end of his time at the Ministry of Health, Chamberlain said, revealingly, that his pleasure was in administration rather than in the game of politics.[7] Lloyd George made the same point in an unkinder way: 'Neville has a retail mind in a wholesale business.'[8] He was not chummy. He expected total efficiency and expedition. There was, when necessary, much consultation, but no genial badinage. Business was brusque and serious. 'Has anybody any objection to that? Very well, thank you very much. We will report accordingly.' He respected efficient subordinates, and if they stayed the pace they respected him. There was much unhappiness within his staff when he was deposed by Churchill in 1940.

The ministry over which Chamberlain presided between 1924 and 1929 established a new relationship between the individual and the state. The steps that the Asquith and the Campbell–Bannerman governments took before the First World War, principally at the instigation of Lloyd George and Churchill, can be seen to be the beginnings of the welfare state, and its detailed articulation was established by the Attlee governments of 1945–51. But there was more traction under Chamberlain than in either the later or earlier periods. The structural and psychological change which took place was seismic. It could have happened without the pre-war Liberal reforms, but Attlee's reforms could scarcely have been effected without Chamberlain's achievements.

At the risk of threatening to diminish the scale of what happened between 1924 and 1929 I shall look at just three of the flagship pieces of legislation.

## Housing

It's important to remember what Chamberlain had to do. In the course of chronicling what Orwell described as the road from Mandalay to Wigan, he catalogued in detail the dwellings he had seen. One-up, one-down houses with two rooms each measuring twelve feet by ten feet. The sink contained in a recess under the stairs. No room for a larder. The floor might be subsiding and no windows would open. Another one-up, one-down flat had its walls coming apart and water coming in. The back windows would not open. There were ten in the family with eight children all close in age. Often there would be eight or ten children living in a three-roomed dwelling. One small room was full – kitchen range and sink and so forth with no room for a bed, so the eight or ten people would sleep in two rooms in at most four beds. Obvious problems arose when there were adolescent children. The lavatory might be seventy yards from the house. There was frequently a queue for the lavatory which could be shared by, say, thirty-six people.

Lack of housing led to the existence of caravan-colonies in Wigan and Sheffield. Orwell said he had never seen such squalor except in the Far East. They were cold and damp. Condensation from the paraffin cookers that were kept on all day to try to dispel the cold added to the humidity. Mattresses were wringing wet. Water was supplied by a hydrant shared by the whole colony. There was no sanitation. Most people constructed a little hut outside the caravan to use as a lavatory and once a week they dug a deep hole in which to bury the refuse. Wigan, with a population of about 85,000 had about 200 caravan dwellings with a family in each – perhaps the whole colony housed, if that is the right word, a thousand people. Throughout the north of England there were perhaps tens of thousands of families (not individuals) who had no home except these insubstantial hovels.

These were the practical problems Chamberlain had to deal with. His first results were achieved in a matter of months. In March, only three and a half months after he had come into office, he had steered two crucial pieces of legislation through the House: the Housing Act and the Rent Restriction Act. The Rent Restriction Act was no Tory measure. Rents now had to reflect the condition of the property. This didn't appeal to landlords, whose powers of eviction were also restricted. The two acts were intended to achieve the rapid completion of modest, decent homes, in tandem with the clearance of slums.

Lloyd George's taxation of tenanted properties had put an end to private building. Neville Chamberlain told his party that housing subsidies had to be renewed; the government would pay £6 a house a year for twenty years for all houses completed before October 1925. The Cabinet wanted private enterprise to get most of the money, but Chamberlain secured the power to make the payments to councils if they could demonstrate that they could do the job. Councils were given increased powers to assist with house purchase and the state met half the cost of slum clearance. By March 1925 nearly 200,000 houses had been approved under the scheme, a full one-third of which were to be built by the councils. Rent restriction had meant that landlords could not afford to maintain or improve their properties and received no return on their investment. The Rent Restriction Act provided for a phased programme of decontrol but with provision for recourse to the courts where necessary. By the time Chamberlain left office in 1929 he had built almost one million houses and set up fifty-eight slum clearance schemes.

## Pensions

Social and economic conditions in the early 1920s were heartbreaking. Agriculture had collapsed at a time when £500 million a year was spent on imported foodstuffs. Only 10 per cent of national income was reinvested, as against 25 per cent before the war. Four hundred million pounds were spent in poor relief and unemployment benefits between 1918 and 1926, and £100 million in rent subsidies. In 1929, 1.1 million people were in receipt of poor relief. Forty per cent of Scots lived in two-roomed habitations. Disease, including tuberculosis and venereal disease, was at a high level and 50 per cent of army recruits were rejected on medical grounds. In 1926 there were two million outdoor poor.[9] A response to this was the Widows, Orphans, and Old Age Pensions Act of 1930. This Act gave a non-means-tested pension to widows, dependent children and orphans of men insured for health; and pensions to insured men and their wives at the age of sixty-five, rather than seventy. The benefits were achieved by a combination of contribution and increased government spending, but the increase in contribution was only an additional two pence a week.

This measure involved close liaison with the Chancellor of the Exchequer, and Chamberlain and Churchill worked companionably on the matter. Churchill prefigured the legislation in his Budget speech, but the Bill was Chamberlain's. He took it through Parliament, winning the applause of the King for his compassion and skill. It represented a principle of compulsory and contributory pension provision on which Beveridge would build. It was in relation to this measure that Churchill declared that Chamberlain, rather than he, could leave a lasting legacy, a monument, a name in history.

## The Poor Law

It may come as a surprise to us today that there are people still alive who grew up in a world where the Poor Law operated, where there were workhouses and Poor Law guardians.

The Poor Laws went back far beyond what we know of them from nineteenth-century novels, back at least to early Tudor times and perhaps beyond. The laws were codified under Elizabeth I and modified by the 'New Poor Law' of 1834. The purpose of this Victorian reform was broadly to address the problem of 'sturdy beggars' which had bothered parliaments in the time of the first Elizabeth. The aim was to ensure that claimants of the nation's bounty should have a much tougher time than the poorest working man. Though relief outside the workhouse, outdoor relief, continued to some extent, relief would principally be given within workhouses whose regime was designedly harsh.

Parishes were combined into Poor Law unions and workhouses were built in each union, all of this financed by a 'Poor Rate' payable by parishioners. The system was unpopular with those who had to pay for it, dehumanising for those who benefitted from it, if that is the right word, and much criticised, and not only by anti-Poor Law campaigners. In 1886, Joe Chamberlain encouraged the Local Government Board to set up work projects rather than use the workhouses (the shadow of Joe was never far behind Neville), but the workhouses persisted into the 1920s.

The introduction of old-age pensions and National Insurance implied that the burden of looking after unfortunate members of society should be shouldered at a national level, but poor relief was paid for locally: the burden heaviest where poverty was highest. This led to the Poplar Rates Rebellion, which the Labour leader George Lansbury led in 1921, and the poverty of these years threw the problem of poor relief into sharp focus.

To Chamberlain, the Poor Law was anachronistic, illogical, inefficient and inhumane: the epitome of what he sought to attack and reform. He effectively abolished it in his Local Government Act of

1929. There had been tinkering with the Act before, but Chamberlain did not adhere to the British tradition of inconsistent ad hoc patches. He had the intellectual energy and logical drive to reform the system wholesale, abolishing the Poor Law guardians and transferring powers to the Councils (as Joe Chamberlain had always urged). The effect of the Act as a whole was much wider than that: it established an entirely new relationship between local and central government. In doing so, Chamberlain was engineering a move from the individualistic, capitalist society of Adam Smith to a corporate state, a society directed from the top down. How very far from traditional Conservatism.

Reform of the Poor Law was a truly radical exercise and involved a structural change in the organisation of local government and the relief of poverty, a switch from a piecemeal, grudging ragbag of measures to a systematic and efficient system, delivered by local government but finally directed by the state. It was effected by two pieces of legislation, the second of which was the Local Government Act of 1929. The first, though, was the Rating and Valuation Act of 1925. This measure, enacted just months after Chamberlain came into office, was a much more meaningful statute than its title would suggest. The Act established a single, standard approach to the valuation of properties for the purpose of establishing their liability to rates, with quinquennial revaluations. That was more important than it sounds, but more important still was that it transferred responsibility for rating from the Poor Law guardians, whose Dickensian title reflects their archaic nature, to the councils.

These changes sound mundane and uncontentious, but they were not. There were many who rejected Chamberlain's idea that the councils – County, Borough and District – were 'the real living bodies of today'. The Rating and Valuation Act reduced the number of rating authorities from 12,000 to 6,000, concentrating power in the hands of these real living bodies of today. These councils were in many cases Labour controlled, and his policies (as also in relation to the abolition of the Boards of Guardians for Poor Law Relief in the 1929 Local Government Act) were not always appreciated by rank-and-file Tories. Tory magnates were horrified at the thought of socialist corporations bringing down capitalism by imposing penal rates. Chamberlain wanted to stimulate industry by derating machinery. Householders and landowners did not welcome a corresponding increase in what *they* were to pay.

Tories might well be uncomfortable, because Chamberlain's legislation owed much to socialist thought. His proposals were based very much on the Report of the Royal Commission on the Poor Law of 1909 – but not the orthodox majority report: the radical minority report, largely written by Beatrice Webb and George Lansbury. It was described by the young Clement Attlee as 'a remarkable document challenging the whole conception of public relief and distress'.[10]

A nepotistic system of Poor Law overseers, thousands of them scattered around the parishes, had no wish to see their comfortable jobs transferred to new authorities. Six hundred Poor Law Unions which had administered poor relief lost powers to the new assessment areas. There was a combination of powerful interests, mostly within the Tory community, who opposed a transformational piece of legislation. It was as well that the Tory Party didn't initially see that Chamberlain was starting to build the big state against which Mrs Thatcher would rail.

There were *some* tensions between Chamberlain and Churchill over reform of the Poor Law but they had to work together. Churchill wanted to relieve industry and agriculture of the burden of rates, and this could only be accomplished through the agency of Chamberlain's new system. He was able to use the new rating system to reposition the national economy *because* Chamberlain had created a unified and modern approach to rating throughout the UK. Joined-up government and national planning was precisely what Chamberlain was aiming for. Rates Reform and Poor Law Reform had to proceed together and the civil servants at the Treasury and the Ministry of Health worked together, even when their principals differed. Churchill thought Chamberlain lacked vision and Chamberlain thought Churchill lacked discipline.

Chamberlain's relations with Churchill were not damaged on any long-term basis, and Churchill in particular was impervious to the rough and tumble of politics. More significantly for the long term, however, Chamberlain's relationship with the Labour Party began to deteriorate.

Before the reform of the Poor Law, some guardians, from the best of humanitarian motives, bent the rules to make special (that is, illegally high) financial provision to alleviate the effect of strikes. Chamberlain used the Guardians (Default) Act to bring the guardians to heel. Similarly he had recourse to the Audit (Local Authorities) Act, which made errant councillors personally liable for unauthorised expenditure. The most notable instances were in Poplar and West Ham. Most of Poplar Borough Council was sent to prison in 1921 because of their failure to make payments required by the London County Council. Council meetings sometimes took place in prison so that the delinquent tribunes could contribute to the deliberations.

Chamberlain had started off in a cordial and sympathetic relationship with the Labour Party and the trades unions. As an employer, he had sought the cooperation of the unions and valued good labour relations. In local government he had not been partisan. As we have seen, he had been criticised for 'socialist' views, which he had not disavowed. Now, however, he became increasingly aggressive towards Labour in the House – indeed he criticised some of his colleagues who seemed to suck up to Labour members. He said that only he and Douglas Hogg really *attacked* Labour: Churchill made jokes and Baldwin was too mild. *He* had no such compunction. He seemed increasingly to find it necessary to be aggressive. He even belaboured the saintly Lansbury who led the Poplar Rates Revolt. This was a new side to Chamberlain. It was perhaps a result of his lack of experience in the House that he adopted an unnecessarily confrontational style, quite the reverse of the conciliatory approach which Baldwin pursued so successfully. Chamberlain would pay the price in 1940, when Labour declined to enter a coalition which he headed.

That crust of self-control did a lot of damage. It disguised his sensitivity. It was a pity that he did not take what were fairly minor attacks more philosophically. In reality he was far more socially progressive than any other leading Conservative and he could have enjoyed a productive relationship with Labour. The problem was that he was an administrator, not essentially a politician. He didn't recognise politics.

Poplarism particularly needled him. His intention was to benefit those whom the Poplar councillors also wished to protect, and his neat logicality found it offensive and unreasonable that mavericks, as he saw them, were standing in the way of the interests of the majority.

The councillors, now faced with having their possessions seized as a result of the application of the Guardians Default Act, appealed against the ruling of the District Auditor. The law was clear enough and the case, which went as far as the House of Lords, was decided against the councillors. Chamberlain had some sympathy for them and when they appealed to him to set aside the surcharge he agreed to do so. His hand was, however, then forced by the rate payers in Poplar, the people who had to pick up the shortfall. They went to the courts, which ruled that Chamberlain had no right to set aside the surcharge, and his order was quashed.

Chamberlain didn't want a return to the situation which had occurred in 1921 when the Poplar councillors had been sent to jail, and he brought in the Audit (Local Authorities) Act of 1927 to allow councillors an appeal against surcharges. The legislation was conciliatory, designed to relieve councillors of the sanctions they faced, but it still provided for disqualification of reckless overspenders. However hard Chamberlain tried to take the sting out of his legislation, the debate was heated, particularly the exchanges with Lansbury. Chamberlain gradually emerged as a caricature of the meanest-minded Conservatives from whom he was so strikingly different. He didn't help himself by his manner, which could be sneering and overbearing. The Webbs said that he attacked self-government and set up a local dictatorship, but for Chamberlain the logic of his actions was inescapable.*

Baldwin asked him to remember that in the House of Commons he was addressing a meeting of gentlemen and said that he gave the impression that when he spoke there he looked down on the Labour Party as if they were dirt. Chamberlain said to his sister, 'The fact is that intellectually, with few exceptions, they *are* dirt'.[11] An astonishing thing to say, not least because it was untrue. In 1928 he wrote to his sister, complaining that Labour allowed dogma to get in the way of efficiency: 'Their gross exaggerations, their dishonesty in slurring over facts that tell against them, and their utter inability to appreciate a reasonable argument, do embitter my soul sometimes, and if I seem

---

* Economists and Fabians Sidney and Beatrice Webb. As has been seen, Beatrice sat on the Royal Commission on the Poor Laws and Relief of Distress, and was the lead writer of the commission's minority report. As a couple, they personified high-minded socialism. They spent their honeymoon examining trades union records.

hard and unsympathetic to them, it is the reaction brought about by their own attitude'.[12]

The Local Government Bill was enormous, with 115 clauses and twelve schedules, and Chamberlain himself took the legislation through the House. He introduced it at its second reading in a memorable speech of two and a half hours. In that speech he enumerated the scope of the responsibilities of the Local Authorities, covering 'tuberculosis, lunatics, mental defectives, maternity provision – and yet every one of these things are dealt with also by the Guardians in the discharge of their duties'. By contrast his bill was 'designed to create locally one single Health Authority whose duty it will be to survey the whole institutional needs of that area'. His assessment of his own legislation was not inhibited by undue modesty: 'When you consider the magnitude of the changes this bill proposes ... it must be reckoned among the greatest measures which have been presented to parliament for many years.'[13]

His speech was received with acclamation – even by Labour members. He had been so closely involved in the drafting of the Bill that he scarcely looked at his notes. He had worked through the night, surviving on almost no sleep. He could have said of the Local Government Act what he said of the Rating and Valuation Act: 'I slaved away at it night and day till one in the morning, so that when the time came I had mastered the beastly thing.' In black morning dress, using his pince-nez to emphasise his points, he dominated the House. 'When I sat down', he recorded in his diary, 'the House cheered continuously for several minutes ... [What] particularly struck and touched me was that Liberals and Labour men ... joined with the greatest heartiness in paying their acknowledgements.'[14] Though later an autocratic and unbending figure in Parliament, his performance was acknowledged to be sensitive and skilful. Even George Lansbury, although against the legislation and offensively treated by Chamberlain, responded to the third reading of the Act by describing Chamberlain as having been 'courtesy itself'.

The Pensions Act, the Rating and Valuation Act and the Local Government Act were solid, practical achievements. They signalled a move from grudging Dickensian charity to an early version of the welfare state. As Roy Jenkins acknowledged, they were designed 'within the framework of financial discipline, to improve the condition of the people, not to win plaudits at party conferences'.[15]

Another experienced parliamentarian, Iain Macleod, said, 'Reading the Hansards of those days there are times when it seems as if there was only one Minister in the government, and it seems incredible that anyone could take the hideous strain.'[16] A correspondent to the *Sunday Times* in 1925 said that a plain man could be excused a feeling of dizziness in seeing the Conservative Party under Mr Baldwin taking up the Social Reform Work of the 1906 government.[17] A. J. P. Taylor: 'He had efficiency, clarity and resolution, qualities marred only by his unsympathetic manner: he did more to improve local government than any other single man in the twentieth century,'[18] and Paul Addison said, 'All in all the social services were the most advanced in the world by 1929 and Neville Chamberlain contributed more than any single figure.'[19]

*Chapter 18*

# Second in Command:
# Chancellor of the Exchequer

George V may never have read Bagehot from cover to cover,\* but he seems to have got to the bit which said that the monarch had the right to advise. He advised a lot. After the general election of 10 October 1931, when the Cabinet came to be formed he told Baldwin that Chamberlain had been so good at Health that he should be kept there rather than be moved to the Exchequer. The King was also a little suspicious about his ultra-protectionist views.

Chamberlain was no keener on the move than the King. When the National Government came together he was very happy to have Philip Snowden remain as Chancellor, and he became Minister of Health for the third time. But only briefly: Snowden decided not to stand at the 1931 general election, and Chamberlain moved to the position which he had never really wanted but could no longer avoid, effectively the second in the pecking order of the offices of state.

The government that took office in 1931 with such a dangerously large majority was dominated and directed more by Chamberlain than by any other man. Baldwin was not an egotist. He was happy that the Prime Minister was nominally MacDonald, in reality the prisoner of the

---

\* Walter Bagehot, *The English Constitution.* George V's tutor (when the King was a married naval officer of twenty-eight years of age) was J. R. Tanner, a Fellow of St John's College, Cambridge. He told his pupil to make a digest of Bagehot's work, but the old Queen Victoria vetoed the idea of studying the views of the irreverent commentator. She told her daughter-in-law to make sure that George concentrated instead on his French and German. It was not fitting that he and Princess May should talk to relatives from abroad in English – 'as I observe you do'. (Kenneth Rose, *King George V*, p. 35.)

Conservative majority. He was equally happy that though he was himself the nominal leader of the largest part of the coalition, the energising figure who dominated policy was Chamberlain. He allowed Chamberlain a wide remit, untrammelled by an interfering chief, embracing almost all important aspects of domestic policy. And from early 1935 onwards he came to dominate equally defence and foreign policy.

While he didn't throw his weight about, Baldwin was not a cypher. He gave the government its character and set its tone. His reassuring, avuncular presence, smoking his pipe, rubbing the pigs' backs on his farm, the frequent and eloquent evocations of an older, tranquil idealised England (not Britain) with its happy cottagers and deferential hog-reeves, was appealing, and when people thought of the government they thought of Baldwin rather than the fey, evanescent MacDonald, his thoughts ever more elusive, enveloped in his beautiful but impenetrable oratory, or Chamberlain's contained efficiency.*

Neville was well aware that his reach extended far beyond his own department. In self-satisfied tones he told his sisters that he found new policies for all his colleagues. His influence was always of a liberal nature, as he promoted agricultural initiatives and intervened in housing policies. He sought, but failed, to modernise the House of Lords by slashing hereditary representation to 100 members balanced by the creation of the same number of Life Peers. Constitutional innovation as radical as this did not meet with Baldwin's approval. Sleeping dogs were a protected species.

On India, the huge preoccupation of the Conservative government between 1930 and 1935, Chamberlain was, however, no liberal. Gandhi, he told his sister, was 'a revolting looking creature without any redeeming feature in his face that I could see'. His attitude to reforming the Indian constitution was to watch and see how provincial autonomy worked, while retaining strong control over the central government of India.

He was then very much at the centre of this government of, as Churchill put it, 'nearly all the talents'. Indeed, he was, as Churchill

---

* Baldwin's evocations of an idealised arcadian world, collected in *On England*, were popular with the public but parodied by the intellectuals. One splendid piece of satire had him referring admiringly to one of his workers clearing his nose 'with the fine untrammeled gesture of his ancestors'. Osbert Lancaster drew an image of this being done by a horny-handed man of the soil in smock and gaiters.

again put it, 'their pack horse': Neville said pretty much the same thing himself. By 1934 he complained in his diary that he was more and more carrying the government on his back. 'The PM is ill and tired . . . and won't apply his mind to problems.'[1] There was some basis for Churchill's 'nearly all the talents' jibe. Churchill himself was not in the ministry, partly because of his views on India – although he was in any event no admirer of MacDonald. Lloyd George was obviously out; Chamberlain made it clear that he would not sit in a Cabinet alongside him. Austen said he would not take the place of younger men, although his brother thought he would have taken the Foreign Office if it had been offered. There were others, such as Leo Amery, who might have expected a place in the government and who would have contributed valuably to it.

As it was, Chamberlain referred to an inner Cabinet of 'the six': MacDonald, Thomas, Simon, Runciman, Baldwin and himself. He himself was showing signs of a disposition which would become dangerously pronounced, a policy of relying on a tight and limited circle of advisers, and cutting himself off from those with whom he did not agree and indeed frequently despised. He had described MacDonald in the past as 'a moral weakling' and had increasingly little time for the soporific miasma of the Prime Minister's beautifully delivered speeches. He felt apart from the younger members of the Cabinet (and even more of the party generally): 'the Boys Brigade', the 'Young Tory Intellectuals'.

It was in this spirit of aloof confidence allied to a great sense of purpose that he returned to the Exchequer. He was never going to take his responsibilities narrowly. To his mind, budgetary and economic policy was inseparably linked to social and industrial policy. He worked closely with Runciman, the President of the Board of Trade. This width of approach was entirely consistent with what he had done when he had been Minister of Health; and the peculiar circumstances of the 1930s, the world economic crisis and the crises in foreign affairs, meant that his brief, as he conceived it, now extended to rearmament and foreign policy, as well as issues about war debts, but more about that later.

One can take a choice about the economy as Britain moved out of the First World War. On the one hand things were bad. The biggest creditor nation in the world was now a debtor. Huge debts were owed to the United States, unemployment was high, and inflation, although at a lower level than that of many other countries, was a cause for great concern. The specialised nature of the war economy had exaggerated the importance and development of heavy industry at a time when economic imperatives dictated another approach.

On the other hand, Britain was still a major power. It dominated the League of Nations; the United States chose not to participate in an institution which was largely its creation. Britain also continued to dominate world trade; having the largest Merchant Navy in the world, and the largest fleet of warships, meant that Britain had access to the world, including the markets of the United States and the Far East, in a way that Germany did not. The economic planners in the interwar years were aware that the Allied blockade had been one of the causes of Germany's defeat in 1918, while Britain had been able to import food, even if only just enough. The fact that more than half of Britain's food was imported was seen as a strength and not a weakness: manpower could be used for fighting and the production of armaments rather than in the fields. Germany and France couldn't do this. Access to global resources was a great advantage.

Germany's reparations had been fixed at Versailles at £6,600,000. Even under the international reparations plan of 1928, Germany would still have been paying reparations in 1988. Chamberlain's preferred policy would have been to cancel reparations altogether; and, reasonably enough, war debts too. He and MacDonald argued for this at the Lausanne Reparations Conference in 1932. The United States were uncompromising to their British and French debtors. 'They hired our money, didn't they?' France, too, found it difficult to be generous. They remembered too well what Germany had done to them in 1870, and again in 1914.

To a large extent because of inflation, but also because they were too absurdly high to be fully enforced, reparations ultimately did less damage to Germany than they might have done, but between the wars Germany's economy was always fundamentally weak and far from advanced. The income level was low, with something like 30 per cent of the male population working in the countryside – there were more people employed in agriculture than in the army – and the rural economy was essentially a peasant one. Chamberlain thought this important.

War with Germany would be unlikely if Britain were economically much more robust. He was not the only one in those years who often referred to a strong economy as the 'Fourth Arm of Defence'. There was thus a delicate balance to be struck: the strength of the economy was part of the preparation for war. Rearmament was needed to fight that war but too much rearmament weakened the economy.

By the late 1920s the worst of hyperinflation was over in Europe, and economies were beginning to settle down. But almost immediately the world was hit by the effects of the Great Depression. It put an end to lending from the United States and led to soaring unemployment. This created slack in the economy, availability of labour, and Germany directed that slack into public works and rearmament. In the very first year of Hitler's regime, defence expenditure rose from 1 per cent of GDP to 10 per cent. While this created the illusion of a dynamic economy and virtually eliminated unemployment, there was no real recovery. Most informed opinion in Germany thought that by the end of the 1930s a period of consolidation was required. Instead, what Hitler embarked on was an aggressive foreign policy aimed at expanding Germany's frontiers to obtain access to fresh resources and materials. This seemed so ill-advised that Chamberlain was inclined to assume Hitler could not be seriously bent on such an economically improbable course.

George V had noticed Chamberlain's interest in protectionism, and observant readers will also be aware of the protection versus free trade theme that has been running through this narrative. The time for the denouement is approaching.

In 1930 Lord Beaverbrook ramped up his empire crusade. There was considerable turbulence within the Conservative Party. Though still a member of the party, Beaverbrook was putting up candidates against the official candidates. Chamberlain took advantage of the policy vacuum. Using the expression his father had famously used, he promoted an 'unauthorised programme', a 'free hand' policy that involved discussing tariffs on non-Empire imports. His position was all the stronger because Baldwin had no clear views of his own and, in any case, was on his annual visit to Aix-les-Bains for much of the relevant time. Chamberlain was able to bounce the party into supporting Canada's desire for reciprocal preferences, with an associated 10 per cent tax on non-Empire goods, including food. A tax on food was abhorrent to free traders and Churchill's position became extremely doubtful. This was one of the reasons that prompted him to say that he would resign from the Shadow Cabinet in 1929. No one – except Austen – particularly tried to persuade him to stay; although Neville did counsel him not to take any irrevocable step, he did so with insincerity.[2]

Churchill's position was slightly obscure. He left the Shadow Cabinet largely because of the government's very mildly progressive policy on India, but his hostility to tariff reform was well known. His first floor-cross, when he left the Tories for the Liberals in 1904, had largely been over this issue. As early as 1907, when Churchill was Under-Secretary for the Colonies, Neville was recorded in the *Birmingham Daily Post* as saying that 'the Colonial Office was represented in the House of Commons by a bumptious youth [Laughter] who thought he could harangue those great self-governing states as if they were a parcel of schoolboys and he, forsooth, their schoolmaster. [Applause]. The sooner ... Mr Winston Churchill was sent as an Ambassador to Timbuctoo the better it would be for the country and the Empire. [Applause].'[3] Chamberlain came to be quite fond of Churchill, whilst still regarding him as flamboyant, lacking in judgement and inattentive to detail. In 1925 he told Baldwin that he liked Churchill. He liked his humour and vitality. He also liked his courage; but 'there is somehow a great gulf fixed between him and me which I don't think I shall ever cross'.[4]

Tariff reform appealed not just to elements within the Conservative Party. The Federation of British Industries, the Economic Committee of the Trades Union Congress, Mosely, Keynes and, amongst the Liberals, John Simon were all toying with the idea. Philip Snowden was against. When Chamberlain heard Snowden introduce his last Budget, he said that he was listening to the last Chancellor of the Exchequer who would always insist on free trade rather than 'something more adaptable to the needs of modern industrial civilisation'. The remark reflects not so much prescience as determination.

The 1931 manifesto contained a wishy-washy endorsement of tariffs. Baldwin said, 'I shall ... continue to press upon the electors that in my view the tariff is the quickest and most effective weapon not only to reduce excessive imports but to enable us to induce other countries to lower their tariff walls.' But there was never any doubt about what Neville Chamberlain wanted. Tariff reform was unfinished business and in it there was a concurrence of filial responsibility and personal belief. Now, manifesto commitment or no manifesto commitment, the 'doctor's mandate' gave the government a free hand, and there was an assumption that, with a growing trade deficit, unemployment and stalling world trade, the doctrine of free trade would remain unquestioned no longer.

The Samuelite Liberals were against protection, as had been Snowden. Other former Labour Cabinet members and the Simonite Liberals took a different view.* Chamberlain might not have been unhappy to lose the Samuelites, but they stayed aboard. On 22 January, Snowdon, Samuel and Sinclair said that they would resign rather than support free trade. MacDonald appealed to them to take account of the straits in which the nation found itself, but what saved the day was an intervention from the former Douglas Hogg, now Lord Chancellor Hailsham, proposing 'an agreement to differ' – a novel break from the principle of collective agreement which has only rarely been repeated. Harold Wilson used the device in relation to the European Referendum of 1975, David Cameron in 2016. Chamberlain was intrigued by the illogical expedient. He wrote to Hilda, 'We are now committed to this extraordinary proceeding under which we go to the country as a united government, one section of which is to advocate Tariffs while the other declares it has an open mind but is unalterably convinced of the virtues of Free Trade . . . I foresee a peck of troubles as soon as the election is over, first in the formation of the government and then in the formulation of policy.'

Chamberlain cracked on. The first assault was in an act harmlessly entitled the Abnormal Importations Act of 1931, enacted just a few weeks after taking office. It subjected 'dumped goods' to a massive tariff of up to 100 per cent. It was only temporary and of limited application, but it paved the way for more. He now became chairman of a Cabinet Committee to formulate means of addressing the adverse balance of trade. The recommendation was for a permanent general

---

* The followers of Herbert Samuel, the mainstream Liberals, were unhappy with the Conservative-dominated National Government and finally left it; Sir John Simon and his followers were more tolerant of the Conservatives and less wedded to the doctrine of free trade.

revenue tariff of 10 per cent with exceptions for certain categories of goods; and for Dominion and Colonial preference, and preference for industries, such as steel, which needed particular protection.

This was the substance of the Import Duties Bill, which went through its stages in just a matter of weeks and was passed on 4 February 1932. Chamberlain described that day as 'the great day of my life'. The sense of theatre was immense. The importance which he attached to finishing what his father had begun shows how sensitive and emotional this man was, behind the control of his public face. He had Hilda in the gallery, along with Mary, Joe's widow, representing the great man and his unfinished business, and he brought his notes to the Commons in the Despatch Box which his father had used for his last speech in the House. The House was well aware of the double significance of what was happening – the personal significance allied to a seismic change in the national political identity, the death of free trade. Chamberlain struggled to contain his emotions as he proposed a 10 per cent tariff on most imports, with power to the Board of Trade to raise the level in the future, subject always to a critical preference for Dominion and Colonial products. His voice was breaking as he made a speech which was famous in its time:

> Nearly twenty years have passed since Joseph Chamberlain entered upon his great campaign in favour of Imperial Preference and Tariff Reform. More than seventeen years have gone by since he died, without having seen the fulfilment of his aims and yet convinced that, if not exactly in his way, yet in some modified form his vision would eventually take shape. His work was not in vain. Time and the misfortunes of the country have brought conviction to many who did not feel that they could agree with him then. I believe he would have found consolation for the bitterness of his disappointment if he could have foreseen that these proposals, which are the direct and legitimate descendants of his own conception, would be laid before the House of Commons, which he loved, in the presence of one, and by the lips of the other, of the two immediate successors to his name and blood.

The bill was passed by a majority of 454 to 78. There were no Cabinet resignations. The other immediate successor, Austen, less of a reformer but a devoted son all the same, knew what his brother had done. He walked to the Treasury bench and shook Neville's hand. The House warmed to the gesture and approved noisily. Members of Parliament, who can be sentimental and forgiving on a good day, knew what was happening. The press described an extraordinary demonstration of enthusiasm in which every non-Labour Member of the House was on their feet.

It was an intensely personal event, and Chamberlain exposed his feelings more frankly than on any other parliamentary occasion. He had put aside his customary reticence and revealed the personal significance of what he was doing when he told the house: 'There can have been few occasions in all our long political history when the son of a man who counted for something in his day and generation has been vouchsafed the privilege of setting the seal on the work which the father began but had perforce to leave unfinished.'[5]

The poignancy of the speech and of what Chamberlain had done, forgotten today, was widely recognised at the time. The Duke of York, later George VI, had Chamberlain write out a long section of his speech in his autograph book.

Britain was moving, it seemed, from being a world economy to relying on her domestic base and her imperial connections. But the concept of an imperial free trade area, a sterling area, couldn't be imposed on the Dominions unilaterally. Canada had been pressing for preferential treatment for some time and in July a strong delegation went to confer at Ottawa. The team consisted of the core of the Cabinet, led by Baldwin, together with industrial advisers, civil servants like Horace Wilson who would emerge in the coming years as almost Chamberlain's doppelgänger, and a clutch of newspaper editors not excluding those noted for the size of their circulation rather than the quality of their advice.

Ottawa was very much Chamberlain's show, despite the strength of the delegation of which he was part. In the course of the voyage, he prepared his team thoroughly for what could have been the realisation of the dreams entertained by Joe Chamberlain and Lord Milner,*

---

* The architect of the South Africa which emerged after the Boer War, he developed a visionary scheme of what a forward imperial policy could do to reinvent and re-energise Britain's international role. As he had inspired his 'kindergarten' in South

the dream of a great British–led institution which would preserve the imperial creation and transform it into a robust and enduring economic superpower. In the event, the conference, which lasted for a full month, was a disappointment. There was no shared sense of vision. Perhaps the conference was taking place thirty years too late for that. The discussions degenerated into technical squabbles in which the different parties sought to protect their interests in relation to zinc, softwood, beef or mutton. Chamberlain found it disheartening and at one point told Baldwin that he would resign if the conference broke down because of Britain's reluctance to put a tariff on non–imperial meat.

He didn't even have the opportunity to relax with some decent fishing. Fishing in Canada was 'a coarse, unscientific affair' and he was reduced to fishing with worm. He was particularly irritated by the Canadian Prime Minister, Bennett, who, instead of chairing the conference impartially sought simply to lead the Canadian delegation. The conference ended with a series of technical agreements brought together by no more than a declaration of intent that they should be seen as steps towards reduction or elimination of trade barriers within the Empire. Roy Jenkins said that 'enough discrimination was achieved to give the Americans a running grievance, but not enough to produce any great stimulation of Empire trade.'[6]

Chamberlain returned to Britain disillusioned, as indeed the founding fathers of the notion of imperial preference would have been. A historic opportunity to create a unique trading organisation had been lost — forever, as it transpired.

But while Ottawa was much less than true tariff reformers would want, it was much more than diehard Liberal free traders could stomach. At the end of September, Samuel and Sinclair resigned along with seven junior ministers. They were replaced by Conservatives and National Liberals. This at least Chamberlain could applaud: there was now a common philosophy in the government which he was certain

---

Africa, so he had an inspirational effect on his followers in the Commons, partly through the periodical *The Round Table*. Although he was never a Member of the Commons, he had about as much influence as anyone on political events in the twenty-five years of which the First World War was the centre. When Joe Chamberlain resigned as Colonial Secretary it was Milner who was offered the job. He declined in order to continue with his work on South Africa.

would lead to the emergence of a National Party without that Conservative label which he so disliked.

Among the passengers who travelled to Ottawa with Chamberlain were some of a group of advisers who were to have great influence over him. Montagu Norman, Governor of the Bank of England from 1920 to 1944, Horace Wilson, and Geoffrey Dawson, editor of *The Times* from 1912 to 1919 and from 1923 to 1941, were a troika of shadowy advisers on whose counsel Chamberlain came to rely during his time at the Exchequer and, even more so, as Prime Minister.

Geoffrey Dawson and Horace Wilson played particularly important parts in the Chamberlain story and they deserve to be briefly sketched here.

## *Geoffrey Dawson*

Dawson was born Geoffrey Robinson but changed his name by Royal Licence and assumed the arms of Dawson, his mother's eldest sister. He was a King's Scholar at Eton and obtained a distinguished degree at Oxford. He was an honorary fellow of Magdalen College and at one time Estates Bursar at All Souls' College.

His real career, however, was at *The Times*. He became editor in 1912 at the age of just thirty-seven. Inevitably, he fell out with the increasingly psychotic proprietor, Lord Northcliffe, and he left the paper in 1919. After Northcliffe's death in August 1922 he returned to the editor's chair and remained there for nineteen years. His second editorship is remembered because of his exceptional closeness to the central figures of government and the influence which he was able to bring to bear on them, not least in regard to appeasement. He was very much a Conservative, a close friend of Samuel Hoare and Anthony Eden. It is said that in the 1930s he knew more about Cabinet thinking than most members of the Cabinet. He was a regular visitor to Cliveden and part of Nancy Astor's pro-appeasement set. Anti-appeasers like Robert Boothby described him as 'The Secretary-General of the Establishment, the fervent advocate of appeasement'.[7]

That is too extreme a view. Various explanations have been put forward for the way he leant towards appeasement. He was not well-informed on European affairs; moreover he didn't regard this as a problem and was not concerned about foreign coverage in his news-paper – he did not appoint a foreign editor to succeed Harold Williams after his death in 1928. His outlook was the expression of his idea of Britain's imperial mission.

Joe Chamberlain had touched him too. He was appointed Joe's assistant private secretary in 1901 and later in the same year was sent to South Africa where he became assistant private secretary to Lord Milner, that visionary imperialist. He was a member of his 'kindergar-ten' and on his return to Britain was one of those who favoured a forward imperial policy and published the periodical *Round Table*. Covering the Versailles negotiations for Northcliffe in 1919 he was already concerned about disturbing the polity of Europe, and complained about his proprietor's 'irresponsible Hun-baiting'. His position on Hitler was that undue concern about Central European issues diverted Britain's attention from what really mattered: over-arching imperial concerns. He told Chamberlain that 'going to war with Germany over Czechoslovakia in 1938 would have been unpop-ular throughout the Empire'.[8]

That this was at the base of his thinking is revealed by his dramatic turnaround as soon as war was declared. He was horrified by Chamberlain's lack of vigour in pursuing the war and criticised him openly. He sacked his military correspondent, Basil Liddell Hart, because of his defeatist stance, but he had done his damage long before then.

## Sir Horace Wilson

Horace Wilson, on the other hand, was not a member of the Brahmin caste which supplied most of the top civil servants of the era. He didn't attend Eton and Balliol; his father was a furniture dealer and his mother ran a boarding house in Bournemouth where he was educated at a local elementary school before becoming a 'night school' student at the London School of Economics. On his death he left estate worth about £185,000 in today's terms. Sir Alexander Cadogan, another mandarin whom we shall meet later, here taken at random for compar-ison purposes, left an estate worth about £4 million in today's terms.

He was clearly very able. Getting from an elementary school to the London School of Economics in the first place reflects ambition, application and brains. Thereafter he was involved in the Industrial

Council, a body established before the First World War for the purposes of conciliation and arbitration. When he went into the Ministry of Labour he was initially the Permanent Assistant Secretary in charge of the Wages and Arbitration Department. In 1921, aged just thirty-nine, he became Permanent Secretary. So at this stage in his career his background was in industrial councils, fair wages committees and arbitration; and just possibly this background informed his later approach to international relations. It may also be significant that at this point he was sympathetic to attempts under Sir Warren Fisher to strengthen the Treasury's control over the Civil Service. But in truth it's not easy to find a consistent philosophical or doctrinal approach to Wilson's thinking.

His rise through the ranks of the Civil Service, already rapid, was boosted by the fact that he was the Chief Official Adviser to the British Delegation at the Ottawa Conference. Three years later he was seconded to the Treasury as the Prime Minister's Personal Adviser, an appointment which, to his surprise, he retained under Chamberlain: in effect he became Chamberlain's principal adviser on foreign policy, an area of which he knew little. What endeared him to Chamberlain was not his expertise, but the fact that the two men shared a similar cast of mind, committed to ignoring the Foreign Office and seeking to conciliate rather than confront Hitler. In addition, Wilson lacked none of Chamberlain's commitment to the cause. It was he who drafted conciliatory (that's to say, pro-German) letters and minutes on Chamberlain's behalf. It was he, and he alone, who was initially aware of Chamberlain's decision to fly to Germany in September 1938.

He lacked none of his boss's thoroughness and was ready to tackle the press and public opinion head on. The Foreign Office's news department was closed, the BBC and the newspapers – particularly *The Times* – were manipulated. He negotiated directly with the German Embassy in London and he, rather than a senior Foreign Office official, accompanied Chamberlain on his three visits to Germany. In September 1938 he went alone to see Hitler between the Godesberg and Munich summits. On the day before the declaration of war, Ribbentrop invited him to come and see him in a last-minute attempt to preserve the peace.

His role as an unelected official who played such a critical role in reinforcing Chamberlain in his beliefs was greatly resented by the anti-appeasers. He had private access to the Prime Minister's private apartments through a door from his adjoining office. When Churchill replaced Chamberlain as Prime Minister, Wilson came through the door to find himself confronting Randolph Churchill and Brendan Bracken, the most loyal of Churchill's acolytes. They sat together on a sofa and simply stared at him, saying nothing, until Wilson retreated through the door. He never reappeared. Churchill banned him from Number Ten saying that if he ever reappeared he would be sent to govern Greenland.

Chamberlain knew his own mind and was certainly not his puppet, but Wilson's reputation has never been rehabilitated. He was particularly attacked in the brilliant polemic, *Guilty Men* (dealt with below): 'Sir Horace Wilson established an ascendancy over Mr Chamberlain which will take its place in history. Neither of the men were fully aware of the position. Yet things came to a point when no major decision of any kind was taken by the British government before Sir Horace was consulted. If the plan did not win his approval it was often shelved.'[9] He was in truth a more deluded appeaser than Chamberlain ever was. Chamberlain, certainly latterly, knew that war was coming and was trying to buy time in order to fight it efficiently. Wilson himself believed that 'redress of grievances would erode support for Nazism and that war could thus be avoided'.[10]

There was an element of snobbery in the way Wilson was viewed by his mandarin colleagues. Orme Sargent, a Permanent Under-Secretary at the Foreign Office, remarked after Wilson retired in 1942, 'He came from Bournemouth and destroyed the British Empire and has now returned to Bournemouth.'[11] The same unappealing assumptions were shared by Lord Hugh Cecil when he said of the Abyssinian crisis that the aristocrats were 'all for singeing Musso's beard', whereas Baldwin, MacDonald, Runciman, Simon and the Chamberlains were 'terrified if he frowns at them. *Conspuez les bourgeois!!*'* Cecil's sister said that Halifax was more to be censured than Chamberlain for seeking to conciliate Hitler: 'a poor old middle-class monster could not be expected to know any better'. Harold Macmillan said Chamberlain was 'very middle class ... very narrow in view' and Harold Nicolson thought him 'no more than an ironmonger'.[12]

---

* 'Spit out the middle classes!'

But the middle-class appeasers were not *emotionally* committed to appeasement. Chamberlain's 'appeasement' was practical, a desire to avoid war if possible but at any rate to buy time. The emotional appeasers, the appeasers by conviction, those who rather liked the pure Aryan doctrine of Nazism were aristocrats, members of the Cliveden Set, anti-communists, men and women who believed in social Darwinism, the idea that survival and indeed progress depended on blood and steel, as opposed to a cosy suburban decline. They were also attracted to Nazism because it protected their financial interests and their privileged social status. Anti-Semitism was not far below the surface.

It is an interesting paradox that the more experience politicians had had of blood and steel, the less they liked appeasement. Eden, Churchill, Duff Cooper and Harold Macmillan had all fought with conspicuous courage in the Kaiser's war (and some of them had been seriously wounded), whereas Baldwin, MacDonald, Chamberlain, Halifax and Simon had either not seen service or at any rate had not served in the front line.[13]

## Chapter 19

# Gold Patches in the Mist

Chamberlain had plenty to do on his return from Ottawa. He relaxed with a variety of hosts in Scotland, shooting and fishing. He also visited the King at Balmoral. George V, the bluff sailor from the quarterdeck, found Chamberlain staid by naval standards and tried, unsuccessfully, to amuse him with some dirty stories. After his usual spring visit to the Dee in Aberdeenshire ('Birches and larches make a purple mist with old gold patches in it') came his first Budget.

He commended the austerity of his predecessor, Snowden, but foresaw a drop of £32 million in taxation income. He calculated that the new tariffs plus a re-imposition of the tea duty, which the paternalistic Churchill had removed, would close the gap. He was uncompromising: there was to be no relief from taxation and no risks would be taken: 'Nothing could be more harmful to the ultimate material recovery of this country or to its present moral fibre . . .' All the same, the highest level of direct taxation was reduced from 66 per cent, where it had been since the end of the war, to 55 per cent. Defence expenditure was reduced from the level at which it had been fixed under Labour. Sir Montagu Norman, the Governor of the Bank of England, wrote to congratulate Chamberlain on almost the first honest Budget since the war.

In May 1932 the gout by which this moderate man was afflicted was so painful that he contemplated having to retire from politics. After a cure of the sort so popular with Stanley Baldwin he was, however, fit to attend the conference in Lausanne to consider the future of the reparations payable by Germany in terms of the peace treaties of 1919. During breaks in the conference he did some sightseeing wearing a gout boot. He also took a few days off to return to London and make a dramatic announcement of which the Cabinet was unaware. The 1932 Budget had spoken of cheap money and currency management. He now added to that a reduction in bank rate to 2 per cent and war debt conversion. He converted £2,000 million of war loan from a coupon interest rate of 5 per cent per annum to just 3.5 per cent. This reduction affected 92 per cent of Britain's outstanding war loans and saved £23 million immediately. A further conversion saved another £40 million. The cut in the war loan coupon was a cruel one for patriotic investors who had bought bonds to help fund war against the Kaiser, but the overall effect of the Budget and these subsequent measures was to stimulate recovery.

The Lausanne Conference was acrimonious. By now the Keynesian view that reparations were counterproductive had been fairly generally accepted. In any event, Germany was pretty well incapable of making the payments, which had been temporarily suspended by the Hoover Moratorium of 1931. The problem was that while the United States were all for ending reparations, they were very clear that repayment of war debt by Germany's creditors to the US Exchequer should not be written off. The conference lasted a long time, as conferences tended to do in those days, from 16 June to 9 July. The unsatisfactory discussions ended with the conclusion that Germany's war debt could be written off if the Allies' debts to the United States were written off too. On that basis the delegates headed home. Given the inward-looking and isolationist approach of the United States, the Europeans cannot have been surprised that in December 1932 Congress rejected a reduction of Allied war debts. The payment of German reparations should theoretically have recommenced but they did not. Germany got away with paying just one-eighth of the debt agreed at Versailles. America's allies were given no similar consideration.

Chamberlain had not been impressed by European liberal democrat politicians in conference and by their failure to face up to reality. He himself probably played a bigger part in the conference than any other individual, not that it amounted to much. He made a particularly favourable impact on the veteran French Prime Minister, Édouard Herriot, who was taken by his insight and lucidity: '*Chamberlain, c'est du cristal.*'*

The 1932 Budget was criticised for its toughness, and that toughness was continued until 1934 when the literary Chamberlain talked

---

* 'Chamberlain's mind is crystal clear.'

of moving from *Bleak House* to *Great Expectations*, reducing income tax and enhancing unemployment benefit. He was able to say in the following year that the national economy had recovered to the extent of 80 per cent from the depths to which it had fallen. He was essentially a pragmatic chancellor, not doctrinaire. This pragmatism excluded even the theories of Keynes. He told Hilda after he had had a meeting with Keynes that 'his ideas were worse than I had supposed'. Spending money had to be on constructive ventures: he thought that it was pointless to fund schemes purely on the basis that they would create employment. Equally silly the Roosevelt New Deal: 'the poorest stuff imaginable, vague rhetorical and containing not a single new idea . . . Idiotic Yankees simply infuriate me'.[1]

His approach was essentially practical; when A. J. P. Taylor described his Budgets as reactionary he was not being critical. He meant that Chamberlain had pragmatically reversed a trend towards direct taxation that had seemed inexorable. He was an interventionist and, as in his days at the Ministry of Health, a social engineer. The power of the state was used to restructure industry. For example he interfered in the organisation of the iron and steel industry and set up and subsidised the London Passenger Transport Board to modernise transport in the capital. By 1937 unemployment had fallen from 2.9 million to 1.3 million and even in the coal mines had been cut from 40 per cent to 18 per cent. New departures in agricultural legislation had increased the acreage under wheat by 44 per cent. Above all, in the area of housing, which meant so much to Chamberlain, progress was made. In 1935–6 local authorities built 52,000 houses and private enterprise 270,000, half of which were bought with the assistance of building society loans. That's not to say that conditions were ideal – far from it. Backbenchers like Harold Macmillan criticised the government for not doing enough. Unemployment was still far too high. Housebuilding had improved, but from a very low base. In 1934 international trade had shrunk to a third of what it had been in 1929. None of this could be compensated for by the sight of a wagtail in the park which Chamberlain reported to the press.

There was a suggestion at the end of 1934 that he should move to the Foreign Office. His reasons for turning the suggestion down are interesting. The Foreign Office was expensive and he could not afford it.

He would loathe and detest the social ceremonies. Above all, he would not want it thought that he had engineered the move in order to avoid budgetary difficulties which lay ahead.[2] Instead, 'Have you considered Eden?'

MacDonald's third premiership lasted only from June 1935 to May 1937 and he no more dominated Chamberlain in that brief period than he had done before. Poor MacDonald soldiered on too long, hurt and bruised by the charge that he had abandoned Labour. He enjoyed foreign affairs, but when he went to the Geneva Disarmament Conference in 1932 he had to be accompanied by his doctor. Chamberlain noted his trembling. His speeches became increasingly incoherent. The press and the political establishment were remarkably tolerant. When he told reporters that he was fit and was only suffering from loss of memory, this was not mentioned in the papers. Finally, he agreed to resign in favour of Baldwin after King George V's Silver Jubilee Celebrations in 1935. He continued in the Commons for a period in 1935, though without a seat in the Cabinet, and King George V died in January 1936. MacDonald had been his favourite Prime Minister and MacDonald regretted the death of his 'kingly friend'. In November 1937 MacDonald died in the course of a sea voyage which it was hoped would restore his health. Much of Baldwin's remaining two years were absorbed by contemplation of the abdication crisis and by seeking to avoid alienating the nation by embracing rearmament.

Unlike the socialist MacDonald, Chamberlain had little time for royalty. Despite his apparent conventionality – he is never what he seems – Chamberlain didn't much like the kings and queens of his time. George V invited him to dine at Windsor when he was Director General of National Service. He was put out by the King's lack of interest in his work:'He hardly mentioned it and talked about anything else that came into his mind, forestry, drink, food control, racehorses etc.'[3] It was fairly predictable that he wouldn't like Edward VIII whose character was much too weak for his liking. In fact, he helped to engineer his abdication. George VI and Queen Elizabeth liked him more than he liked them.* He did like talking to Queen Elizabeth ('not

---

* They were upset that he was forced out and replaced by Churchill. Queen Mary told Jock Colville, who had been Chamberlain's secretary, that he should decline to become Churchill's secretary.

intellectual') but found George VI uninteresting. Robert Rhodes James held that Chamberlain deliberately kept George VI in the dark and indeed misled him: there were few instances 'of a Prime Minister treating a monarch with greater duplicity than the way in which Chamberlain dealt with George VI'.[4]

In the Baldwin years Chamberlain had plenty of scope for pursuing his non-Treasury interests: an Education Bill raising the school-leaving age to fifteen, an Act extinguishing tithes, a Cotton Industry Bill, unemployment insurance for agricultural workers, subsidies for air transport and special areas, extensive reorganisation of the Unemployment Assistance Board.* He caught record trout on the Test and suffered his worst attack of gout. On the other hand, the Beethoven quartets took him 'into another world'.

When he introduced his 1936 Budget, he took pleasure in reflecting that as a result of tariff reform a negative trade balance of £104 million had been transformed into a positive balance. Thirty-four million pounds had flowed into the Treasury and there had not been the rise in commodity prices which critics had foreseen. He had also made money cheap, saving interest charges of £40 million and allowing the building of 1.25 million houses. Unemployment had fallen from 22.4 per cent to 14.4 per cent. The critical view of Chamberlain's time at the Treasury, the caricature of an unimaginative book-balancer, entirely unaffected by the Keynesian inspiration is inaccurate. He was not highly imaginative or innovative, but under his stewardship the economy began to grow again, sterling recovered and unemployment, although high, was reduced by 48 per cent between 1932 and 1937.

Rearmament will be dealt with separately, but in the context of his Chancellorship it is worth remembering that in the 1936 Budget speech he referred to a White Paper on the largest programme of defence ever undertaken by this country in peace time. In February 1937 he announced that there would be defence expenditure of not less than £1,500 million over the next five years. By now he was

---

* In 1934 Chamberlain initiated the 'Special Areas' Policy, with two commissioners, one for England and Wales and one for Scotland, who would seek to initiate and promote schemes to facilitate economic development and social improvement in four areas of Britain. This was the basis of a policy which would remain in force until Mrs Thatcher's time and would indeed be toyed with even afterwards.

convinced of the need for rearmament, particularly for the Royal Air Force. The defence budget for 1936–7 was £186 million, £50 million more than in the previous year. To pay for all this, he would raise income tax and introduce what he called a National Defence Contribution, a graduated tax on businesses. He faced fierce criticism. He considered that he was doing the bravest thing he had done in public life, risking his claim to the premiership.[5] When Churchill spoke at a party meeting on 31 May 1937, he generously conceded that when the government had at length become convinced of the urgent need to rearm, no one had been more active than Chamberlain.

In March 1937 Austen died, and Neville was much affected. He stood behind the Speaker's chair listening to the tributes rather than reveal his emotions on the benches. On 29 March he wrote to the Archbishop of Canterbury in moving terms: 'From my earliest days I have looked up to Austen with perhaps much more deference, as well as affection, than is usually the case where the difference of years was so small. He was a rare, good brother to me, and the only one I had.'

Baldwin had decided that he would resign after George VI's Coronation in 1936. He promised that after his departure he would neither spit on the deck nor speak to the man at the wheel; he bravely bore the self-denied loss of these pleasures. Chamberlain accepted office as Prime Minister the day after he wrote his letter to the Archbishop. He declared that he had achieved an office which he could never have done without his wife and that it had come to him without his raising a finger to obtain it.

*Chapter 20*

# Prime Minister

If the new Prime Minister, on his way to Ten Downing Street, had done such an un–Chamberlain thing as to wander into the path of one of those big red buses, he would have been remembered by history as a great reforming domestic politician, more radical in a way than Radical Joe – certainly more *effective*; of the three Chamberlains the one who had decisively modernised society, vastly changing it for the better.

Mean-minded historians of a socialist disposition might have dwelt on his intemperate language towards his opponents and his treatment of overspending councils, but their more generous and better-informed colleagues would have chronicled the extent of his changes – the abolition of the Poor Law, the end of free trade, the extension of the role of the state in health care, provision of public housing, the creation of a modern system of pension and benefits. He was a *sport*, the political equivalent of a botanical phenomenon, genetically different from the stock which surrounded him, and historians would not have been able to resist reflecting that he would have been far more at home in Attlee's great reforming post-war government than in Baldwin's smug and inward-looking administrations.

But that is not how Neville Chamberlain is remembered. A thoughtful Fortune, thinking of his place in history, might better have directed his feet into the path of that oncoming bus so that he would be judged not on the last three years of his adult life, but on the forty-seven which preceded them.

Chamberlain's appointment as Prime Minister in succession to Baldwin was pretty well inevitable, but there was no sense of acclamation. It was even said that many Conservatives would have preferred Sir Thomas

Inskip, whose appointment as Minister for the Co-ordination of Defence was compared with the appointment of the Emperor Caligula's horse as consul.

Chamberlain's sheer ability and capacity for work meant that there were no competitors for the job, but that did not make him popular. His rise to the top of the party had been very fast. All the same, because of his late arrival in the House, at the age of sixty-eight, he was one of the oldest holders of the office of Prime Minister and it was assumed that he would be a short term stopgap, to be succeeded probably by Anthony Eden. He may have thought that he could 'do the affable', but he had none of the easy geniality that tends to mark traditional leaders of the Conservative Party. He had not been to Oxford or Cambridge, or spent time in the army. He was not part of the metropolitan or aristocratic elite. He didn't try to look like an engaging amateur or to disguise his contempt for those who truly were amateurs. He had always had confidence in his abilities, and by now he took no pains to disguise that confidence or his contempt for those who were less able than he was.

The comparison between Baldwin and Chamberlain is instructive. G. M. Young was Baldwin's official biographer, and wrote thus:

> Knowing them both, I always felt that, of the two, Chamberlain had the clearer mind, Baldwin the larger vision; Chamberlain, within his own circle, the warmer heart, Baldwin the wider affection. Instinct, insight, the most sensitive response to what others were feeling or thinking – as dimly perhaps he did himself: all that was Baldwin; and to Chamberlain all that was at times exasperating. Yet there were heights to which Baldwin could rise and he could not; while, on the other hand, Chamberlain could carry burdens – departmental burdens, party burdens of organisation and research – which Baldwin was only too willing to devolve on any other man's shoulder.[1]

Someone else more succinctly said that Chamberlain had no antennae and Baldwin had nothing else. Aneurin Bevan described the change of Prime Minister: 'In the funeral service of capitalism, the honeyed and soothing platitudes of the clergyman are finished, and the cortège is now under the sombre and oppressive guidance of the undertaker.'

Chamberlain *enjoyed* the fact of power. It meant that he could get things done. Much as he had relished the range of his authority as

Chancellor of the Exchequer, he now said 'As Ch of the Ex I could scarcely have moved a pebble: now I have only to raise a finger and the whole face of Europe is changed.' [2] But with power could come delusion. In the same letter to his sister Hilda he talked about 'the extraordinary relaxation in tension in Europe', a bizarre insight as Spain dissolved into a vicious Civil War in which the different factions were proxy agents of great powers. And with power could come paranoia. He resented criticism from the followers of Churchill and Eden, and complained to his sisters that the House of Commons did not give him the deference he received from the outside world. He suspected that Churchill was in direct communication with Jan Masaryk, the Czech spokesman in London. He tapped the phones of his critics: 'They of course are totally unaware of my knowledge of their proceedings. I had continual information of their doings and sayings.' [3]

Chamberlain's reach, his control of politics, was remarkable. He came with extensive experience and he had a prodigious memory and mastery of his brief. His managerial approach was entirely novel. It was different from that of his predecessors,* and most of his successors until Mrs Thatcher. From the start, he required Cabinet ministers to inform him about all their departmental plans for the following two years. He read and remembered all the Cabinet papers. He chaired all the major Cabinet committees. He was briefed by Sir Horace Wilson on what was going on in the different departments of government.

In Cabinet, ministers made their pitches unaware of his view and waited in trepidation for his summing up. His abilities were great and he was aware of that. His confidence meant that he did not see that he needed to court favour or work the tea rooms. But though he cared far too little about the opinion of Members of Parliament, it would be wrong to imagine that he was unconcerned about public opinion in the country at large. Part of his concept of management was that government policy should be presented clearly and consistently. He talked well on film newsreels, and was well aware of the importance of broadcasting. He used it to get the government's message over; he also did his best to make sure that the government's

---

* Except perhaps the Duke of Wellington. 'The most extraordinary thing happened this morning [at his first Cabinet]. I gave them their orders and they wanted to sit around discussing them!'

work was not undermined by criticism. Broadcasts that attacked Germany, for instance, were censored. His press office, under George Steward, was even more effective than Tony Blair's under Alastair Campbell, and journalists were supine in following the government line in a way of which his successors could only dream of.

On 8 December 1935 Chamberlain had written to Ida, mulling over his political future:'I suppose ... that I know no one that I would trust to hold the balance between rigid orthodoxy and a fatal disregard of sound principles and the rights of posterity. And, perhaps, when I come to think of it, I don't really care much what they say of me now, so long as I am satisfied myself that I am doing what is right.'[4] Being free from doubts, being convinced that one is right is all very well, but not if one is blinded to other views. Then the means are justified by the ends. This is the problem with Chamberlain's years as Prime Minister.

I tried earlier to suggest the character of the man when he entered Parliament. He wasn't a particularly attractive personality then: buttoned-up, shy, prickly and rather self-satisfied. Not someone we'd really choose to spend the evening with. But well-meaning, all the same, with a range of endearing interests. Not an unpleasant man. But by 1937 he was different. His less appealing characteristics were more marked and his more human ones less evident. He had been given great responsibilities and had discharged them with efficiency. He knew he had done well and he had done it when the clubbable amateurs had achieved much less. He was reinforced in a self-confidence which had become impenetrable.

In his period as Prime Minister Chamberlain remained involved in domestic matters. In 1938 coal mining royalties were nationalised, a substantial step towards nationalisation of the mines themselves. There was legislation in relation to factories, housing, slum clearance, overcrowding and physical training. Civil aviation was nationalised. In these and many other ways, the state continued to grow bigger and the assumptions of capitalism were challenged.

But I have said enough about Chamberlain as a radical reformer in social matters to establish that part of my case. We now turn to appeasement, the part of Chamberlain's political life that has most shaped his image. The charge against him is that he was weak, dangerously – even pathetically – credulous, that Hitler rang rings round him, that he was culpably blind to the explicit aims of Nazi Germany.

There have been four views about what Chamberlain did. The first, the reaction at the time, was overwhelmingly favourable. Most people thought he did wonderfully well in his negotiations with Hitler. The immediately subsequent reaction was the polar opposite. He was reviled and excoriated for spineless caving in, for a failure to resist and prepare. This view is most memorably set out in the book *Guilty Men*, already referred to and dealt with more fully later. That interpretation persisted until well after the war. There was then an attempt at revisionism, what Roy Jenkins called 'the low case for Chamberlain'. This recognised that Britain was not in a position to take Germany on, and that while Chamberlain talked on with Hitler he was also preparing for war as fast as he could and rearming in readiness for that war. Revisionsim was followed as always by post-revisonism, and a vague assertion, never very carefully articulated, that preparing and rearming was fine, but in some sort of way it just wasn't enough.

That's too sloppy. Even if we find the appeasement years pretty nauseating we have to look at them analytically and to be a little more precise. Hitler and all he stood for was revolting, but Chamberlain didn't create him. He had to deal with him. I am very far from approving of every aspect of Chamberlain's approach to the dictators, Hitler and Mussolini, and I am very critical indeed of the way he ran his government and the Tory Party in these years. Robert Skidelsky says that a biographer has to be a mixture of counsel for the defence and judge; but justice has to be done and I shall set out the evidence against him as well as in his favour.

What I suggest is that although he did some things and said many things that were extraordinarily wrong, overall he could have done nothing that would have averted war and that in the meantime it was his achievement to prepare for it so that Britain would not be defeated when it broke out. I do not attempt to minimise the case against Chamberlain, and his twin policies of seeking to avert war while preparing for it have to be placed in the context that informed his premiership: reliance on a small band of confidants who were not responsible to Parliament; control of his party by bullying; and the manipulation of news and propaganda through a compliant press. It is a deeply unpleasant world, and I shall begin with the press.

*Chapter 21*

# Chamberlain's Press

The distinguished political journalist James Margach studied the relationship between Downing Street and the media. He called his book *The Abuse of Power*, and opens his chapter on Chamberlain uncompromisingly:

> Neville Chamberlain was the first Prime Minister to employ news management on a grand scale. His aim had nothing remotely to do with open government, access to information and the strengthening of the democratic process; it had everything to do with the exploitation of the Press to espouse and defend government thinking. From the moment he entered Number 10 in 1937 he sought to manipulate the Press into supporting his policy of appeasing the dictators.[1]

He cites Cabinet minutes of 13 April and 3 November 1939. The first recorded that the Prime Minister had sent for the chairman of the *News Chronicle* and had protested in the strongest terms againsst the attitude which his paper had adopted in a particular instance. The second minute recorded the Cabinet's agreement that Chamberlain should approach the proprietors with a view to securing a cessation of 'the present Press campaign against the government'.

Margach was a young lobby correspondent at the time and was able to draw in detail on his own experience to support his argument that Chamberlain 'made the most misleading and inaccurate statements which he was determined to see published so as to make its policies appear credible and successful. Quite simply, he told lies.'[2]

The lobby had been in existence since 1885, but George Steward, Chamberlain's Press Secretary, changed the free-for-all atmosphere to what Margach called 'a fraternity of organised insiders'. Steward did the briefing, and journalists were not allowed direct access to ministers. Chamberlain (and indeed other ministers) noted Steward's effectiveness, and they began to direct their own unattributable briefings to the compliant insiders and not to the fifty or sixty members of the wider lobby.

What was new and crucial was that the journalists, in exchange for information that they thought useful, surrendered any critical faculty. Everything that was said by or on behalf of the Prime Minister was reported as objective fact. By 1939, the tractable lobby correspondents transcribed Chamberlain's words verbatim.[3]

From his time as Chancellor, Chamberlain increasingly acted to influence and control the press with the twin objectives of getting the government's case across and silencing any other case. He worked not on the larger lobby but concentrated on just three or four representatives of Conservative papers who were given private meetings usually over lunch at the St Stephen's Club opposite Westminster Bridge. There the host would usually be Chamberlain, Steward or Sir Robert Topping, the Director General of Conservative Central Office. If Chamberlain sensed criticism, he dealt with it at once. His mildest response would be a sneer. The next step up would be meaningfully to ask the correspondent his name and that of the newspaper he represented, with the implication that he would be speaking to the editor.

Any dissent was met with cold distain:

> [Chamberlain] was surprised that 'such an experienced journalist was susceptible to Jewish/Communist propaganda'. When asked a question which he resented he would attempt to snub the correspondent with frozen silence; after an eloquent pause, staring contemptuously at the questioner without saying a word in reply, he would turn aside, look in a different direction, and snap: 'Next question, please'. He was the only Prime Minister in my experience who could use this weapon of the total freeze. He was completely immobile, not merely for a fleeting second but for a long pause: an extraordinary show of silent intimidation.[4]

The favoured few, when Chamberlain, Steward or Topping were unavailable, often met Sir Joseph Ball, the Director of the Conservative

Research Department. Ball was one of Chamberlain's few friends; they even spent fishing holidays together. He had been Head of the Investigation branch of MI5 and had been recruited from MI5 in 1924 to 'run a little intelligence service' for the Tories by J. C. C. Davidson, the chairman of the Tory Party. The little intelligence service included planting agents in Labour Party headquarters and tapping the telephone wires of Chamberlain's opponents: he infiltrated Labour Party Headquarters in the same way as he had infiltrated the Communist Party when he was with MI5. Davidson later described Ball as having had 'as much experience as anyone I know in the seamy side of life and the handling of crooks'.[5] He tapped, for instance, the telephones of Eden's supporters and manipulated the way in which the government's policies and Chamberlain's image were presented.

Ball regarded as deviant even the acquiescent press such as the *Daily Mail* and the *Daily Express* and regretted that although 'admirable' the *Daily Telegraph* and *The Times* circulated too few copies to influence public opinion significantly. He accordingly acquired the publication *Truth*, originally a radical publication, established by Henry Labouchère in 1877, as a propaganda vehicle. All its files, like Ball's own papers, have been destroyed. Who controlled the periodical was carefully disguised, but Chamberlain was indubitably aware of what it was and what it was doing. Sir Robert Vansittart, who is discussed below, instigated a private enquiry into *Truth* in 1941 which concluded that it was run by the 'hard Munich core' of the Conservative Party. In his study of Chamberlain and the press, Richard Cockett writes that '*Truth* became stridently anti-Churchill, anti-Semitic, and anti-American and pacifist and, as such, accurately reflected the real state of Ball's and Chamberlain's minds'.[6] Harold Nicolson referred in his diary to a 'rude article about me in *Truth* saying that I have the "mincing manner of a French Salon", that I lack virility and should retire from public life …'[7]

The Foreign Office news department was independent of Steward, Ball and Chamberlain. It was run by Rex Leeper, who became head of the department in 1935. He attempted to centralise the flow of diplomatic news, much as Number Ten manipulated the lobby. He regarded journalism as inimical to diplomacy: the journalist had to be transformed into a 'willing collaborator'. Chilling. Leeper was not, however, an appeaser. His views were those of Sir Robert Vansittart and he admired Eden. When Sir Alexander Cadogan succeeded Vansittart* as Permanent Secretary in 1938 he was disappointed to find that Leeper was 'still "hypnotised" by [Anthony Eden] and very anti-Chamberlain'.

Leeper started to lean closer to Chamberlain, but by the summer of July 1938 Downing Street was concerned all the same that the Foreign Office news department was leaking information which the Prime Minister did not wish disseminated. After Munich, Sir Horace Wilson rang Leeper to tell him that Cabinet members thought he was being disloyal. Wilson saw Sir Alexander Cadogan about Leeper on 4 October 1938 and Cadogan decided that Leeper must go. He was taken away from dealing with the press and put in charge of propaganda, and shortly afterwards shunted off to Bucharest.

Soon afterwards the Foreign Office news department was subsumed into an amorphous Ministry of Information which came into being in 1939. Downing Street now stood alone and supreme in its control of the lobby. The degree of governmental control of the press caused concern in Parliament. James (later Lord) Milner, the Labour Member for Leeds South East and nothing to do with the great imperialist, raised the matter in March 1938, but Halifax dismissed the charge of formal interference without venturing into the area of informal influence.

The threat to tell tales to proprietors and his opportunity for doing so were real. Chamberlain kept closely in touch with proprietors and leader writers. Every Friday at 3.30 p.m. the editor of the *Sunday Times*, for example, went to Downing Street to be briefed. There were just one or two of the Conservative press which were outside the fold: the *Telegraph* and the *Yorkshire Post*, both favourable to Eden, with the *Telegraph*, under the proprietorship of Lord Camrose, also supportive of his friend Winston Churchill.

The closest contact was with *The Times* where the editor, Geoffrey Dawson, not only suppressed parts of his own foreign correspondents' despatches but inserted glosses of his own, with the effect of turning the despatches on their heads in order to mollify the Fascist leaders. Chamberlain even intervened in the minor matter of making sure that Hitler was always referred to as Herr Hitler and Mussolini as Signor

---

* More of both later.

Mussolini. Any marks of disrespect, however trifling, were censured. The dictators were not the enemies: the enemies were communists and Jewish propagandists. Geoffrey Dawson met the Foreign Secretary, Lord Halifax, almost daily and would never have criticised him. *The Times*, like the *Daily Express*, was the government's plaything.

Eventually, even supine editors became worried by the gap between the sunny reports which their correspondents submitted to them and what the dictators were actually doing. A number of lobby correspondents arranged a private lunch with Chamberlain and told him that their credibility was under threat. Chamberlain retorted that he was astounded that they could be taking such a self-centred view of their responsibilities. Herr Hitler and Signor Mussolini resented attacks in the press and appreciated his efforts to improve the atmosphere. The real threat came from Russian Communism.[8]

It's difficult not to conclude that, by now, in the isolated bubble in which he conducted foreign policy, Chamberlain was clinically detached from reality. He was particularly angry when the papers accused him of being dictatorial. James Margach records one occasion when he, amongst others, was summoned to Downing Street

> where we found [Chamberlain] in the Cabinet room, trembling and white with fury. He thumped the table many, many times as he snarled out his protest: 'I tell you that I am not dictatorial, I am not autocratic, I am not intolerant, I am not overpowering. You are all wrong, wrong, wrong, I tell you. I'm the most relaxed and understanding of people. None of you, I insist, must ever say I am dictatorial again. I tell you.' It was a saddening performance. In this angry outburst, which must have seriously depleted his sorely sapped nervous and physical resources, he looked and acted himself as the complete dictator.[9]

What Margach describes is rather like Charlie Chaplin's performance as Hitler in the film *The Great Dictator*.

It should be remembered that Margach was a trusted, long-term member of the lobby establishment who was respected for the measured, dispassionate quality of his reporting. He was not particularly hostile to Chamberlain. Throughout his long career he was best known for his moderate commonsense. What he says is supported by what others have revealed about Chamberlain's relationship with the press. Alastair Campbell – and perhaps even Dominic Cummings – were pussycats compared to their 1930s predecessors.

The cohesive support of the press for Chamberlain and appeasement puzzled those who thought about it, particularly after the publication of *Guilty Men*. A Royal Commission on the press was set up immediately after the war to explore what had happened. It had been assumed that there had been conscious collusion, but the Commission's report in 1949 found no evidence of that.

As usual, conspiracy theories were too sophisticated. What had happened had more to do with personal contacts than anything else. George Steward worked on what he called the 'human element'.

The *News Chronicle* and the *Daily Herald* became increasingly critical of Nazism, but they were exceptional and those involved did not go unpunished. Great pressure was put on the *News Chronicle* over the years and occasionally leader articles were modified. Arthur Mann, the editor of the *Yorkshire Post*, was a staunchly independent provincial journalist who stuck to his line in the face of criticism from the leadership of the Yorkshire Conservative Newspaper Association, but he was exceptional.

Also exceptional, not only in opposing Chamberlainite orthodoxy, but in the way they stood apart from the main press, were Stephen King-Hall and Claud Cockburn. Commander Stephen King-Hall, MP, started a periodical, *The King-Hall Newsletter*, in 1936 with an initial list of 600 subscribers ('members'). It was enormously successful and by November 1937 had 37,500 members, 53,017 by May 1939. Its message, as King-Hall said, was to repeat 'with what now reads like monotonous regularity that unless measures were taken to deal with the Nazi menace it was as certain as anything can be in this world that there would be a war'. He even circulated *The Newsletter* in Germany to put heart into Germans who opposed Hitler. Needless to say, it was abominated by the appeasers and particularly by Sir Neville Henderson at the Berlin Embassy. Claud Cockburn, who had worked in Germany as a foreign correspondent for *The Times*, resigned in 1933 to start his newsletter, the *Week*. The periodical was critical of Chamberlain – Cockburn claimed that most of the information in the *Week* had been leaked to him by Sir Robert Vansittart. He was clear that he was kept under observation by the Security Services.

## Chapter 22

# A Foreign Office Quartet

In foreign affairs Chamberlain worked closely with a limited number of men. They were not necessarily from the Foreign Office: he was probably most influenced by Geoffrey Dawson and Horace Wilson, who, as we have seen, came from quite different backgrounds, but there were one or two others who did come from King Charles Street and whose advice shaped his personal policy.

## Edward Wood, Lord Halifax

When Chamberlain became Prime Minister he took on Baldwin's Foreign Secretary, Anthony Eden. Eden was charming, opinionated and febrile. He can, however, be dismissed too easily, as Mussolini did in describing him as the best-dressed fool in Europe; while not an intellectual he had a good grasp of policy. He tended, however, to be inflexible, and he and Chamberlain separated increasingly until he resigned in February 1938 in circumstances that will be explored later. He was succeeded by Lord Halifax, whom the Prime Minister found more congenial.

Halifax was at the centre of politics in the first half of the twentieth century. His was a complicated character, very difficult to analyse, which has fascinated historians. Even his name confuses. He started out as Edward Wood, but then went to India as Viceroy and needed a title, so became Lord Irwin. His father died in 1934 and he became Viscount Halifax. In May 1944 he was created the first Earl of Halifax.

His nickname, the 'Holy Fox', was a pun on the name 'Halifax' but it also pointed to the different strands that make him such an intriguing character. The 'holy' element reflected a real piety. He inherited a strong Christian commitment from his father. After gaining a first in

Modern History at Oxford he was elected to a fellowship of All Souls' College. His first book was a biography of John Keble. 'Fox' alluded to two things. One was his love of hunting: in England he was Master of the Middleton Hunt, and he also hunted when he was in India and in the United States when he became Ambassador there. It is of some relevance to the history of appeasement that in 1937 he accepted an invitation from Göring to attend a hunting exhibition in Berlin and to *shoot* foxes in Pomerania. The combination of the macho outdoor world of hunting with his spiritual commitment is improbable. The foxiness also alludes to his ability, without compromising his idealism, to advance his political career.

He had occupied important ministerial offices before he was appointed Viceroy in October 1925, and on his return from India, where he had a productive relationship with the equally spiritual Gandhi, he returned to various high offices before succeeding Eden in 1938.

He might have gone further. He could have been Prime Minister in 1940 if he had even chosen to *hint* that he wanted the job. The King and the Royal Family wanted him; Chamberlain wanted him and the Tory Party wanted him. As Chamberlain discussed with him and Churchill who should be his successor, he put the critical question, 'Can you see any reason, Winston, why in these days a peer should not be Prime Minister?' Churchill turned his back, looked out on Horse Guards Parade and maintained that silence which he described as seeming 'longer than the two minutes which one observes in the commemoration of Armistice Day'. It wasn't Churchill's studied silence that denied Halifax the keys to Number Ten. It was Halifax who broke the silence to say that as a peer he could not carry out the responsibilities of Prime Minister. Earlier in the day he had told his Parliamentary Under-Secretary that he thought he could do the job, but when it came to the bit he literally didn't have the stomach for it. He had felt sick at the prospect and when the Chief Whip couldn't decide between himself and Churchill, 'My stomach ache continued.'

Halifax is often superficially written off as an appeaser. He was certainly no warmonger,* but his approach was not doctrinaire

---

\* There is a little cameo that I rather like. Halifax was so anxious not to distress German sensibilities that he even made a point of meeting the brilliant cartoonist David Low so that he could ask him to tone down his criticism of Hitler.

– certainly less so than Chamberlain's. He tended, as the drama played out, and as Hitler's untrustworthiness became clearer, to be less credulous than Chamberlain, but to Chamberlain's credit, after war had broken out and Hitter's blitzkrieg had conquered Western Europe, it was not Chamberlain but Halifax who wanted to enter into negotiations and, as we shall see, sign a humiliating peace treaty. It was Chamberlain who came to Churchill's side and argued for continuing the war.

## Sir Robert Vansittart

Sir Robert Vansittart, 'Van', was Permanent Under-Secretary at the Foreign Office from 1930 to 1938. He came from a family that had grown rich on the profits of the East India Company, riches that had been substantially dissipated by his father's enthusiasm for the stock market, but on his second marriage in 1931, following the tragic death of his first wife, Van found himself at the age of fifty very comfortably off. He and his second wife (whose income was £40,000 per annum, a huge sum at the time) lived in a magnificent William and Mary manor house in Buckinghamshire with a hundred acres of gardens modelled on Hampton Court. They employed a staff of twelve servants and five gardeners.

Vansittart was very intelligent. He was top of the diplomatic examination list in 1903. He also had considerable literary skills and sometimes contemplated giving up the diplomatic service to be a full-time writer. In his early twenties, a third secretary at the Paris Embassy, he wrote a play in French which ran for six weeks at the Théâtre Molière. In 1933 he published *The Singing Caravan* which ran to several editions and was admired by his kinsman, T. E. Lawrence. His posthumous autobiography, *The Mist Procession*, is written with charm. Its final sentence reflects on how he saw his life: 'Mine is a story of failure, but it throws light on my time, which failed too.' His time, the diplomatic world of the interwar years, failed, in his view, because the rest of the world failed to restrain Germany. His obsession, as some saw it, with

---

'Very well', said Low, 'I don't want to be responsible for a world war.' (But after the annexation of Austria, Low felt that the outbreak of a world war wouldn't be his responsibility, and he returned to his superb depictions of Hitler.)

the nature not just of Nazism, but of the country which embraced Nazism, finally resulted in his being kicked upstairs from the Permanent Under-Secretaryship to which he had been appointed at the age of just forty-eight, to a meaningless sinecure as Chief Diplomatic Adviser to the government.

His opponents, who included Eden and Chamberlain, by now tended to write off his views as almost paranoid (he didn't do himself any good during his time as head of the American Department at the Foreign Office in the mid-1920s, by referring to the American people as 'this untrustworthy race') but his views on Germany were based on a close examination of the country and its history. Before entering the diplomatic service he travelled on the Continent for over two years, and in Germany he saw for himself the intense anti-British feeling that was born of colonial and naval rivalry and had crystallised around the South African War. He also visited France and fell in love with that country. His hostility to one and his affection for the other of the two European rivals polarised his European policy. During the First World War he was in charge of the Prisoners of War Department. He was in no doubt that Germany was fundamentally barbaric and had committed innumerable atrocities, and was deeply affected by the death of his younger brother who was killed at Ypres. In *The Mist Procession* he said: 'The personal elements should not affect the policy, but one cannot help prevent experience from confirming conclusions already reached. Why ask for strength to reverse them?'

By May 1930, now Permanent Under-Secretary and having spent two years as Assistant Under-Secretary as Private Secretary to Baldwin and MacDonald, he was convinced that Hitler was bent on the same aggressive militarism as the Kaiser and his advisers in 1914. In a minute of 6 May 1933 he wrote: 'The present regime in Germany will, on past and present form, loose off another European War just so soon as it feels strong enough ... We are considering very crude people who have very few ideas in their noddles but brute force and militarism.'[1] His reaction was very simple. Germany had to be explicitly recognised as a danger to Britain and Britain's top priority must be to build up defences against her.

The Hoare–Laval Pact, designed to create an Anglo-French-Italian alliance against Germany by acquiescing in Italy's 1935 landgrab in

Abyssinia, was engineered very much at his instigation. The Cabinet initially approved of this secret agreement but when its details were leaked it was disavowed by both the British and the French. Hoare resigned and George V made a joke: 'Well that's it. No more coals to Newcastle and no more Hoares to Paris.' The King was pleased with his joke. He even told it to Hoare: 'The fellow didn't even laugh.' Hoare went and although Vansittart didn't, his position was never the same again. In January 1938 he was succeeded by Sir Alexander Cadogan.

Vansittart was patronising about Chamberlain: 'An earnest and opinionated provincial who was bound to err if he plunged into diplomacy.'[2]

## Sir Alexander Cadogan

Cadogan grew up in grand surroundings – the family home was Chelsea House on the corner of Cadogan Square and was described by Harold Macmillan as 'a kind of baronial castle'. There was also a family estate of 11,000 acres near Bury St Edmunds. But the dominating influence in his upbringing was not wealth and pomp, but a sense of duty and application. To that he added very great intellectual ability. When he entered the Civil Service he was top of the list in the diplomatic service examinations. His abilities were recognised throughout his career. He was Permanent Under-Secretary to the Foreign Office for an unusually long period of eight years, was very seriously considered for the Foreign Secretaryship in 1944, became the first UK representative at the United Nations and was the first civil servant to receive the Order of Merit.

His time at the United Nations was prefigured by work at the beginning of his career with the League of Nations, and indeed he was asked, but declined, to become its Secretary General in 1933.

His position on rearmament and appeasement was subtle. He was frequently compared with his predecessor, Vansittart. The comparison, when anti-appeasers made it, was usually to Cadogan's disadvantage. He did not have the flamboyant and extrovert character of Vansittart and was cold and restrained – though much later the publication of his diaries would reveal him to have a satirical sense of humour and no sense of deference towards his political masters.

At the League of Nations, where, incidentally, he much approved of Austen Chamberlain – who encouraged the forward movement of his career – he did believe that the pursuit of disarmament could lead to long-lasting peace, but he was not dogmatic in his views. Vansittart saw the deterioration in the European situation in the same black and white terms as did Churchill, but Cadogan, who was also pessimistic about Germany's intentions, was aware of the limitations of what Britain and her leaders would tolerate. This sense of realism resulted in the conclusion, shared with Halifax, that Britain was too weak to do much about the problems in Central and Eastern Europe and had to recognise that and concentrate instead on repairing the dangerously weak defences on the edges of the Empire.

Cadogan's approach was that if Germany was bent on Britain's destruction, the best that could be done was to '*put it off*' [the emphasis is his]. 'Therefore we *must* try and talk with some of them and encourage some of them. It's no use … doing nothing. If our rearmament is backward, we must have time … It's no good, as Van does, forming no policy and merely saying "Rearm" … I've endured nearly a year of loyalty to the F.O., but there are other, and more important loyalties, and I think Van is rushing us to disaster.'[3]

A month later Cadogan wrote a minute to record the details of Lord Lothian's interview with Hitler and Göring, a minute which was annotated by Vansittart. The comments of the two men reflect their differences. Vansittart believed that Germany's demand for redress of grievances was spurious and that the more was conceded the more would be asked. Both men agreed that Germany should be pressed for an explicit statement of what her ambitions were, but Cadogan rejected the argument that a premature removal of grievances would simply result in the production of more 'legitimate claims'.[4]

Chamberlain, Halifax, Vansittart and Cadogan all dealt with the same British representative in Berlin: Sir Neville Henderson was the British Ambassador to Germany from 1937 until the outbreak of war.

## Sir Neville Henderson

Henderson was on occasion described in the press as 'our Nazi Ambassador in Berlin', but he was known to respond to the '*Heil*

*Hitler!'* salute with 'Rule Britannia!' He was vain, fastidiously dressed and self-important, but underneath self-conscious and lacking in judgement.

His father, a Director of the Bank of England as well as of the family business of R. & I. Henderson in Glasgow, died when Neville Henderson was just thirteen. He was brought up by his mother, a very powerful lady. She had travelled round the world at the age of twenty-four and it was she who decided that her son should enter the Diplomatic Service rather than the army, his preference. He served at the Paris Embassy from January 1916 until October 1920 and it was there that he became convinced, first, that the Versailles settlement was unfair to Germany and, secondly, that French diplomats were not to be trusted. He still adhered to these views when he was appointed as Ambassador to Berlin.

Even before his appointment he had disconcerted Eden with his ideas about what he would do when he got to Germany. Once there he wrote a memorandum arguing that Britain should acquiesce in the annexation of Austria and in Germany's right to recover colonies and to dominate Eastern Europe. He let Austria know that he was in favour of *Anschluss*, its annexation by Germany. He made a speech in which he said that there was much misunderstanding in England about what Nazism really stood for. The Foreign Office, including Vansittart and Orme Sargent, head of the Central Department, were taken aback by these policy departures. He soon went further and started attending the Nuremberg Rallies as his predecessors had not and the French and American ambassadors did not. Since he thought that Versailles had been unfair, he believed that Germany had a valid claim to the Sudeten part of Czechoslovakia.

He was prejudiced against the Czechs and their president, Edvard Beneš. After Munich he wrote to Chamberlain: 'Millions of mothers will be blessing your name tonight for having saved their sons from the horrors of war.'[5] All this disconcerted the Foreign Office, but it did little damage to Henderson, who was assured that his views were entirely those of the Prime Minister.

History has tended to regard him as a committed arch-appeaser, but although he was more emollient to Germany than his predecessors, Sir Eric Phipps and Sir Horace Rumbold, he was not in favour of Nazism and was opposed to annexation of Czechoslovakia by force.

He thought that Hitler, who referred to him as 'the man with the carnation', was unpredictable to a clinical degree and he had no time for Ribbentrop.*

He suffered from cancer of the throat from 1938 onwards and after Munich asked Halifax to move him somewhere else. He never wanted to work with Germans again, but, for reasons that are still not clear and despite his poor health and despite the fact that Halifax and Cadogan had no confidence in him, he remained in post to deliver Britain's ultimatum to Germany on 3 September 1939 and only returned to England a few days later.

The plus points don't outweigh the minus ones. His judgement, affected by his predisposition towards Germany, was not impartial. As a result of a meeting with Chamberlain in April 1937 he regarded himself as the enforcer of Chamberlain's policy rather than that of the Foreign Office. He believed that he had been specially selected by providence to help to preserve the peace of the world.[6]

In the early part of 1938, Henderson repeatedly told the Foreign Office that if there were to be a positive follow-up to a visit to Germany by Halifax there had to be a 'propaganda-truce'. He was embarrassed by what Germans regarded as the vilification of Germany by the British press, particularly by the *News Chronicle* and the *Manchester Guardian* which the Germans complained were Jewish newspapers infected by Soviet Bolshevism. Henderson was assured on behalf of the news department of the Foreign Office that the proprietors of the *Manchester Guardian* were 'entirely Arian' and that the *News Chronicle*, at any rate, was 'free from all Jewish influences'.[7] These responses say a lot about establishment values.

---

* Joachim von Ribbentrop, latterly the German Foreign Minister, had been German Ambassador to Britain and Chamberlain's tenant at Eaton Square. Chamberlain had described Ribbentrop as 'so stupid, so shallow, so self-centred and self-satisfied, so totally devoid of intellectual capacity that he never seems to take in what is said to him'. He was amused to find himself Ribbentrop's landlord: 'I think it is very amusing considering my affections for the Germans in general and R. in particular.'

*Chapter 23*

# Foreign Affairs:
# The Landscape and the Fog

Given that it was on Chamberlain's watch that his country entered the Second World War, something that can't just be brushed aside, it is pretty inevitable that it's usually on his 1,050 days as Prime Minister that he is judged and on them alone. But foreign affairs didn't start in 1937. Nor did Chamberlain's involvement in them.

We've seen that his ambitious concept of his role as Chancellor extended to defence preparations. As a senior member of the Cabinet, he was also involved in the formulation of foreign policy. At a dinner in 1936 Austen Chamberlain tried to silence his half-sibling: 'Neville you must remember you don't know anything about foreign affairs.' Anthony Eden, who quoted the remark said that Neville 'smiled wryly and remarked that this was rather hard on a man at his own dinner table'.[1] Austen was being jocular. Chamberlain had already taken far more interest in foreign policy than his departmental responsibilities required, and had twice been asked to be Foreign Secretary.

He was very far from an insular man. He was very much more travelled that most politicians of his time. From his earliest days he had been a traveller, and an observant and inquisitive one. He was familiar with the language and culture of Europe, as well of that of the wider world, and spoke both French and German reasonably well.

The pivotal issues of the years running up to his time as Prime Minister arose from the settlement at Versailles in 1919. The savage terms of the financial punishment of Germany have already been mentioned, but Versailles caused many other problems for the future. Many books have been written about what happened at Versailles, about how out of the heterogenous arbitrariness of the old Habsburg and Hohenzollern Empires the American President Wilson sought to create a new Europe, based on principles of self-determination. It was an impossible project and it was frustrated by Wilson's increasing detachment from Europe, by the special concerns of many of the participants and because very soon the leaders of Europe had run out of time and interest. What was left was a series of quick-fixes: frontiers that ran across ethnic boundaries, new concoctions, like Czechoslovakia and a redrawn Poland, that yoked together disparate and hostile communities. Of those who complained about the settlement, Germany had the greatest and most justified set of grievances.

The overarching charge against Chamberlain is that in relation to Germany he was gullible and weak and followed a policy of unilateral concession. That policy is what is described as appeasement. It was a policy that failed in its aim of averting war.

It is important not to use hindsight. 'Appeasement' in the early 1930s had no derogatory connotation. It was a technical Foreign Office term. It did not imply weakness, buying off aggressors or paying Danegeld. It was thought to be a constructive policy of maintaining the peace of Europe by identifying territorial wrongs and righting them by negotiation rather than war. It was the continuation of the Congress policy which had been used to keep the peace in continental Europe from 1815 to 1914.

Appeasement wasn't Chamberlain's creation. It was first suggested in 1931 by Orme Sargent, the important Foreign Office official who ended his career as Cadogan's successor as Permanent Under-Secretary.* He was no appeaser in a pejorative sense, and was very much aware of Hitler and his dangers. The policy was approved by his boss, Vansittart, despite his hostility to Germany.

Although Chamberlain is rightly associated with appeasement, all the Foreign Secretaries of the time – Simon, Hoare, Eden and Halifax – accepted the policy to greater or lesser extents. Redressing grievances in order to establish a new, fair basis to European polity seemed perfectly reasonable.

That doesn't in itself exonerate Chamberlain and his fellow appeasers. The question is whether the policy was applied in a robust and

---

* In the interwar period he had particular responsibility for Central Europe and then Germany. He had been part of the British delegation to the Versailles Conference.

realistic manner or whether the appeasers were unduly credulous and disposed to surrender. With hindsight we may conclude that Chamberlain, in his proper desire not to see a return to the tragedy in which Norman and so many men of his generation had needlessly died, strained to the limit to avoid that disaster. I argue that he did not allow the desire to take him beyond that limit.

As we saw, there had been talk of a move from the Exchequer to the Foreign Office in December 1934 ('Have you considered Eden?'): Chamberlain was Foreign Secretary material. Despite turning the job down, he was increasingly directly involved in foreign policy from about then onwards. MacDonald had opposed the First World War,* and now worked for peace and disarmament, enjoying the great international conferences, 'resort diplomacy', of these years. Chamberlain had little confidence in the Foreign Secretary, Sir John Simon, who seemed, to him, too much of a lawyer, too inclined to see both sides of a case and fail to take a strong lead.

Hitler came to power as Chancellor of Germany in January 1933. It was not immediately obvious how serious a threat he would be, but many in the Foreign Office did think that he was looking for an excuse for a war, though possibly a limited one. He was certainly starting to rearm despite the provisions of the Treaty of Versailles. In the debate which developed in Britain between those who wanted to build up the national defences and those who did not, Chamberlain was distinctly on the side of those who wanted to make realistic preparations. At this stage, he envisaged the development of what he called a limited liability force, 'an international police force'.[2] Germany would not be part of it.

As 1934 went on, Hitler's intentions became clearer. The Night of the Long Knives consolidated his power and clarified the nature of domestic Nazism. In July, the Nazis in Austria murdered the Chancellor, Engelbert Dollfuss, no democrat but an opponent of Nazism:

What an ominous tragedy [wrote Chamberlain], with Austria once again the centre of the picture, with another murder almost on the

---

* As a result he was unpopular and accused of cowardice. But he had visited the front and when he was there found himself under fire. He displayed impeccable coolness and never mentioned the episode.

anniversary of that of the Archduke, and with Germany once more behind, instigating, suggesting, encouraging bloodshed and assassination for her own selfish aggrandisement and pride. I felt terribly upset about poor little Dollfuss ... that those beasts should have got him at last, and that they should have treated him with such callous brutality, makes me hate Naziism and all its works, with a greater loathing than ever.[3]

His reaction was that Britain had to prepare herself for hostilities with Germany – rather, that is, than with the other potential antagonist, Japan. The keynote of his approach from now was that while still working with France towards a general settlement 'the western nations should simultaneously prepare for armed resistance'. Thus: 'Hitler's Germany is the bully of Europe; yet I don't despair.'

When Hoare ('No more coals to Newcastle') stepped down in 1935, Chamberlain was pleased enough to see him replaced by Anthony Eden, a former Lord Privy Seal and Minister for the League of Nations. He respected his skills in negotiation, but relations between them were tested over Italy.

In 1935 Mussolini began Italy's annexation of Abyssinia. Italy had made always made it very clear that this was on the agenda, and Mussolini even announced when it would happen. Britain's position was awkward. Relations with Italy had been good; Rome and Berlin were not yet an axis and indeed Italy had renewed her commitment to the Locarno Agreements and to Austrian independence, even taking precautionary military measures to deter annexation of Austria. Not much was known about Abyssinia – though it was a member of the League of Nations and entitled to assistance in the event of aggression. Different politicians weighed these conflicting considerations in different ways. There was no great appetite in Britain for taking any dramatic steps to defend a country of which most people had never heard. George V himself said to Lloyd George that if there were any prospects of intervening over Abyssinia, he would go to Trafalgar Square himself, waving the red flag.

And yet Abyssinia presented a real challenge to the principles of the League of Nations. The Covenant of the League required its members collectively to protect the frontiers of every member state. This was a clear-cut case where the League should have intervened. There was no question here of redressing grievances imposed in the Peace Treaties; instead Italy was engaged on a good, old-fashioned piece of imperial adventuring. But there was absolutely *no* suggestion that Britain – or any other power – would go to war for the sake of the Abyssinians. Chamberlain's initial position on Abyssinia was to favour oil sanctions against Italy. That was, in fact, more than most of his colleagues would have done; they were in favour of sanctions providing they didn't hurt. But sanctions were problematic. Since the Japanese invasion of Manchuria in 1931, sanctions had been judged pretty ineffective. Many, like Baldwin, thought that sanctions could develop into war.

Chamberlain had thought that if Britain and France held together they could stop Mussolini. If they did not – and after the disavowal of the Hoare–Laval Pact they did not – Britain couldn't be expected to maintain the peace single-handed. He recognised that the League was going to be shown to be valueless. Italy renewed her attacks, now using poison gas, and the war ended in May 1936. It was, too, pretty much the end of the League.

While Eden didn't falter in supporting sanctions against Italy, there were many who took a different view. Austen Chamberlain and Churchill were quite clear that the real threat was not from Mussolini but from Hitler, and saw no value in dealing with what they regarded as a minor problem. Neville, however, neither wanted to punish Mussolini, as Eden did, nor to see Hitler as inescapably hostile. He did not want sanctions to be prolonged unduly. He wanted, rather, a rapprochement with Mussolini so that he would become an ally in mollifying rather than confronting Hitler.

As always, when Chamberlain had decided on a policy he wasted no time in implementing it, and he was prepared to ruffle feathers. Despite the fact that Baldwin and the bulk of the Cabinet had yet to take a position on the issue, he rejected a demand by the League of Nations Union and the opposition parties in Parliament for increased sanctions against Italy. At a well-attended meeting of the Conservative Dining Club on 10 June 1936 he described the idea as 'the very midsummer of madness'.

He had intervened on a foreign policy issue, Eden's province. That was a breach of protocol and he apologised for having done so (but he admitted in his diary that he had deliberately avoided prior consultation because Eden would have objected to what he intended to say). His tactics worked and seven days later the Cabinet agreed to begin lifting sanctions. Harold Macmillan resigned the whip. Chamberlain had displayed leadership and made the weather.

Chamberlain had nothing to be ashamed about over Abyssinia. Others had. There were unappealing examples of racial prejudice. Even Churchill said that 'no one can keep up the pretence that Abyssinia is a fit, worthy, and equal member of a league of civilised nations'.

Quite apart from the Abyssinian dimension, Mussolini from the outset was a target of Chamberlain's diplomacy, in part because he couldn't establish much of a dialogue with Hitler, in part because Mussolini might act as a link with the more dominant dictator and in part because of the importance of the Mediterranean. Vansittart dismissed the importance of Mussolini, the 'dictator minor', and Eden regarded him as no more than an opportunistic thug. None of that bothered Chamberlain.

The Spanish Civil War started in 1936, Chamberlain stating: 'The Bolshies are the limit'.⁴ When it broke out, Eden was on holiday, and didn't bother to come back. Lord Halifax, who deputised for him, said that government policy was 'to localise the disturbance . . . and prevent outside assistance from prolonging the war'. There can be debate on how far that policy was successful. There certainly *was* outside assistance, notably from Germany and Russia, but things could perhaps have been worse. The Civil War further clarified Chamberlain's position on Mussolini. He was anxious that whichever way it ended, and he didn't think it much mattered how it ended, it should be a Spanish victory and not an Italian or a German one: it should be a local affair. He thought he could persuade Mussolini to refrain from intervention in Spain and to persuade Germany to do so also.

His favourable view of Mussolini and his delusion that he had a particular rapport with him was greatly encouraged by the close relationship he had with the Italian Ambassador in London, Count Grandi. Grandi told Chamberlain in June 1937 that 'all Europe [was] looking to him as the only man who could get us out of our troubles'.⁵ This was exactly the thing to say to Chamberlain. He loved flattery and he loved to be reinforced in his consistent view that he had a special chemistry in foreign relations, that he could see into the hearts of his interlocutors and bind them to him with hoops of steel. It was a bizarre and dangerous conceit, far removed from his usual logical processes. It was the weakness of a man whose experience had been in negotiating with union officials on the factory floor. As long as Austen was fully involved in foreign affairs Neville had, out of deference to him, tended to avoid that area of policy, but this restraint ended with Austen's death. He promoted himself to a role for which he was not qualified.

Hitler took advantage of Western preoccupation with Abyssinia. In March 1936 his armies marched into the Rhineland, remilitarising it in defiance of the provisions of the Versailles Treaty. Hitler could have been stopped when, as he said, with his heart in his mouth and ready to call them back, he ordered his troops into the Rhineland. By 1938 and the Czech crisis it was too late. But there was no real prospect of action. The fault for that had nothing to do with Chamberlain – he wasn't even Prime Minister. Inertia was endemic in the Western community generally. Maybe the damage was done when Hitler saw how the Allies failed to react over Abyssinia. Or even back nearly twenty years when the world stood back and watched the Turks massacre 1,500,000 Armenians. 'Who remembers Armenia?', Hitler would ask.

In 1936 Hitler guessed rightly that neither France nor Britain had the stomach for a war over the arcane issue of whether the Rhineland, wherever it might be, was demilitarised or remilitarised. His judgement was impeccable: Britain and France did not even consider a military response. So he went on his incremental way.

But there was no escaping the fact that there was a real threat from Germany. Chamberlain was clear that in the circumstances it was better to have one enemy than two. He resolved to conciliate Italy. It was now that he made his midsummer of madness speech. He was certainly turning his back on the League, and to spurn an institution which the *bien pensants* still regarded as the embodiment of good sense and decency was to invite criticism. He *believed* that Eden was with him, but it was Chamberlain, rather than the Foreign Secretary or the Prime Minister, who took the initiative in courting Italy.

'General mood of the House is one of fear,' said Harold Nicholson about the Rhineland. 'Anything to keep out of war.'[6] The reaction of *The Times* was crystallised in a leader, 'A Chance to Rebuild'. A League of Nations meeting at Stratford-upon-Avon voted 197 to 3 in favour of negotiating with Hitler.[7]

The Rhineland was a long way from Stratford, but it was on France's eastern border. The French took a different view from *The Times*. They certainly didn't mobilise to repel the marching Germans, but did ask Britain to join in opposing the German move. Nothing came of this. The more pacific amongst the British had long regarded France as unreasonably hostile to Germany,* and many were concerned that if Germany were humiliated over the Rhineland the result would be to strengthen communism not only in Germany but also in France itself. Communism was always a bigger fear than Hitler in these years. On 19 March 1936 the League Council declared that Germany was in violation of Versailles and Locarno but did not even demand that Germany withdraw from the Rhineland: all it suggested was the establishment of a demilitarised zone.

At length, staff talks began between Britain and France, but the Conservative Party, though not Eden, was against military commitments to France. Military commitments, and not treaty obligations, had effectively taken Britain to war in 1914. The Minister of Health, Kingsley-Wood, was representative of the party: 'The boys won't have it,' he told Baldwin.[8]

The appeasers' automatic response to the remilitarisation of the Rhineland was to look for a grievance to justify what Germany had done. One of the grievances of which Germany complained was the seizure of her colonial possessions at the end of the First World War. A Cabinet committee was set up to consider this matter, and concluded that if a general settlement were to be achieved, the German colonies should be returned. Eden was against this, but again it was Chamberlain, not the Prime Minister, not the Foreign Secretary, whose views prevailed in Cabinet committee. No final decision was reached. Chamberlain arranged that the matter be left open. Policy and a piece of unfinished business remained for future discussion. As Prime

---

* In 1923 France had occupied the Ruhr in retaliation for Germany's reparation failures. Britain strongly deprecated the action and the former allies, just five years after the war in which they had uncharacteristically been comrades-in-arms, arrived at a *rupture diplomatique*, just one notch away from hostilities. It was a return to a traditional stance: Britain and Germany *versus* France. Everyone felt much more comfortable.

Minister, Chamberlain would continue to pursue this notion of a general settlement; Hitler preferred to nibble away.

Chamberlain was no pacifist. He accepted the need for wars and weapons. It has been noted that if he had had his way he would have deployed oil sanctions against Italy and not just have gone through the motions. But most of the country and most of the Cabinet were not with him. Pacifism was abroad in the land.

Pacifism wasn't just a wishy-washy sentiment in these years. It was mobilised and organised and its effects quantifiable. In 1934, Lord Robert Cecil undertook a national survey of public opinion and in June 1935 the League of Nations Union ran a Peace Ballot. The questions were framed tendentiously: 'Are you in favour of an all-round abolition of National Military and Naval Aircraft by International Agreement?' Result: 'Yes', by nine to one. The purpose behind the polling was to rally support round the League. While there was some opposition to the Peace Ballot – from the Beaverbrook papers, for example – the conclusion of most Conservatives, including Austen Chamberlain, was that a failure to take note of its findings would lead to electoral disaster. Eleven and a half million people had voted for an all-round reduction of armaments and the abolition of military aircraft. It would have taken a brave politician to ignore them.

In a famous speech Baldwin said that he gave his word that there would be 'no great armaments'. A year later he admitted that he had been worried about the turn of international events in Europe in 1933, but that given the mood of the country, fighting a general election on a rearmament ticket would have been a disaster for the Conservatives.

In the course of his first few months as Prime Minister, Chamberlain, turning his attention increasingly to Germany, continued to hope that conflict could be avoided and should certainly not be precipitated by an aggressive stance, and he was reassured by the weakness of the German economy. He thought the Foreign Office unimaginative and too wedded to tradition. For his part, he increasingly warmed to the idea of personal contact with the dictators. At the same time, he stressed to Neville Henderson in Berlin that Britain must continuously rearm. His policy remained a combination of hope and realism.

He remained committed to a General Settlement and to avoiding divisive alliances.

Given that, his relationship with Eden deteriorated. Eden remained preoccupied by Italy more than Germany. Chamberlain had little interest in Italy for its own sake: 'If only we could get on terms with Germany I would not care a rap for Musso.'[9] There was a minor disagreement when Eden suggested that *he* should write a personal letter to Mussolini to try to improve relations. Chamberlain agreed with the idea of a personal letter, but decided that he would be the better person to write it.

There was also some petulance over a visit to Germany by Lord Halifax, then Lord President of the Council. This visit centred round the hunting exhibition to which he had been invited by Göring. Eden had initially been even more enthusiastic about the visit than Chamberlain, but he became worried by Foreign Office views about protocol. Vansittart was very much against the meeting and Eden's private secretary, Oliver Harvey, thought that the visit cast Britain too much as the petitioner. Chamberlain, on the other hand, thought that the visit would show the Germans that Britain wanted to be friends.

Downing Street briefed the press, stoking up hopes of what might be achieved. Eden was ill, in bed and resentful. He took himself to the telephone to speak to Chamberlain and the conversation ended with the Prime Minister telling the Foreign Secretary to 'go back to bed and take an aspirin'.

In the event it was Hitler who risked being slighted. When Halifax arrived at his residence, Hitler met him at the door. He was wearing black trousers, silk socks and patent leather shoes and Halifax took him for a footman preparing to help him up the snow-covered steps. He started to hand him his coat and hat. The situation was only saved by the German Foreign Minister, von Neurath, who insistently told him it was '*der Führer, der Führer*'.

Chamberlain resolved to poke the Foreign Office 'with a long pole'.[10] It was now that Vansittart was shunted out of his role of Permanent Under-Secretary and replaced by Sir Alexander Cadogan, whom Chamberlain found a congenial adviser and confidant – and who was enthusiastically behind the policy of direct contact with the dictators.

Soon, Eden too left the scene. He resigned in February 1938. His resignation was not, as it is usually portrayed, over a major principle – to do with facing up to the dictators; it related not to one large issue but to two much smaller ones. The first was the fact that Chamberlain was discouraging about a suggestion of a conference with Roosevelt; the second was that Chamberlain was, in Eden's view, being unnecessarily conciliatory to Mussolini. It is far from clear which of these considerations was more important in causing the resignation, which may largely have been based on the incompatible styles of the Foreign Secretary and the Prime Minister. What didn't cause it at any rate, was any headline issue – certainly not, as is often assumed, the Munich Agreement, which took place seven months later.

One of those on the Conservative benches who applauded Eden's departure was the politician and diarist, Chips Channon: 'Chamberlain's stock soars. I think he is the shrewdest Prime Minister of modern times; and it is a pity he did not drop Anthony months ago.'[11] Cadogan did not lament Eden's departure. He thought that Eden's policy of standing up to Mussolini was wrong-headed, and that the critical matter was to engage with Hitler.

'And yet ... the manner and timing of Eden's resignation have defeated the reconstructive powers of historians as much as it baffled contemporaries. Nobody at the time was precisely sure why Eden resigned and no one since has been able, quite, to offer a satisfactory explanation.'[12] Chamberlain didn't particularly want to get rid of Eden. It may well be that the failings and weaknesses which were to manifest themselves so markedly at the Suez crisis were at work. He seemed confused and unreasonable. Halifax thought 'His judgement was not at its best ... [He was] no longer seeing it straight'.[13] Duff Cooper was also critical, and, as Neville Chamberlain liked to say of the resignation afterwards, 'scarcely a dog barked'.

Halifax succeeded as Foreign Secretary. Eden very weakly led the dissident group of Conservatives known as the Glamour Boys, always critical of the Prime Minister but never daring to strike. Because of his resignation and because of his ill-judged aggressiveness over Suez in 1956, Eden has always been seen as having been against appeasement and an opponent of Chamberlain. In reality he was not critical of appeasement in principle. He knew what war was like. He had served with distinction in the First World War, where he won the Military

Cross and, at the age of nineteen, was the youngest adjutant on the Western Front. These experiences had a powerful impression on him, and he no more wanted another world war than did Chamberlain.

The foreign policy issues that Chamberlain would deal with in his short time as premier were already evident before he got there. So was the line he would take. It was equally clear that he would be at the front of foreign policy. Even before Chamberlain moved into Number Ten Downing Street he told Nancy Astor that he 'meant to be his own foreign minister and also to take an active hand in co-ordinating ministerial policy generally, in contrast with S[tanley] B[aldwin]'.

## Chapter 24

# Talking of Peace and Preparing for War

Reaction to the German threat involved diplomacy but also rearmament, and Chamberlain's diplomacy can't be attacked for being weak if while he talked he was rearming as fast as he could. As fast that is, as public opinion would let him.

Although Chamberlain was obliged by financial constraints and by the weight of public opinion to regulate the pace of rearmament, he was not an innocent in terms of policy. He was no pacifist. We have seen that even as a young man, living with his father, he had supported the Territorial Army. He was chairman of the board that ran Birmingham's Territorial units, had been involved in the Committee of Imperial Defence for many years and was fully aware of defence and foreign policy matters. He responded not only to European defence issues, but also to emergencies in the Far East. We have seen that in the years after 1935 he accepted the need to allocate money to defence that he would rather have spent on social improvements.

Of all the myths that surround Chamberlain none is greater than the idea that he was lax in providing for Britain's defence against Germany. However hard he strove to believe that Hitler would be susceptible to logic and reason, he never deviated from a long-held belief that it was the duty of the nation's leaders to make their country strong. In relation to defence expenditure he was a hawk when others, including, surprisingly often, Churchill, were the doves.

A. J. P. Taylor, a historian slightly to the left on the political spectrum, held that the country, under Chamberlain, 'was marching consciously towards a war on which she was all along resolved'.[1] That may be going too far. But the diplomatic half of what he called his 'double policy of rearmament and better relations with Germany and Italy' certainly didn't preclude the possibility of war.

The late twenties and the early thirties were marked by a flood of anti-war literature: this was the period that saw the publication of *Journey's End*, *Goodbye to All That* and *Memoirs of an Infantry Officer*. At the Oxford Union in February 1933 the famous motion, 'This House will under no circumstances fight for its King and Country' was passed by 275 votes to 153 (not in fact as an expression of the true opinions of the members, but in response to a powerful speech from the philosopher C. E. M. Joad). In October 1933, at the Fulham East by-election, the Labour candidate campaigned on the issues of disarmament and pacifism, and turned a Tory majority of almost 50,000 into a Labour majority of almost 5,000.

In July 1936 Baldwin spent two days receiving a deputation led by Austen Chamberlain and Lord Salisbury, but with Churchill very much behind it (and speaking for a full hour from a prepared speech) arguing for a forward defence policy. Baldwin declared, 'I am not going to get this country into a war with anybody for the League of Nations or anybody else or for anything else. If there is any fighting in Europe, I should like to see the Bolshies and the Nazis doing it.'[2] His 'appalling frankness' or 'party before country' statement, very briefly mentioned above, referred back to Fulham, and was made to Parliament in November 1936:

> I put before the whole House my own views with an appalling frankness. From 1933, I and my friends were all very worried about what was happening in Europe ... [Y]ou will remember at that time there was probably a stronger pacific feeling running through the country than at any time since the War.
>
> That was the feeling in the country in 1933 [at Fulham] ... Supposing I had gone to the country and said that Germany was rearming and that we must rearm, does anybody think that this pacific democracy would have rallied to that cry at that moment? I cannot think of anything that would have made the loss of the election from my point of view more certain.[3]

This was the remark to which Churchill referred in his *History of the Second World War* with the index entry: 'Baldwin, Stanley, Puts party before country'. Churchill was not rising to the level of events. It was a cheap jibe: if the Conservative Party had lost the general election of 1935 (as it was its majority was reduced) there would have been far less rearmament under Labour than the Tories planned. Churchill's animosity against a man who had been remarkably generous towards him was surprising and uncharacteristic.

The Labour Party was pacifist in the early post-war years. When he was its leader, George Lansbury said, 'I would close every recruiting station, disband the army and dismiss the air force. I would abolish the whole dreadful equipment of war and say to the world, "do your worst".'[4] Though pacifism did not endure as Labour Party policy, the pacifist element in the party remained significant. In the last year or two of peace, Labour was against appeasement and accused Chamberlain of a quasi-fascist sympathy for Hitler; but they always voted against defence increases.

Chamberlain's initial position was to subscribe to the Liddell Hart view that 1914–18 had not been 'The British Way of War'. Involvement in a huge land campaign in the First World War had been an aberration. Britain had historically avoided that sort of war. It had subsidised allies and concentrated its own efforts on an essentially naval war. Britain should not repeat the First World War anomaly. France would supply a large army, Britain would add air war to traditional sea power. This was the reaction of many theorists to the experience of the First World War, and it was a reaction which accorded with his own observation of what had happened in that conflict and what he had learned from Norman's letters: what Norman had suffered could only be justified if it never, ever happened again.

In 1932, in his first Budget, Chamberlain's primary job was to get the economy under control and defence expenditure was reduced from the level at which it had been fixed under Labour. Hitler was not yet in power and the need for high defence spending wasn't evident.

What *was* worrying was not even on the European continent. Japan had invaded the Chinese province of Manchuria in 1931, and the League of Nations was incapable of doing anything about it. The result was a sudden awareness in Britain of how vulnerable British possessions in the Far East – particularly Singapore and Hong Kong

– would be to Japanese attack. The Chiefs of Staff told the Committee of Imperial Defence in 1932 that *all* of Britain's possessions in the Far East were at risk, and even India and the Dominions. From now right through to 1939 the perception was that the imperative was defence of the Empire rather than resistance to Hitler. For the defence chiefs and the military planners this was a given, and Chamberlain had to overcome the bias whenever he looked at the German threat.

The safety of the Empire was a one-sided concern. Imperial priority remained in place despite the fact that the Dominions repeatedly made it clear that they would not feel themselves bound to support Britain in another European war. Logic should have dictated therefore that Britain would prepare for a war in which she would not have Dominion support rather than for a war in which she would have it. Nonetheless, the Cabinet decided to build up facilities at Singapore, so that the Royal Navy could protect Australia and New Zealand.

To the primacy of imperial defence was added the certainty in defence thinking that Britain could not *simultaneously* defend herself and her Empire. A choice had to be made. The Chiefs of Staff ensured at regular intervals that this was understood. Churchill would be painfully reminded of the problem when the *Prince of Wales* and the *Repulse* were sunk by Japan in December 1941. Britain was almost defenceless in the theatre, as Churchill noted: 'In all the war I never received a more direct shock ... Japan was supreme and we everywhere were weak and naked.'

Chamberlain was aware, more than most of his colleagues, of the fact that a choice had to be made. As early as 1934 he tried to persuade the Cabinet to enter into a ten-year non-aggression pact with Japan. Perceptively, he told Hilda in July of that year that 'we ought to know that the USA would give no support to Britain against aggression by Japan unless Hawaii or Honolulu were attacked.'⁵ Pearl Harbor is in one of the Hawaiian Islands.

It is ironic that one obstacle to rearmament that Chamberlain and others faced was the legacy of Winston Churchill. As Secretary of State for War and Air in 1919, Churchill had established that defence spending should be based on the assumption that Britain wouldn't be involved in a major war for the next ten years. Even at the time there was opposition on the grounds of the message that was given to Britain's enemies, but Churchill's arguments won the day and the assumption was renewed year by year until 1928. At this point Churchill again, but now as Chancellor of the Exchequer, proposed that the rule should be permanent and renewed *automatically* each year. There was opposition, but again Churchill had his way.

As a result, defence spending of £766 million in 1919–20 had fallen to £102 million by 1932. Part of the problem with an automatically renewing rule of that sort is its sheer inertia: the need for a novel review to displace an assumption. The rule was eventually abandoned in March 1932, a year after the First Sea Lord told the Committee of Imperial Defence that naval strength was now so diminished that if the navy were required to defend interests in the Far East it would be incapable of protecting the Merchant Navy, of keeping sea communications open, of protecting the British Isles or of ensuring the security of any port in the whole Empire.

Air power was little better. Despite Britain's ranking amongst the great powers, there were four of five national air forces bigger than the Royal Air Force. In 1923 the RAF said that they were disastrously ill-equipped to defend Britain from attack.*

In 1933 a subcommittee of the Committee of Imperial Defence was established, the Defence Requirement Committee (DRC). It calculated that £76 million was needed for defence. This was far beyond anything that Chamberlain as Chancellor could contemplate. Chancellors of the Exchequer don't like spending money and Chamberlain was particularly keen on good housekeeping, but by now, the autumn of 1933, he was at any rate no longer looking at cuts. He had entirely changed his position, but didn't give the DRC all they wanted. Baldwin suggested creating a Defence Loan, but Chamberlain dismissed that as 'the broad road that leads to destruction'. It was necessary to cut the coat according to the cloth.[6] He supplied only £50 million of the £76 million, but what is important is that from now on, again and again, he *did* authorise the spending of money on rearmament. Circumstances had changed and Chamberlain's opinions changed with them. In 1935 he would argue for increasing the number of RAF squadrons to eighty.

---

* The attack envisaged in 1923, interestingly, was from France, and not from Germany. The necessary action was not taken.

There was no coordination of defence.* The Committee of Imperial Defence was advised separately by the three Chiefs of Staff and if there were any coordination it was collectively provided by the Cabinet. Chamberlain had very substantial input into the DRC, via Sir Warren Fisher, Permanent Secretary at the Treasury and head of the Civil Service, and from February 1934 onwards he arranged that proposals for defence expenditure only reached the Cabinet when they had been reviewed and filtered by himself as Chancellor. Quite a remarkable extension of his territory.

A Disarmament Conference convened by the League and the United States in 1932 collapsed in January 1934. The great gear-change in relation to defence spending that now took place was associated with the rise of Nazism in Germany and Mussolini's intervention in Abyssinia. Since Locarno,† defence spending had been reducing every year. The navy had fewer personnel than in the past forty years; nine cavalry regiments had been disbanded along with sixty-one batteries and twenty-one infantry battalions. The Territorial Army was 40,000 below strength; the air force was then fifth of six in Europe; the defences of Singapore had not been completed.[7] The public were not unhappy with this, and the Peace Ballot of 1935 showed that.

Now the DRC concluded that Germany, no longer France, was the most likely source of trouble and an attempt was to be made at diplomatic rapprochement with Japan. Chamberlain recognised the German threat and the services' lack of funds. In March 1934 he was envisaging 'the staggering prospect of spending £85 million on rearmament'.[8] Another increase in defence spending was made in the Defence White Paper of March 1935 and was followed in 1936 by the huge increase he had referred to in 1934. He also talked of

---

* A vacuum of which Churchill was aware. By appointing himself Minister of Defence in 1940 he was able to control the whole conspectus of the direction of the war in a way which had been significantly absent in the First World War.

† The series of treaties in 1925, which Austen Chamberlain negotiated for Britain, designed to stabilise the post-war settlement by rehabilitating defeated Germany, making some frontiers negotiable and others not, and by bringing Britain and France together again. Locarno created a great sense of relief. Austen was awarded the Nobel Peace Prize in 1925, and the other two principal negotiators, Aristide Briand for France and Gustav Stresemann for Germany, in 1926. The Locarno settlement effectively lasted for just eight years, until Hitler came to power, and was demonstrably ended when he invaded the Rhineland in 1936.

participation in the international police force mentioned above, a 'limited liability force' which would protect mutual frontier guarantees by 'say, Germany, France, Italy, UK, Poland and Czechoslovakia'.

What was interesting was that he dismissed the professional advice, which was to spend almost entirely on the army. He was still thinking about the British way of war. He concluded that the money should be spent almost entirely on the air force: 'Our best defence ... I submit ... is most likely to be attained by the establishment of an air force based in this country of a size and efficiency calculated to inspire respect in the mind of a possible enemy.'[9] He was, remember, Chancellor of the Exchequer, not Minister for War or Defence. He was going far beyond his departmental brief.

Significant change took place in 1935. Chamberlain was principally responsible for writing the Conservative Party manifesto for the general election of that year. He wanted to make national defence the government's primary concern, but wasn't allowed to do so. He accepted that Baldwin's reassuring approach was what the electorate wanted, but his own approach would never have resulted in the damning reproach of putting party before country.

He agreed with the DRC that Germany should be seen to be Britain's principal adversary and that from the starting point of 1935 it would take five years for national defences to be brought up to strength. When he met Hitler in 1938 he knew that Britain was not yet in a position to win a war with Germany, but was, however, doing what he could to make sure that she would be in a position to win a war as soon as possible. He was advised by the Chiefs of Staff that while Britain would in time be strong enough to face Germany, it would not be strong enough to face Japan and, say, Italy as well. This informed his policy of seeking to remain on good terms with those countries.

The Peace Pledge Union and the League of Nations Union deprecated a return to militarism. The Peace Pledge Union had 407,000 members, 3,000 branches and more than 4,000 corporate affiliates including trades unions, women's institutes and even Boy Scout troops.[10] When the air force was expanded in 1934, the Liberals and the Labour Party opposed it, and in the following year Attlee moved a vote of censure on the Defence White Paper. Chamberlain had chaired the DRC which produced that White Paper.

Baldwin tended to defer to this enormous national aversion to defence spending. Chamberlain did not. Even Churchill acknowledged that Chamberlain took the lead in advocating rearmament. In the 1935 general election campaign, as has been mentioned, Baldwin gave the public his word that there would be 'no great armaments' and reassured electors that they should not 'fear or misunderstand when the government say they are looking to high defences'.[11] Chamberlain only broadly took the same line. In the manifesto which he wrote he said that 'We must in the course of the next few years do what is necessary to repair the gaps in our defences.' That was enough for him to be branded as a warmonger: a Labour poster showed a baby in a gas mask. That was the measure of the sensitivity engendered by even the mildest reference to rearmament.

Whereas Baldwin promised that there would be no great armaments, Chamberlain made sure there would be. In 1936 he pressed for an enquiry into the way in which defence policy was framed and into the establishment of a new ministry. While he did so he took time to meet Professor J. Dover Wilson to discuss the significance of particular speeches in *Hamlet*, and he recorded how much he enjoyed seeing the redwings in the park and a glorious Constable painting at Hadleigh Castle.

Chamberlain was responsible, more than anyone else, for the policies put forward in the Defence White Papers of 1936 and 1937. These two Defence White Papers provided for rearmament costing £1,500 million over a five-year period. They involved laying down five new capital ships, twenty cruisers and four aircraft carriers, together with a replacement programme for destroyers and submarines. They provided for four new infantry battalions together with modernisation of equipment and expansion for the Territorial Army. For the air force there was the promise of a front-line strength of 1,750 aircraft, exclusive of the Fleet Air Arm. Provision was made for factories to construct aircraft and manufacture ammunitions as well as a local government scheme for air-raid precautions, an echo of what he'd done in Birmingham in the Great War.

The remilitarisation of the Rhineland demonstrated the breakdown of the Locarno and Versailles treaties. Chamberlain said there should be a Minister for the Coordination of Defence. He himself was so identified with recognition of the need for preparation for war that he was Baldwin's first candidate for the post. Chamberlain declined. Churchill and Hoare were considered before Sir Thomas Inskip was appointed. Inskip was a remarkable choice and that wonderful jibe that his was the strangest appointment since Caligula had made his horse consul will always be remembered rather than the fact that he was to do better than anyone expected.*

From now onwards Chamberlain was increasingly bullish about rearmament spending. DRC planning in 1934 was for £620 million to be spent over five years; in 1936 the sum was increased by £400 million and then raised again to £1,500 million over five years: that was increased two years later to £1,650 million. Financial prudence was not abandoned, but the sums being spent on rearmament were enormous – even though there was a financial recession in 1937.

It was a huge change. In 1922, as the ten-year rule started to bite, defence spending was 2.8 per cent of GDP (a bigger proportion than it is now). By the outbreak of war in 1939 defence expenditure was over 4 per cent. The ten-year rule did not end until 1932, so all the accelerated spending occurred under Chamberlain, either as Chancellor or as Prime Minister.

Chamberlain's last Budget in April 1937 subordinated fiscal objectives to preparation for war. It called for widespread economies and proposed a new tax on company profits (subsequently dropped by his successor, Sir John Simon). This was the policy of a man who was not

---

* His career before his appointment had mainly been in the law. He had been Solicitor General and Attorney General, but he wasn't regarded as an impressive lawyer despite having been entrusted with these offices and offered the Mastership of the Rolls. He was, rather, outstanding in a literal sense: he was six feet four inches tall. He was also courteous and likeable, and these qualities served him well as Minister for Coordination of Defence, where he had no power to command, only the opportunity to persuade. This he did effectively, resolving tensions, for example, between the Admiralty and the air force which resulted in the establishment of the Fleet Air Arm. He also contributed to the evolution of strategic priorities. He pleased Chamberlain by agreeing that effective defence required a strong economy but displeased him by coming to the conclusion by the end of 1938 that appeasement hadn't worked and that war was inevitable. He was dismissed in January 1939. In September of that year he became Lord Chancellor. In May 1940 he went to the Dominions Office and became Leader of the House of Lords. He was moving around fast now and just five months later became the first former Lord Chancellor to be appointed Lord Chief Justice. Not bad for someone whom nobody thought much of a lawyer.

putting all his money on appeasement. He was building up strength for negotiations and for war if negotiations failed.

The scale of activity was immense. By the outbreak of war the government had established twenty Ordnance Filling Factories, most of them away from major cities and the South East of England. The largest were ROF Chorley and ROF Bridgend. Chorley was bounded by a nine-mile perimeter fence, and had its own private railway station, ROF Halt. In September 1939 it employed over 1,000 production workers which had increased to 15,000 by June 1940 and over 28,000 at its peak. In the Midlands, car firms were subsidised to establish facilities for building tanks.

Of the three services, the army was the one which Chamberlain favoured least. A vast army was not part of the British way of war. It was the means by which a war would degenerate into the stalemate of the Western Front and the slaughter which had taken the lives of Norman and his generation. As Prime Minister he initially planned for only two army divisions for operations on mainland Europe.

He was in part motivated by what he considered to be the poor quality of the War Office and the generals. In 1937 he replaced Duff Cooper as Secretary of State for War with Leslie Hore-Belisha, who had previously been an effective Minister of Transport.* Chamberlain told him to stir up the War Office. He encouraged him to read the works of Basil Liddell Hart, and the argument for minimal army involvement in Europe. Hore-Belisha got under way with the stirring. He dismissed the Chief of the Imperial General Staff, the Adjutant General and the Master-General of the Ordnance. Gort, the new Chief of the Imperial General Staff, proved a disappointment. Hore-Belisha and his reforms met with little cooperation. There was an unpleasant whiff of anti-Semitism in the hostility, both amongst the military and Conservative Members of Parliament.

By degrees, Hore-Belisha came to accept that the limited, 'British way of war' approach would not address the increasing threats he saw from Germany. In February 1938 he obtained a major increase in spending to enable the army to operate on a continental scale. He also pressed for doubling the size of the Territorial Army. In May 1938 he

---

* Still occasionally remembered for the 'Belisha beacons' which he introduced.

brought in the Military Training Act, the first instance of peacetime conscription in Britain. The Liberal and Labour Parties opposed the measure. All of this was done with Chamberlain's approval, despite that it ran counter to his original policy of favouring naval or air force expenditure.

In the course of the 1930s, the bomber threat was an increasing concern amongst politicians and defence experts, with Baldwin famously and lugubriously telling the people that 'the bomber would always get through'. Chamberlain presided over the creation of a British bomber fleet which could get through to Germany in the same way as the Luftwaffe would get through to London. Subsequently, it was recognised that monoplane fighters, reinforced by the newly developing science of radar, might stop the bombers getting through at all, and fighter production was increased.

Aircraft were new technology, and initially Chamberlain's interest was supporting the old technology of the navy. He had argued against naval cuts even before the First World War. He was involved again in this debate in 1924, when Churchill, who had fought for increased naval spending ahead of 1914 when he was First Lord, was now Chancellor of the Exchequer and arguing for his ten-year rule. Sometimes a twenty-year rule seemed appealing: with the German fleet scuttled at the end of the First World War, the only navy that Britain could conceivably have to fight would be the Japanese Navy and that would only arise in the outlandish event of a Japanese attack on Australia. Accordingly, planning should be on the basis that there would be no naval war for twenty years. (He got that very wrong: just six years later Japan attacked Manchuria and Shanghai, when Britain was in no position to protect her Far East possessions.)

In December 1937 the important decision was taken to switch aircraft production from an emphasis on bombers to that of fighters. The initiative came from Inskip in the face of opposition from the Air Minister, Sir Philip Cunliffe-Lister, and the air staff. Chamberlain supported Inskip and dismissed Cunliffe-Lister. In May 1938, Attlee, departing from criticising warmongering, pointed out that not only did Britain not have parity with Germany, but she was getting further away from parity week by week and month by month. Chamberlain could see that it was important not only that Britain could withstand a knockout blow, but that it should be *known* that she could withstand it.

Rearmament had been proceeding slowly and fitfully and sometimes in the wrong areas in the four or five years leading up to the Czechoslovakia crisis, but how strong militarily was Britain in 1938? In 1938 Britain's air defences were seriously lacking. Only twenty-nine out of a necessary fifty-two fighter squadrons were ready. France was also markedly inferior in air power.

In October 1938 Britain could only put two fully armed divisions in the field. By September 1939 it comprised about five divisions.*[12] These five divisions were not adequately equipped and in the summer of 1940 Chamberlain wrote to his sisters acknowledging that training and equipment was woefully inefficient, even if there was plenty of manpower.

On the other hand, in 1938 the Germans had not yet reached *their* desired strength. They had only three lightly armoured tank divisions and ammunition for only six weeks of heavy fighting. Although the Luftwaffe had 2,700 aircraft, only two-thirds were operation ready and half of them were fairly elderly aircraft.[13] But Britain was not well informed on the state of German preparedness and tended to overestimate Hitler's military resources.

At the time of Munich, despite all the preparations, Britain was far from ready for war. The worries focused on an air war and particularly these bombers which would always get through. New anti-aircraft guns were in production, but were not yet deployed. Only a quarter of commissioned searchlights and barrage balloons were available. In the whole of London there were only sixty fire pumps. Of twenty-nine active fighter squadrons, only five were equipped with Hurricanes and only one with Spitfires, and the Hurricanes were at this stage incapable of operating above 15,000 feet because of problems with their Browning guns. The Ministry for the Coordination of Defence considered that in September 1938 Britain could only have sustained a war in the air for three weeks. The front-line air force was a façade without reserves or organisation.

Between Munich in 1938 and war in 1939 things improved greatly. But Munich wasn't the catalyst. A lot was already in the programme

---

* Exactly what was initially deployed in 1914.

– and at the instigation of Chamberlain. Heavy bomber production was underway, though it would not achieve delivered results until 1940. Air parity with Germany would be regained in 1941, and that was to Chamberlain's credit, because parity was achieved before Beaverbrook's productive work as Minister for Aircraft Supply had time to bite.

In 1939, Britain and the United States produced more aircraft than Germany and Italy combined. By the end of the following year the Axis powers were only producing 60 per cent of the aircraft that the neutral United States and Britain under the Blitz were building. Before the fall of France the Allies had 4,000 more artillery pieces and 1,000 more tanks than Germany. During the Battle of Britain, the UK produced 2,354 new aircraft, against Germany's 975. Unlike Germany, Britain was also producing far more ships. In particular, Germany simply didn't have the economic resources to create a viable carrier fleet.[14]

The only alternative to buying time until 1939 or, ideally, 1941, would have been to defeat Hitler in, say, 1936, which was out of the question for various reasons which have been touched on and with which Chamberlain had nothing to do. Shortly after Churchill succeeded him, Chamberlain wrote:

> Whatever the outcome, it is as clear as daylight that, if we had had to fight in 1938, the results would have been far worse. It would be rash to prophesy the verdict of history, but if full access was obtained to all the records, it will be seen that I realised from the beginning our military weakness, and did my best to postpone, if I could not avert, the war. But I had to fight every yard against both Labour and Liberal Opposition Leaders who denounced me for trying to maintain good relations with Italy and Japan, for refusing to back Republican Spain against France, and for not 'standing up to Hitler' at each successive act of aggression.[15]

'No minister . . . had done more, no one had done as much, to make the Country ready,' said Iain Macleod.[16] Chamberlain's problem was that he started from a very low level, in the most difficult of circumstances and with little support.

## Chapter 25

# The Darkening of the Eastern Sky

Chamberlain became Prime Minister confident that his general settlement could be achieved by a combination of rearmament and better relations with Germany and Italy. He was convinced, however, that the Foreign Office was frustrating his efforts. The Foreign Office had to be reinvigorated and by poking it with his long stick he attempted to do that.

On his return from his trip to Göring's hunting expedition and the side-trip to meet Hitler, Halifax reported that a general settlement might well be possible if it involved satisfaction of Germany's colonial grievances. Chamberlain put a scheme of this sort to the Cabinet Committee on Foreign Policy on 24 January 1938. Colonial satisfaction was to be promoted, but not independently of a general settlement that truly was general. The general settlement scheme was finally put to Hitler by Sir Neville Henderson on 3 March 1938. This was the only time that a general settlement was formally put to him and the scheme wasn't *said* to be a general settlement: but it was self-evidently a comprehensive deal and he didn't want that when he had a shopping list with lots of items on it. He didn't bite. He had no intention of buying into any general settlement in exchange for a return of colonies.

One of his aims was the *Anschluss*, the annexation of Austria and her incorporation into the Reich, and the planning for that had already been completed. The operation was carried out just a few days later. The Sudeten Germans, those living in the Bohemian and Moravian parts of Czechoslovakia, were being actively encouraged to campaign for separation. Poland too was on the agenda.

All the thought that had been given to this general settlement had been a waste of time, but Chamberlain found it very difficult to accept that. His undying confidence in the philosophical beauty of a general settlement allowed him to move through these crises with his confidence undimmed.

The Prime Minister spoke in the House on 24 March 1938, two weeks after the *Anschluss*. He was critical of the annexation of Austria, but instead of saying anything to discourage a grab for the Sudetenland, he referred to the demands of the German minorities there as a worrying issue which required resolution. He ruled out a British guarantee of Czech independence, saying that 'if war broke out, it would be unlikely to be confined to those who had assumed [legal] obligations'.[1] He meant that there was no saying what would happen if war broke out. The government's policy would then not rest simply on its legal obligations. The speech was intended to be a warning, and this was confirmed by Lord Lothian,* but the message wasn't clear: it wasn't read as a threat; all that came across was that Britain would not guarantee Czech integrity.

Chamberlain dismissed a Churchillian plan for a 'Grand Alliance'. He said that he had talked about it to Halifax and the Chiefs of Staff but the conclusion was that nothing Britain or France could do would save Czechoslovakia if the Germans chose to attack her. If Britain went to war with Germany, he could not see any prospect of defeating her in a reasonable time.[2]

Czechoslovakia would preoccupy Western diplomats shortly, but right now what was to be done about the *Anschluss*? German troops had marched into Austria on 12 March 1938, creating a Central European power that was more unified and threatening than the alliance of Germany and Austria-Hungary before 1914, when the Habsburg Empire had its own independent existence. The West did nothing.

Chamberlain should have reacted more forcefully. It was a bloodless annexation, but a stage-managed one and a clear precursor to other annexations which would not be bloodless. Chamberlain just

---

* Lothian wasn't in political office at the time. He had been a notable appeaser, 'Lord Loathsome', one of David Low's 'Shiver Sisters', dancing along with Chamberlain to Hitler's tune. He visited Hitler in 1935 and 1937, reporting back in credulous and favourable terms. His endorsement of Chamberlain's threat carried all the more weight because of his dovishness at the time. By March 1939 he had become disillusioned by Hitler and mostly remained so.

complained to his sister about 'these wretched Germans'. Gandhi described his reaction as 'indignant resignation'. Sounding rather like a nanny trying to restore order in the nursery, Chamberlain told Hilda that the Führer had been very naughty and that he would have to tell him that 'it is no use crying over spilt milk and what we have to do now is to consider how we can restore the confidence you have shattered'.[3]

On 16 March 1938, days after the *Anschluss*, Churchill dined in Pratt's Club with Randolph Churchill, Harold Nicolson and Bob Boothby. He reflected on what Chamberlain had inherited from his predecessor: 'Never has any man inherited a more ghastly situation than Neville Chamberlain.'[4] First the military reoccupation of the Rhineland, now the annexation of Austria. Next would be Czechoslovakia.

Hitler's attention had been homing in on Czechoslovakia long before the *Anschluss*. Ostensibly he was concerned about the German-dominated part of the country known as the Sudetenland, but from the outset he really wanted to annexe the whole country. It was hardly surprising that he wanted to recover for Greater Germany territories which had been part of the Austro-Hungarian Empire until 1918. Now that Austria had been subsumed into Germany it was logical that her former possessions should follow.

There was no constituency of support for Czechoslovakia in Britain. The Conservative Party, apart from the usual anti-appeasers, Churchill, Boothby, Vyvyan Adams and so forth, who did ask for a British guarantee for Czechoslovakia after the *Anschluss*, was pretty clear that Czechoslovakia was of no interest to Britain. Alan Lennox-Boyd, a junior government minister, told his constituents that if Germany absorbed Czechoslovakia Britain's security would be unaffected.[5] The Postmaster General, George Tryon, was against guaranteeing the independence of a country 'which we can neither get at nor spell'. Michael Beaumont, MP for Aylesbury, wrote to Rab Butler, Under-Secretary of State for Foreign Affairs, saying that he would rather be tortured at the stake than fight for 'that beastly country'.[6] These voices were representative of Conservative Party feeling. Oliver Stanley, President of the Board of Trade, said that there was not 'a soul in this country' who would support a guarantee for the Czechs, and Malcolm MacDonald, Secretary of State for the Dominions, reported that the Commonwealth would break up if there were war over Czechoslovakia.[7] The belief that the Empire would fracture over a European war was a powerful part of Chamberlain's thinking throughout his time in power.

For Churchill and the non-appeasers, Czechoslovakia was the same as Belgium in 1914, a minor country in which Britain had little direct interest, but which had to be defended in order to maintain the balance of power. But Chamberlain and the appeasers did not see Czechoslovakia as requiring defence in the interests of maintaining a balance of power. They saw it as a component in the Eastern European confusion which resulted from the Versailles settlement.

British policy was confused. Chamberlain himself was inclined to leave Germany with a free hand, but Cadogan and others took a more robust position. The Foreign Office wanted to give a formal warning to Hitler about the consequences of an attack on Czechoslovakia, but Henderson was convinced that if the warning were given to Hitler – and it would have been given to him at Nuremberg, the heart of Nazism, of all places – war would be all the more certain. His advice was accepted.

In May 1938 two Sudeten farmers were shot by a Czechoslovak frontier guard. There were demonstrations amongst the Sudeten community, instigated by the Nazi Party. German troops moved toward the border and the Czech army was mobilised. On 22 May Halifax sent a warning to Germany that if there were conflict and if France intervened, Britain could not be relied upon to stand aside. Not an unequivocal promise of action, but what kind of threat could Britain really make? Of her fifteen capital ships only ten were fully operational. The RAF had almost none of the new eight-gun metal monoplanes in service. The army could only send a token expeditionary force to France, and France's own inadequacies were becoming increasingly evident. Russia was still assumed to be a potential ally, but her army had been weakened by Stalin's purges.

In the event, Germany didn't invade. It had been a false alarm, and it is now known that Germany was not ready to invade in May, but at the time it looked as if Britain's quick reaction had paid off. Chamberlain was applauded and as usual the applause went to his head. Germany had lost an opportunity that would never recur. On the contrary, Hitler's decision after this, the first Sudetenland crisis, was to 'wipe Czechoslovakia off the map'. But what Chamberlain, flattered by the comments of ambassadors all over Europe, took out of it was that more than ever he had the opportunity and the personality to pacify the continent.

Chamberlain built on his diplomatic initiative with a mission. The sixty-eight-year-old Lord Runciman was brought out of retirement and sent to Prague to resolve the Sudeten problem. Leo Amery didn't know whether Runciman's appointment was 'comic or a stroke of genius ... it may well be that his bland, invincible ignorance and inca-pacity even to realise the emotions and aspirations on both sides may help to bring down the temperature and so contribute to a peaceful solution'.[8] *The Times* may have been saying the same thing when it referred to Runciman's 'able and unbiased mind'. Lloyd George said that Runciman could make the temperature drop, even at a distance.

Runciman is always described as 'a businessman', parachuted into public life when Halifax asked him to go to Prague. In fact, he was in the Commons on and off for thirty-eight years, entering in 1899 as one of the two members for Oldham. Another candidate in the elec-tion of that year was Winston Churchill, but he failed to get in. Runciman certainly followed a business career, and did so very successfully. But in parallel he didn't do too badly in politics and held a variety of Cabinet appointments. By the time he was appointed to the peerage in June 1937 he had received honorary degrees from at least three universities, so when Sir John Wheeler-Bennett described his arrival in Prague on 3 August 1938 as 'A stooping, bald-headed man with a clean-shaven, beak nosed face emerged, carrying a brief-case'[9] it was a rather facile write-off. In any event it isn't really clear what was wrong with being clean-shaven, bald or carrying a briefcase. That the mission did not go well was not really his fault. Chamberlain hadn't helped by telling him that the demands of the leader of the Sudeten Nazis, Konrad Henlein, a 'moderate and sensible' man, had to be met. Chamberlain did not know that Henlein was not working for the rational elimination of real grievances but had been instructed to create a narrative which would justify German intervention.

Runciman did extract some concessions from the Czechs, but Hitler had never wanted the negotiations to work and they didn't. It's slightly sad for Runciman and his briefcase that he should appear to carry the can.

## Chapter 26

# Berchtesgaden: Fly, Fly, and . . .

It was now that Chamberlain decided on the dramatic event which created the image by which he has been irretrievably defined: Plan Z, the deliberately theatrical, last-minute announcement of a flight to Germany to meet Hitler. When Chamberlain was contemplating his flight to see Hitler – 'so unconventional and daring that it rather took Halifax's breath away' – he was aware that he was dealing with an opponent who was dangerously unpredictable: 'Is it not positively horrible to think that the fate of hundreds of millions depends on one man, and he is half mad?'[1] What he was doing was certainly very unconventional. The idea of Chamberlain setting off as a petitioner to Hitler was criticised by the civil service as lowering the dignity of the Prime Minister.

Chamberlain wasn't troubled by this sort of pettiness. Despite his age (which was regarded by the standards of the day as more advanced than it would be today) he was quite prepared for the travails of flight and a long journey at the far end, and for any indignity implied in being required to wait upon Hitler at his residence, if that was the cost of averting war.

He was well aware that Britain had stood back from events in 1914. It can be argued very plausibly that the Great War took place because Asquith and Sir Edward Grey, the Foreign Minister, had been woefully negligent in not defining what action Britain would take if Germany and Austria-Hungary went to war with France and Russia. Britain hung back while the Central Powers mobilised. Germany had every reason to think that France could be knocked out in a matter of weeks, as it had been in 1870, and that Britain would do nothing, as it had then. It wasn't until the Commons debate of 3 August 1914 that it became clear that Britain would fight; and even then, when Grey bumped into the French ambassador, Paul Cambon, as he left the House, he could not tell his ally whether Britain would be committing troops or just naval support, the British way of war.

If Asquith had jumped on a train, rather than a plane, gone to see the German Chancellor, Theobald von Bethmann-Hollweg, and made Britain's position clear, things might have gone very differently. When Britain did declare herself, Bethmann-Hollweg broke down in tears and the Kaiser morosely said that his grandmother, Queen Victoria, would never have allowed this; but it was too late.

Chamberlain was not going to pursue a policy of such purposeless drift, and Plan Z was very much his project. Unusually, the Foreign Secretary, Halifax, wasn't invited to accompany him. His only official companion was Sir Horace Wilson, technically still Chief Industrial Adviser to the government.

The Foreign Office and Number Ten debated about whether Germany should be given advance warning of Chamberlain's descent from the skies. He wanted the prospect to be kept secret until after Hitler had spoken at Nuremberg, whereas the Foreign Office was afraid that in that event Hitler might have already committed himself to action before Chamberlain arrived. Vansittart was wholeheartedly against the idea of going to meet Hitler. He said it was like the Holy Roman Emperor Henry IV going to submit himself to Pope Gregory at Canossa.* Chamberlain listened to him with his head in his hands.[2]

Chamberlain was boning up on more recent history. As he prepared to meet Hitler, he was reading a biography of the nineteenth-century Foreign Secretary, George Canning. He wrote to Ida that it was a basic principle for Canning that threats should not be made unless they could be implemented and that the advice that he was receiving from his military advisers was that Britain was not in a position to undertake hostilities.

The news of Chamberlain's decision was described by Chips Channon 'as one of the finest, most inspiring acts of all history'. The Labour *Daily Herald* ran a page one headline: 'Good Luck Chamberlain'. Government bonds rose by £250 million. Seventy out of one hundred

---

* Diplomats remembered that during his fight with Pope Pius IX, Bismarck told the Reichstag, 'We will not go to Canossa' ('*Nach Canossa gehen wir nicht*').

people interviewed by Mass Observation approved Chamberlain's actions.[3]

When he left Heston Aerodrome for Berchtesgaden on 15 September 1938 at the age of sixty-nine it was the first time he had flown, and he took to the air despite a rooted dislike of the idea of flying. That very autumn he'd been shooting with George VI at Balmoral when the King tried to persuade him to stay on for an extra day. He offered to fly him down to London afterwards in time for a Cabinet meeting, but Chamberlain declined, saying he hadn't ever flown, didn't like the sound of it and hoped he would never have to fly. Just two weeks later he took off.*

He thought it inadvisable to use a Royal Air Force aeroplane: inappropriate for a man of peace to arrive in a war plane. The Air Ministry was unable to find a civil machine manufactured in Britain, and an American Lockheed Electra was used. In the urgency of the arrangements, it was forgotten that the permission of the King was required before the Prime Minister could leave the country.

On his arrival Hitler was initially very aggressive. He affected to be determined to settle the Sudeten question immediately. 'I do not care whether there is world war or not.'[4] Chamberlain responded indignantly, saying that there had been little point in his coming all the way to Berchtesgaden if Hitler had already made his mind up. Hitler backed off and appeared to accept Chamberlain's suggestion that the Sudeten Germans could be separated from the rest of Czechoslovakia. Chamberlain said he'd have to discuss this with the Cabinet and the French, and they parted on good terms. 'I am very sorry you should have had to make two journeys,' said Hitler. 'I got the impression', Chamberlain noted, 'that he was a man who could be relied upon when he had given his word.'

That statement is often used to demonstrate Chamberlain's credulity, but he was far from the only man to be taken in. Hitler had of course a magnetic personality and could be very charming. Eden, who later prided himself on the way he had faced the dictators,

---

* After an earlier visit to Balmoral, he reflected on how he and Baldwin differed in their reaction to its country charms – and how inaccurate their public images were. 'I know every flower; S.B. knows none. I know every tree; S.B. knows none. I shoot and fish; S.B. does neither. Yet he is known as the countryman; and I am known as the townsman.' (Kenneth Rose, *King George V*, p.289.)

reported after meeting Hitler in 1934 that he found it hard to believe that he wanted war.[5] Lloyd George too had been impressed. The civil servant Thomas Jones noted in his diary on 1 March 1934 that, 'Rightly or wrongly, all sorts of people who have met Hitler are convinced that he is a factor for peace.'* It is thought to be partly for this reason, and to avoid making the same mistake as Lloyd George, that Churchill consciously avoided any meeting with the Chancellor.

Back home, Chamberlain met the Cabinet, and Daladier, the French Prime Minister, and his Foreign Minister, Bonnet. It was agreed that the cession of the Sudetenland to Germany should take place. The Czech President, Edvard Beneš, initially and understandably rejected the Franco-British betrayal but gave way when Britain and France told him he would be on his own if he didn't acquiesce.

The first trip to meet Hitler at his house, the Berghof,† above Berchtesgaden in Upper Bavaria had involved a flight to Munich and then a 120-kilometre rail journey. Hitler had said he would make it easier for Chamberlain by arranging that their next meeting would be at a more convenient location. The second trip was to Godesberg on the Rhine.

Chamberlain was thrown to find that Hitler's position had entirely changed since Berchtesgaden and there was not simply to be a formal approval of what had been discussed a week earlier. Unsettling changes of position of this sort were frequently part of Hitler's negotiating technique. Now the Sudetenland was to be evacuated by the Czechs; and Polish and Hungarian claims on parts of Czechoslovakia were also to be satisfied. Pretty much the dismemberment of the country. He was no longer prepared to countenance delaying occupation of

---

* Thomas Jones, always known as 'TJ', was a remarkable man with a series of successful careers. His time at the centre of government from 1916 to 1930, latterly as Deputy Secretary to the Cabinet, was just one of them. He was very close to Stanley Baldwin, and although a convinced free trader himself had to write speeches advocating protection. This was described as being 'as bizarre as a confirmed teetotaller writing advertising copy for the brewers'.

† Hitler had bought the house in 1933 with the royalties from *Mein Kampf*. It is often confused with the Eagle's Nest, which is further up the mountain, and the Wolf's Lair, his headquarters in East Prussia. Hitler did visit the Eagle's Nest, which was popular with Nazi officials, but didn't like it because of his fear of heights.

the Sudetenland until details had been arranged. It was to be occupied immediately, within a matter of days. The Czechs were to withdraw their army, police and the whole apparatus of government from the German-speaking areas.

Chamberlain immediately said that there was no point in talking further. He left for his hotel on the other side of the Rhine, the Petersberg Hotel, leaving Hitler in the Hotel Dreesen. Chamberlain sent a letter over to the Dreesen: 'In the event of German troops moving into the areas as you propose, there is no doubt that the Czech government would have no option but to order their forces to resist.'

Late the following afternoon he received a long message from Hitler. He had not changed his position, and his letter simply set out what he had demanded on the previous day. But Chamberlain's position had weakened overnight. Halifax had accepted Cadogan's view that Czechoslovakia couldn't just be abandoned, but while the Foreign Office was accordingly urging Chamberlain to stand firm, the army was telling him that it would be crazy to accept annihilation for the sake of the Czechs. However, it wasn't this realpolitik argument that weakened the resolve that had caused Chamberlain to withdraw to the Petersberg Hotel. What mattered, Cadogan confided to his diary, was that Chamberlain still believed that Hitler wouldn't go back on his word and would be satisfied if he was given what he was asking for.

Chamberlain didn't like Hitler. When he met him for the first time he reported that the Führer looked 'entirely undistinguished', like 'the house painter he once was'.* After Godesberg he told the Cabinet that Hitler was frightful and 'the commonest little dog you ever saw', but he didn't retract what he had said after Berchtesgaden: Hitler 'was a man who could be relied upon when he had given his word'. He replied to Hitler, saying that he was prepared to act as an intermediary with the Czechs.

Later that day he went back across the Rhine and had a long meeting at the Hotel Dreesen. Hitler was in a much more jovial mood and agreed with the Prime Minister that he would set out his requirements in a memorandum which Chamberlain could circulate with

---

* In fact he hadn't been a house painter, though many people in Britain thought, or liked to think, he had.

his allies. There was expansive talk about how further European problems could be sorted out by meetings of the two of them. It was just what Chamberlain wanted to hear.

Hitler even made an allowance: 'You are the only man to whom I have ever made a concession.' He would not act before 1 October. In truth he was not militarily ready to move before then. Chamberlain felt that something had been accomplished and that his belief in his capacity for personal negotiation had been vindicated.

But Hitler's memorandum when it came put an end to optimism. The occupation of the Sudetenland should begin on 26 September and should be completed three days later. The evacuated territory was to be handed over as it was, without the removal of a single cow. The precise frontier would be settled by plebiscite in November. This was his last word.

Transferring populations into Nazi Germany from the Sudetenland had only been palatable to the British side because of the stipulation that it was to be an 'orderly' cession with international supervision, exchange of populations and so forth. Now Hitler was going to seize an arbitrary area and talk about safeguards later. When the British party got back to London, Cadogan drove Halifax home. He pulled no punches. He told Halifax very emphatically that the memorandum had to be rejected. The following day Halifax sent for him and told him that he had given him a sleepless night but that he had come to the conclusion that Cadogan was right. So, at an afternoon Cabinet meeting on 25 September (a Sunday), Halifax said that Hitler's proposals had to be rejected. Chamberlain's position had not altered in the same way and he passed a note to Halifax: 'Your complete change of view since I saw you last night is a horrible blow to me.' Halifax replied: 'I feel a brute – but I lay awake most of the night, tormenting myself.'[6]

Cadogan was dismayed to learn that Chamberlain had been preparing to surrender. He considered that Chamberlain had been hypnotised by Hitler, and Halifax had been hypnotised by Chamberlain. For him the worrying feature was Chamberlain's belief that he had established some degree of personal influence over Hitler and believed he would not go back on his word.

But Cadogan had got Halifax on board, and the mood of the meeting was clear. Hitler's proposals were rejected and on 26 September the Foreign Office put out a communiqué saying that the German claim to the transfer of the Sudeten areas had already been conceded but that if an attack were made upon Czechoslovakia, France would be bound to come to her assistance and Great Britain and Russia would stand by France. The mood in the country was of acceptance that war was now inevitable. The Labour Party, formerly pacifist, was now for resistance, as were the trades unions. Slit trenches were dug in the London parks and basic air-raid shelters were constructed. Thirty-eight million gas masks were distributed. The fleet was mobilised and the Auxiliary Air Force called up.

On 27 September, Chamberlain made a broadcast. To be fair to him, he was exhausted. Just before going into the Cabinet room to make the broadcast he said, 'I am wobbling about all over the place,'[7] but that is no excuse for the notorious words he used. Instead of rising to the occasion, asserting the rights and liberties of small countries, he sounded peeved at the domestic inconvenience: how repugnant it was that 'a quarrel which had already been settled in principle should be the subject of war . . . How horrible, fantastic, incredible it is that we should be digging trenches and trying on gas masks here because of a quarrel in a faraway country between people of whom we know nothing.'

The Czechs had of course rejected the Godesberg memorandum, but Chamberlain spectacularly failed to understand that Hitler was an unprincipled opportunist and not a logical Birmingham businessman. Despite everything, he still believed that the matter could be resolved on the basis of the Berchtesgaden formula, and was quite prepared to pay a third visit to Germany if he thought it would do any good.

He was prepared; but neither he nor anyone else really thought that there would be a third visit or that war could be avoided. He did keep trying. On 26 September, the day before the dismal broadcast, Horace Wilson had gone to Berlin to make a fresh appeal to Hitler. Initially Hitler remained obdurate, but as so often he vacillated. He wrote a personal letter to Chamberlain, giving some ground on details. He offered to join with others as a guarantor of the frontiers of the new Czechoslovakia, a poacher offering to become a gamekeeper. Chamberlain replied, proposing to come to Berlin to discuss the matter further. It was what he described as 'the last desperate snatch at the last tuft of grass on the very edge of the precipice'. Usefully, he communicated separately with Mussolini, asking him to tell Hitler that he was willing to be present at a further meeting and to urge Hitler to agree to such a meeting for the sake of the avoidance of war. The wooing of Italy, of which Eden had disapproved, had culminated in a recent Anglo-Italian Agreement, and because Chamberlain had held his nose and courted the Duce, Mussolini advised Hitler to postpone mobilisation for twenty-four hours and to accept Chamberlain's proposal for an international conference.

On 28 September Chamberlain went down to the House of Commons to advise members on how matters stood. This was a highly charged meeting, the equivalent, it seemed, of the meeting on 3 August 1914 which led to the outbreak of the First World War. The House was full, filled with distinguished visitors from the Dowager Queen Mary down. Chamberlain received a warm reception, and reported precisely on the events of the preceding few days. It was assumed that he would end by saying that no agreement had been reached with Hitler and that war therefore seemed inevitable.

What happened has frequently been described. Halifax, sitting in the Peers' Gallery, passed a piece of paper to the Foreign Office staff in the civil servants' box, close to the Treasury bench. An official passed the note to Chamberlain's parliamentary private secretary who, in turn, passed it to Sir John Simon, sitting next to the Prime Minister. Just as Chamberlain reached the point of the narrative dealing with his contact with Mussolini, Simon was seen to pull Chamberlain's coat-tails. Chamberlain read the paper, which narrated the contents of a telegram just received from Berlin. He was seen to smile and was heard to whisper, 'Shall I tell them?'

When he did tell them that he had now been invited by Hitler to meet him in Munich on the following day along with Mussolini of Italy and Daladier of France, the atmosphere of sombre crisis suddenly dissolved. There were tears. There was clapping, forbidden by the rules of the House. Tension dissolved into hysteria.

On the following morning, Chamberlain flew again from Heston. 'If at first you don't succeed, try, try and try again' he said, although this was frequently parodied as 'fly, fly and fly again'. More poetically, and at the suggestion of his wife, he quoted from *Henry V*, hoping that on his return he would be able to say, 'Out of this nettle, danger, we pluck this flower safety.'

*Chapter 27*

# . . . Fly Again

Since the agreement that was reached at Munich on 29 September would not stand the test of history, it is unnecessary to study the detailed negotiations, which lasted fourteen hours. Mussolini purported to act as a mediator, but in reality read from a text prepared for him by the German Foreign Ministry. An international commission was to be set up to deal with boundary details, and the Czechs were given ten days to withdraw from the Sudetenland, instead of the even more precipitate timetable envisaged at Godesberg. Otherwise, Hitler got precisely what he had wanted. There would be a four-power guarantee of Czechoslovakia's boundaries, but only when questions about the Polish and Hungarian minorities had also been settled. When the agreement was ready for signature it transpired that the ornate ink pot was empty, an inappropriate omen.

The coda was the 'piece of paper' which Chamberlain produced to Hitler when they met at his flat on the following morning. When Hitler understood what the piece of paper contained, he signed it immediately without a moment's thought or concern. Well he might, as it amounted to absolutely nothing: 'We regard the agreement signed last night and the Anglo-German Naval Agreement as symbolic of the desire of our two peoples never to go to war with one another again.' Consultation would resolve any questions that might concern the two countries.

Hitler told Ribbentrop not to take the piece of paper seriously. He said that he had only signed it 'to please the old gentleman'. But the old gentleman took it very seriously. He waved it in front of the crowds at Heston later in the day. 'I've got it!' he said. He told Lord Dunglass, his parliamentary private secretary, that if Hitler broke the agreement, he would demonstrate his untrustworthiness to the world. On the other hand, if Hitler kept the bargain then 'well and good'.

Nowadays we think Chamberlain looks very silly in newsreel footage of his arrival at Heston, grinning and waving that piece of paper, but he was giving the crowds what they wanted. He told Dunglass that there was no certainty about peace in view of the 'volatility' of Hitler, 'without question the most detestable and bigoted man with whom it had been his lot to do business'.[1] The piece of paper was for the historical record. It would 'ensure that if war did break out the international community would know on which nation the responsibility fell'.[2]

That measured judgement was swept aside by what happened when he reached London. At the aerodrome there was a message from the King, with the constitutionally improper request that Chamberlain should come straight to the palace to receive his congratulations, which he did on the palace balcony.

At Godesberg and at Munich, and in the interval between these meetings, Chamberlain displayed a pathological blindness to reality and a desire to believe the unbelievable. But he was very far from being the only person who surrendered their critical faculties in their wish to believe that war could be averted. The mass of the British people was as much to be criticised as he. Those who were to denigrate Chamberlain so viciously just a year or two later, even to burn him in effigy, chose to forget how they and their fellow countrymen received Chamberlain on his way from Heston to the palace and then to Ten Downing Street. The crowds sang again and again 'For he's a jolly good fellow'. Chamberlain wrote to his sisters, describing how his route was 'lined from one end to the other with people of every class, shouting themselves hoarse, leaping at the running board, banging on the windows, and thrusting their hands into the car to be shaken'.

When he reached Downing Street he was faced by more crowds, more 'For he's a jolly good fellow'. Under some pressure he made a mistake. It was Annie's fault. She had been a very active Prime Minister's wife, much involved in public activities, unlike Mrs Baldwin, and she came into her own during the Sudetenland crisis. While Neville was away on his visits to Germany her movements were reported in detail by the press. She spent time praying in Westminster Abbey. She received thousands of letters. So many gifts arrived for her and Neville that additional secretarial staff had to be taken on. Women waited outside Ten Downing Street and ran alongside her car. She was invited by the King and Queen to come to Buckingham Palace to meet Chamberlain on his return from Heston.

On the day before his final trip to see Hitler, Annie had told him, 'I want you to come back from Germany with Peace with Honour . . . you must speak from the window like Dizzy [Disraeli] did'. Chamberlain said, 'I'll do nothing of the sort. I am not in the least like Dizzy.'[3] But he gave way. As he acknowledged the cheers from an upper window someone told him he must say something. He didn't want to ('I don't do that sort of thing'), but he did, and he regretted it almost immediately. As Annie had suggested, he used the words that Disraeli had done in a slightly similar situation in 1878, when he too had returned from Germany. 'This is the second time in our history that there has come back from Germany to Downing Street peace with honour. I believe it is peace for our time.'

It was not peace with honour, and as he had revealed to Dunglass he wasn't even sure that it was peace for our time. He retracted what he had said in the Commons within the week: it had been a remark made in 'a moment of some emotion, after a long and exhausting day'. But it was a remark which more than any other thing he said or did has settled how he would be seen in history. When the perspective of history altered – only months after Munich – those who excoriated him were not only conniving in the creation of a caricature, but in an interesting psychological turnaround, dissociating themselves from a mood which almost all had shared. Newsreel coverage, the press, the Palace and above all the public were overwhelmingly behind what he had done. He received 52,000 letters of thanks, gifts that ranged from fishing rods and umbrellas to 4,000 tulips from Holland and cases of wine from France. There was a request from Greece for a piece of his umbrella to be used as a relic in an icon. The British monarch was not alone in his adulation; the King of the Belgians wrote to him in fulsome terms: 'You have done a wonderful piece of work.' The ex-Kaiser sent a letter of congratulation and relief to Queen Mary.

The manipulated press was ecstatic. Lord Rothermere had been shocked by the Godesberg terms yet on 1 October he telegraphed to tell Chamberlain that 'You are wonderful'. The *Daily Mail* reported on the same day that the Prime Minister had returned from Munich 'with peace at the summit of his valiant endeavours'. On the same day the *Express* ran its notorious headline: 'There Will Be No European War' – which Charles Peake of the Foreign Office news department said bore 'all the marks of official inspiration from Number 10'.[4]

When Chamberlain returned to the House of Commons, there were, said Dunglass, 'a lot of appeasers in the House that day'. The anti-appeasers in the Conservative Party faced extraordinary opprobrium. Their local parties were minded to disown them and they were threatened with deselection. Even Churchill was threatened in this way. Leslie Hore-Belisha, although a minister, admitted that 'the Conservative Party machine was even stronger than the Nazi Party machine ... [I]t is similarly callous and ruthless. It suppresses anyone who does not toe the line.'[5]

When the Duchess of Atholl was told that the Kinross and West Perthshire Conservative Association would seek a new candidate, she immediately resigned her seat and stood as an independent. 'The Red Duchess' had already been in trouble because of her support for the Republicans in the Spanish Civil War. The Conservative Party put up an official candidate against her while Labour and the Liberals put up no candidates of their own. Churchill alone on the Conservative benches sent her a public letter of endorsement. The party directed the full force of its considerable resources against her. Any Tory who spoke on her behalf would be deselected. Central Office sent up innumerable senior politicians to endorse the official candidate, a local farmer. It was described as 'one of the dirtiest by-election campaigns of modern times, from which only the Duchess emerged with any distinction'.[6] Chamberlain wrote to the Chief Whip, saying that he was 'overjoyed' by the Duchess's defeat.

That Chief Whip was David Margesson, and in order to convey something of the unpleasant nature of the Conservative Party in these years and the military discipline which permeated its organisation it's worth injecting a few paragraphs about the man who enforced that discipline. Margesson had been appointed Chief Whip in 1931 at the age of just forty-one, and remained in that position until 1940. He served four Prime Ministers – MacDonald, Baldwin, Chamberlain and Churchill. He had volunteered for the army at the outbreak of war in 1914 and joined the Worcestershire Yeomanry. In 1916, at the age of twenty-six, he became adjutant. He was awarded the Military

Cross for 'helping to pull the line together'. As Chief Whip he ran the Conservative Party, very many of whose MPs had served as officers in the First World War, exactly as an adjutant would.

At an anecdotal level, it is a little difficult to form a view of Margesson. He was certainly in general regarded as a fearsome disciplinarian who terrified new Members of Parliament. Sir George Harvie-Watt, a junior whip, a brigadier himself and not easily intimidated, described him as 'a real dictator'. He was an impressively tall and formally dressed man. His presence was reinforced by his powers. Under Chamberlain he and Sir Horace Wilson had a large element of say in who would be promoted and who would be demoted in the Tory Party.

There were those, however, who took a gentler view. Harold Nicolson, at this time no favourite of the whips, spoke favourably of him, and Churchill, also on the other side of the party, admired him and retained him as his Chief Whip when Margesson declined a Secretaryship of State.

But leaving aside the anecdotes, he was a bully who valued only obedience, and it was as a result of his efforts that the Tory front benches by 1939 were filled by supine creatures of the party establishment.[7] Bribes and threats were used to force Chamberlain's critics into the correct lobby. The regimental atmosphere of the party and the merits of blind loyalty were accentuated, so that at the time of the Norway debate, which ultimately brought Chamberlain down, veterans of the Somme could only bring themselves to vote against their leader with tears pouring down their faces. Margesson bellowed obscenities at one young rebel and described him as 'a contemptible little shit'.*[8] Margesson was conceived to merit a whole chapter in *Guilty Men*.

---

* The rebel was John Profumo. In view of what happened much later some will say that Margesson got his character right, but not in the way he meant. Profumo had a very distinguished career in the war, fighting through Italy. He was mentioned in Dispatches, awarded a military OBE and a US Bronze Star, reached the rank of brigadier and was offered the post of second in command of the British Military Mission in the Far East at the end of the war. Margesson told him in May 1940 that for the rest of his life he would wake up feeling guilty about what he had done. Profumo said he never did. It had taken courage to vote as he did, and he showed the same strength of character to seek to atone for lying to the House over the affair to which his name is given.

There were a few, of course, who saw Munich as an abject act of betrayal. Duff Cooper, the First Lord of the Admiralty, resigned, saying that Britain should have gone to war, not just for the sake of Czechoslovakia but to avoid one nation, by brute force, dominating the whole European continent. He was using almost the same language that Sir Edward Grey had used at the outbreak of the First World War, itself a restatement of Gladstonian principles. Later, but only later, Duff Cooper's position was adopted by most middle-of-the-road commentators. That position was not remotely typical of the immediate reaction at the time. In the Commons debate Duff Cooper received no support and although thirteen Conservative Members abstained, they did not vote with the opposition. And Eden and Amery, although abstaining, only did so with great difficulty and kept their options open until the last moment.

It is important to remember that there was this huge emotional desire to believe that Hitler *could* be relied on. This was the mood of a country which had only twenty years earlier emerged from the multiple concussions of the First World War. Almost anything was better than a return to Flanders. By 1938 everyone knew Hitler was an opportunist gangster. Many, perhaps most, knew something of how he treated Jews and his political opponents. The Night of the Long Knives, which he had directed from the Petersberg Hotel, had been fully reported in Britain as had the existence of camps in which not only Jews but his domestic enemies were confined. Munich may have been a selfish betrayal of an ally, a faraway country and a people of which we knew nothing, but it was a betrayal in which the whole nation colluded.

The betrayal was the expression of two views. On the one hand, Chamberlain still clung to hopes that were not based on realism, hopes that the Munich Settlement would be part of a new system of resolution of disputes by negotiation. On the other hand it was a profoundly realistic recognition that Britain was far from ready for war and that much needed to be done. Chamberlain ratcheted up rearmament after Munich. He was never wholly deluded, unlike the masses who cheered for him. On 3 October he told the Commons that there would be plenty of critics who would accuse him of facile optimism, but that he did not believe that more had been done than to lay the foundations of peace. 'The superstructure is not even begun.'

After Munich, Halifax can be seen to move away from appeasement. He even made the odd dig to Chamberlain about 'his German
friends'. He had come to regard Hitler as a 'criminal lunatic' who had
to be confronted. In 1963 Cadogan looked back on the events of 1938.
He suspected that Chamberlain had taken longer to understand the
truth about Hitler than Halifax. But he had his doubts:

> I cannot be sure. Hitler's open atrocities against the Jews in the
> autumn of 1938 certainly deeply impressed Chamberlain . . . And of
> course Halifax was no less shocked. Many people who did not
> know Chamberlain personally had the impression that he was a
> gullible and obstinate old man. During all that ghastly time I saw
> almost as much of him as I did of Halifax and I will say, from my
> observation of him, that nothing could be further from the truth.
> He was haunted day and night by the prospect that he saw clearly
> enough. He gave everything of his strength to try to avert it. Many
> people thought he was a cynic. Cynicism was a virtue with which
> he was perhaps not sufficiently equipped, or he would not have
> been taken in by Hitler's rather transparent 'piece of paper'. On the
> other hand he had quite a streak of the sentimental and emotional
> in him, which betrayed him into uttering those unguarded words
> to the crowd in Downing Street after his return from Germany.[9]

*Chapter 28*

# After Munich

What happened afterwards shows that, for all the public euphoria, Chamberlain saw Munich more as buying time than as a deliverance. Sir John Anderson was now put in charge of civil defence, and expenditure on air-raid precautions was increased from £9.25 million to £42 million for the ensuing financial year. Walter Elliot, the Health Minister, constructed plans for the evacuation of school children and created emergency beds and hospitals. Extensive work took place on radar and other technology for air defence.

Chamberlain continued to woo Mussolini. With Halifax and Cadogan he travelled to Italy by train, arriving in Rome on 11 January 1939. The British party was warmly received both by the Roman populace and by the Duce and his entourage. As usual, Chamberlain saw what he hoped to see. He wrote afterwards that he was satisfied that his journey had strengthened the chances of peace. Mussolini, he reported, was straightforward and considerate and had an attractive sense of humour. He wanted peace and was ready to use his influence to get it.[1] Mussolini's impression was quite different: 'These . . . are the tired sons of a long line of rich men, and they will lose their Empire.'[2] Ciano, his son-in-law and Foreign Minister, phoned Ribbentrop in Berlin saying that the visit was a fiasco (literally, 'a big lemonade'), 'absolutely innocuous'.[3]

Chamberlain had been irritated that reports appeared in the British press of booing when he had visited Paris and he wanted none of this when he saw Mussolini. To this end, 'The press office in Downing Street and the less antagonistic Leeper-less news department at the Foreign Office orchestrated the most complete set-piece of news manipulation yet attempted by a British government.'[4]

The nexus between Halifax and Chamberlain continued to be strained. The Foreign Office was not advised about a semi-official visit to Germany by the Governor of the Bank of England, Montagu Norman, in January 1939. Other visits were arranged of which the Foreign Office was unaware and these amateur diplomats were encouraged by Göring and others to think that Hitler was still anxious to achieve some sort of general settlement. Thus, Chamberlain made a serious of optimistic statements in the course of February and March 1939, telling Ida, on 12 March, that he was still confident that he could save the country.

But Czechoslovakia was disintegrating, the fault line being the division between the Czechs and the Slovaks. And on 15 March, just three days after Chamberlain had told his sister that he could save Czechoslovakia, German troops moved into Prague. From Prague Castle, Hitler declared that Bohemia-Moravia was now a German protectorate. The richest parts of the country were in Germany's control, including the Skoda Munitions Works. The dismemberment was completed when Hungary, with Hitler's approval, seized sub-Carpathian Ukraine.

That was the end of Chamberlain's optimism. There could scarcely be clearer evidence of the emptiness of Munich. On 18 March, Chamberlain told the Cabinet that he had concluded that 'It was impossible now to negotiate as before with the Nazi regime. No reliance could be placed on any of the assurances given by the Nazi Leaders.'⁵ It had taken him a long time to get there. At a Cabinet meeting on the morning of the invasion he said that the Anglo-French guarantee to defend Czechoslovakia was now meaningless since there was no Czechoslovakia to defend. This dismal piece of sophistry was too much even for the Conservative benches and within a couple of days, at Halifax's prompting, Chamberlain's posture became a little more belligerent, although that belligerence was confined to what Britain would do in the event of *further* challenges, not in retaliation for what had just happened.

What Hitler was doing was no longer camouflaged by the idea of recovering parts of Germany: he was overtly breaking the promise that Munich would be his last demand. As he tended to do, Chamberlain descended from the level of events to personal petulance: 'Surely as a joint signatory of the Munich Agreement I was

entitled, if Herr Hitler thought it ought to be undone, to that consultation which was provided by the Munich Agreement?' Russia
proposed a six-power conference amongst nations which had
common cause against Hitler. Chamberlain was instinctively biased
against Russia and declined. His proposal was a declaration of
common action by Britain, France, Russia and Poland. This was
stymied by Poland's distrust of Russia.

Just two days after the occupation of Prague, Romania declared
itself threatened by Germany. This threat proved to be spurious, but a
flurry of diplomatic activity took place all the same. The outcome was
a series of interlocking agreements by which Poland would come to
the aid of Romania if need be, and Britain and France would come
to the aid of Poland.

The Polish guarantee looked likely to need early implementation.
On 29 March 1939 the *News Chronicle* correspondent, Ian Colvin,
expelled from Berlin, arrived at the Foreign Office with detailed
information about a strike on Poland, to be followed by annexation
of Lithuania and an alliance with Russia. There was a great deal of
dithering about whether a declaration of support for Poland should
be given. In a spectacular statement of the obvious, Chamberlain said:
'If we take no action, there is a risk that we shall find that Poland has
been over-run. On the other hand, if we utter a warning such as is
now proposed, we shall be committed if Germany persists in aggression.'[6] The Chiefs of Staff thought that Poland would be destroyed in
a campaign of two or three months but that if Britain were going to
go to war with Germany, she would be better to do it with Polish
allies than without. If Britain were to fight, then Germany should be
made to fight on two fronts.

Near the end of his life, Cadogan read through his diary for the first
three months of 1939. He said that it left

> The impression of a number of amateurs fumbling about with
> insoluble problems. It is necessary to try to recall the situation of
> those times. Our own military capabilities were deplorably inade-
> quate. We were being swept along on a rapid series of surprises
> sprung upon us by Hitler with a speed that took one's breath
> away ... And it was that in the end that drove Chamberlain to take
> a sudden and surprising decision to guarantee Poland. Of course

our guarantee could give no possible protection to Poland in any imminent attack upon her. But it set up a signpost for himself. He was committed, and in the event of a German attack on Poland he would be spared the agonising doubts and indecisions.[7]

Chamberlain wrote out in his own hand a unilateral guarantee on behalf of Britain and France: if Poland's independence were threatened the guarantors would lend them all the support in their power. To save Polish face, the undertaking was subsequently converted into a reciprocal agreement. The problem was that, whatever the case for France, Britain could not bring military force to bear directly on Eastern Europe. At most an Expeditionary Force could be deployed on Germany's western frontier. If Poland were to be supported directly, Chamberlain would have had to hold his nose and cooperate with Russia. A Russian alliance might have provided a mechanism which would have avoided the invasion of Poland which was the cause of war in September 1939.

On 31 March Chamberlain publicly announced the Franco-British guarantee to Poland. Hitler was furious: 'I'll brew them the devil's potion', he said. The directive for 'Case-White', the invasion of Poland, was issued on 11 April. Annexation would take place any date after 1 September 1939.

In the aftermath of Germany's occupation of Bohemia and Moravia, Chamberlain worried that he might have to forgo his Easter Scottish fishing holiday. But he was rather proud of his speech about the guarantee and the warning to Hitler which had been inserted at Halifax's initiative. He had moved from what he called the 'guessing game', keeping Germany in the dark about his intentions, and was using 'the carrot and the stick'. He thought that he had checked Hitler, and decided to go fishing after all.

No sooner had he arrived in Scotland than he received news that his friend Mussolini had invaded Albania, behaving towards him 'like a sneak and a cad'. He was greatly shocked to find that his personal relationship with Mussolini meant so little. He accepted that further rapprochement with Italy was now impossible. The seizure of Albania threatened Eastern Europe and British control of the Mediterranean (it was thought that Italy was about to invade Corfu). The Foreign Policy Committee recommended that the integrity of Greece should be guaranteed. The Italian connection, an essential strand of Chamberlain's foreign policy, was at an end.

Chamberlain's authority over the Conservative Party lessened as his control of the international situation was seen to be illusory. Nick Smart argues that 'his political position was never so vulnerable as it was in the weeks following Hitler's and Mussolini's Czech and Albanian springtime 1939 coup'.[8] To say, however, that his critics 'could have seamlessly engineered' his departure and that an 'ideal solution' of Halifax as Prime Minister in the Lords and Eden leading the House of Commons might have come about is wildly improbable.[9] There was no concerted desire to push Chamberlain out. The critics, for all their readiness to wound, were astonishingly loath to kill. Halifax, as he was to show in 1940, probably didn't want to be Prime Minister; who knows what Eden wanted.

But there was, as the opinion polls showed, a strong popular desire to have Churchill back in the Cabinet. The bulk of the press – the *Daily Telegraph*, the *Observer*, the *Manchester Guardian*, the *Yorkshire Post*, the *News Chronicle*, the *Daily Mirror* and even the Communist *Daily Worker* – supported him too. Three hundred and seventy-five academics, including seventy professors, wrote a letter to *The Times*, urging his recall. But on 4 July, the day after a pro-Churchill leader in the *Daily Telegraph*, its proprietor, Lord Camrose, had a conversation with Chamberlain. Chamberlain said that in the event of war he would indeed ask Churchill to come into government, but he still thought that war would be avoided. His reason for excluding Churchill was that he continued to think, as he always had done, that Churchill's judgement was 'notorious' and that he would seek to dominate Cabinet discussions as he had done when he had been Chancellor in Baldwin's government. Chamberlain tended not to have a great interest in political history except so far as it related to Joe, but he amused Camrose by recalling that when in 1886 Lord Salisbury, then Prime Minister, had been asked to recall Lord Randolph Churchill, Churchill's father, to the Cabinet, he had replied, 'If you have once got rid of a carbuncle do you make an effort to get it back?'

As the year went on, Hitler's attention was increasingly absorbed by Poland. He focused on the free city of Danzig, which he maintained was not technically part of Poland and therefore not covered by the

Anglo-French guarantee.* Mussolini wanted a Polish Munich, another four-power conference: he wanted Danzig to be treated in the same way as the Sudetenland. This time round Chamberlain was more sceptical. By now he was feeling that Hitler had outmanoeuvred him at Munich, and he didn't want a repeat of that. Even if in theory an acceptable way could be found of meeting German claims to Danzig without weakening Poland's independence or economic security, he no longer believed Germany would act reasonably. By mid-July he thought war the likelier outcome.

Russia, however, did not think that Britain would go to war with Germany and accordingly began the negotiations which would result in August in their agreement with Germany on how Poland was to be carved up. On 23 August 1939 the news broke like a bomb-burst that in Moscow, Ribbentropp and his Soviet counterpart, Molotov, had signed the pact which is now known by their names. The explosion blew apart the diplomatic framework of Europe and all the assumptions on which Britain and France had based their thinking. The two great tyrannies, apparently at opposite ends of the political spectrum, resolved publicly on non-aggression and privately on the dismemberment of Poland. The Molotov–Ribbentrop Pact marked the final failure of Chamberlain's plans and policies. He could not avoid seeing that. Germany was now free to attack Poland without a war on two fronts. Everything that his foreign policy was designed to do had failed. The American Ambassador, Joseph Kennedy, met him on 23 August 1939: 'He said he could think of nothing further to do. He felt that all his work had come to naught.'¹⁰ His reaction to great events was always solipsistic.

It's a mark of the fact that Chamberlain was essentially a courageous man that he didn't flinch. He immediately issued a statement saying that the pact did not alter Britain's obligations. He wrote Hitler

---

* There was something in this. Danzig (now Gdańsk) had been carved out of Germany as part of the Versailles settlement and, with the surrounding area, established as a free city. The designation harked back to what it had been called when Napoleon seized it from Prussia, which had taken it from Poland in 1793. When it was re-established in 1920 it wasn't returned to Poland, so Hitler was right: it was, however, recreated for Poland's benefit, in order to give Poland a decent Baltic seaport. Poland had extensive rights over Danzig, which was for practical purposes part of Poland.

a very blunt letter – the weather was not the same as it had been at Munich. He could not have been clearer in spelling out Britain's determination to meet its obligations in regard to Poland. He stressed that if war started, it would be a long war and would not be determined by victory on just one front. It 'would be the greatest calamity that could occur'. He stressed that the Nazi–Soviet pact, whatever its details, which were still unknown, made absolutely no difference. Neville Henderson was sent to deliver this warning to Hitler at Berchtesgaden without delay.

Hitler hesitated briefly. He called Henderson back and made reassuring noises about respecting British interests. He made similar vague statements to France. But on Poland he did not budge. There was a proposal for a highly secret visit to Britain by Göring, which came to nothing. There were vague suggestions of a conference to be convened, as a year before, by Mussolini. That too came to nothing. He told Henderson that if Britain did not interfere with his solution to the Polish problem he would guarantee the British Empire, and to this end would even go to the length of making the armed forces of the Reich available to Britain, who would in return accept Germany's limited colonial requirements. He was so carried away that he even said that he had no wish to end his life as a warmonger. Once the Polish matter was out of the way he would return to the world of art, which was his true métier. Then he spoke to his generals. He told them that they had nothing to worry about. He had met the 'umbrella men', Chamberlain and Daladier, and there was nothing to fear from them.

In Britain the Cabinet called up that part of the coastal defence and anti-aircraft units which had not already been mobilised. The naval reserves, like the auxiliary air force, had already been called up. A large number of merchant ships and fishing trawlers had been requisitioned. The air-raid warning scheme was put on standby. Chamberlain spoke to the Commons. Nothing could make him an orator and his far from stirring speech was listened to in silence. The mood of the House was, however, resolute and calm. The panic of the earlier crises had disappeared.

There were no further serious negotiations. Hitler dithered a little bit about when the invasion would take place. There was some toing and froing between London and Germany by a Swedish intermediary,

Birger Dahlerus (whom the Foreign Office referred to as the 'Walrus'). In the course of these final conversations Henderson found himself shouting more loudly at Hitler than Hitler had been shouting at him. He apologised later to Halifax but explained that he thought that Hitler needed to be given some of his own medicine. All of this was taking place after the point of no return had been passed, but Hitler may have thought that even now he could get away with a further annexation without going to war. He said that for the sake of his friendship with England he would delay action if a Polish plenipotentiary arrived in Berlin within twenty hours; and indeed Henderson recommended agreeing to this.

It was to the credit of the British Ambassador in Warsaw, Sir Howard Kennard, that there was no hint of another Munich. He said that the Poles would rather fight and die than submit to humiliation. Halifax agreed, while Henderson continued to urge that the Poles should negotiate with Hitler or that the Pope should intervene. The Poles' sense of honour and self-respect was, however, immensely impressive. The British government was reminded what backbone amounted to. At 4.45 a.m. on Friday 1 September the outbreak of the Second Great War was announced as the guns thundered over Poland.

On the same day, Chamberlain asked Churchill to join his government in the event of war. Churchill agreed but expressed his surprise that Britain was not already at war. On 2 September, Chamberlain went to the House of Commons, not, as it transpired, to announce that an ultimatum had been given, but simply to say that Britain and France were discussing an appropriate time limit for German withdrawal from Poland. He was heard in silence and sat down without a cheer. When Arthur Greenwood rose to speak for Labour in the absence of a sick Attlee, Leo Amery* shouted, 'Speak for England!', a rebuff to Chamberlain for his failure to rise to the occasion. Greenwood did indeed speak for England as the Prime Minister had not done.

Chamberlain's performance had been appalling. Halifax later said that he had never heard him so disturbed as when he described what he had been through in the Chamber. He believed that the

---

* Devoted all his life to Joe Chamberlain, Amery would later precipitate his son's downfall in the Norway Debate in May 1940.

government was likely to fall within a couple of days. Churchill was disconcerted by Chamberlain's behaviour. He had heard nothing about joining the government since their talk on the previous day. In his flat on the evening of 2 September 1939 Boothby told him that he was being double-crossed. Churchill wrote to Chamberlain asking him to confirm that he had been sincere in his offer.

Chamberlain continued indecisive. He was reluctant to issue an ultimatum until France had done so, and France proved to be very dilatory. Pressure built up as the evening went on. He held private meetings with the Labour Party leaders. A number of Tory Ministers, Simon, Hore-Belisha, Anderson, De La Warr and Elliot met in a cabal. On their behalf Simon went to see Chamberlain in Downing Street and told him that the Cabinet must meet again that very night and declare war. The Cabinet met at 11 p.m. and only now, forced to do so, did Chamberlain at last say that an ultimatum would be given.

Henderson presented Britain's message to the German government at 5 a.m. on 3 September with an ultimatum of 11 a.m. France's ultimatum expired six hours later. The German leaders seem to have been stunned. At 11 o'clock in the morning of that Sunday 3 September, Chamberlain made his broadcast to the nation, another solipsistic, ill-judged, self-regarding speech: 'Everything I have worked for, everything that I have hoped for, everything that I have believed in during my public life, has crashed in ruins.'

## Chapter 29

# The Continuation of Diplomacy
# by Other Means

A complete change came over Chamberlain once Britain was at war. Having sought to the limit of his powers to avoid war, he was now unequivocally committed to fighting. His view of the nature of the war developed over the months. He was not very good at waging war, but he was determined to win it, and there was no talk of the negotiated peace that others hoped for. To begin with he thought, as many others did, that what was required was a victory over Hitler and Nazism, rather than the defeat of Germany. He had tried to believe that Hitler could be worked with, but after 3 September he never again indulged in that delusion – even when Halifax did. He who had compromised so much was now uncompromising. He had always hated Nazism, particularly its anti-Semitism, and he never weakened now in his determination to destroy it.

Though he was reluctant to commit Britain irretrievably to war if circumstances altered, he did not ever discern a change in these circumstances. He was a compromiser, an appeaser, a negotiator only when he thought there was a basis for negotiation. He may have thought that for far too long, but his change in position once war was declared was absolute. He told the Archbishop of Canterbury that the war could not end as long as Hitler remained in power. Hitler had to go, although possibly only to St Helena. He thought that there could be no return to civilisation while Nazism existed. He was not prepared to accept any proposals that Hitler might make after the fall of Poland.

Soon, Hitler made just such post-Poland proposals, and, on 6 October 1939, he addressed the Reichstag. Since Britain and France had failed to save Poland, they might as well now conclude a peace. He proposed a European Conference – an idea which America favoured. On the following day, the War Cabinet debated how they should reply. The terms of the reply took a long time to agree. Chamberlain would have nothing to do with further parleying, but presentation was important. He was reluctant to alienate reasonable German opinion by spelling out that there must be a change of regime. The final British reply was that there was no question of negotiation. On the other hand, it was not British policy to exclude from her proper place in Europe a Germany able to dwell in friendship with others. This attempt, like many subsequent ones, to speak over the heads of the German government failed. Berlin re-presented the response as a calculated rejection of the hand of peace held out by the Führer. On 14 November Ribbentrop said there could only now be a war of annihilation between England and Germany.

The 'phoney war,' the 'funny sort of war' as the French called it, was what its name suggested. Very little offensive action went on except in and around Poland. There was a war of propaganda and vast quantities of leaflets were dropped over Germany by the RAF. The Chancellor of the Exchequer, Kingsley Wood, famously argued against bombing German factories because they were private property. The BBC would not allow Sir Horace Rumbold to deliver a broadcast on the grounds that he was too anti-Nazi.

Chamberlain, far from alone in this, remained convinced that Germany could not economically cope with the consequences of war, so he positively welcomed a waiting war, free from offensives, in which Britain could outlast Germany. He was quite pleased with himself and the way he was directing the war. He believed that by keeping up economic pressure and building up munitions the war would be won by the spring of 1940 without the need for any great offensive action. Basil Liddell Hart emphasised the strength of the defensive, claiming that a successful German offensive in France would require a superiority of three to one throughout the country.[1] Chamberlain was cheered by the fact that the winter of 1939/40 was an exceptionally hard one on mainland Europe. He made notably uninspiring weekly statements to Parliament and continued to surround himself with the appeasers.

When he unimaginatively appointed the former Home Secretary, Sir John Gilmour, as Minister of Shipping, Violet Bonham-Carter, Asquith's daughter, wondered whether he was really trying to win the war. He was, but he thought victory could be won by letting the German economy implode. When Hitler had made his grandiose October proposal for a peace conference, Chamberlain's comment was that the Germans were deluding themselves: they had yet to be convinced that they could not win.

It's easy to see things in retrospect. Our view of the war is seen through the events of 1940 and onwards: blitzkrieg in the west, the fall of France, the Battle of Britain, the Blitz, Britain standing alone, the offensives on the Eastern Front, North Africa, D-Day, Normandy and so on: a heroic clash of civilisation against the forces of darkness. The war wasn't seen like this in 1939. It was a limited war in parts of Europe of which the man in the street knew nothing. It wasn't and wouldn't be another world war.

Chamberlain was in fact more aggressive now than many of his countrymen. He said he was more afraid of a peace offer than an air raid because it would encourage the 'peace-at-any-price people'.[2] In one week he had received 2,450 letters, of which 1,860 wanted him to bring the war to an end.[3] His readiness to ignore public opinion on this issue at that time underlines the fact that he had always been a practical appeaser and not an emotional appeaser.

There was a considerable momentum for emotional appeasement. A meeting took place at the Duke of Westminster's house on 12 September 1939. It was attended not only by the Duke of Westminster but also by the Duke of Buccleuch, many members of the House of Lords, influential journalists and others. A manifesto was produced, attacking those newspapers 'controlled by the left and the Jews' that called for the destruction of Nazism. The British and the Germans were brother races and should not be fighting each other – particularly as the Polish issue was now settled. Even Lloyd George, the man who had won the war in 1918, was arguing for peace. The Deputy Chief Whip, James Stuart, thought he was quite right and wrote to the Duke of Buccleuch to say so.

By now Chamberlain and Halifax – although the latter would wobble in May 1940 – were aware of the dense web of peace feelers. There was an odd belief that Göring could well supersede Hitler.

Göring was often seen as a sympathetic and emollient fellow, with an interest in shooting like a good aristocrat, who could be relied upon to do the decent thing. His role in the Night of the Long Knives appears to have been easy to overlook. The Duke of Buccleuch kept raising his head. Chamberlain wrote to him at great length on 12 February 1940:

> My dear Walter . . .
> You fear that a war begun as a war against Hitler has now become a war against Germany. I would remind you again that what we are fighting is aggression . . . [N]othing could be worse than an inconclusive peace or a reversion to an armed truce and . . . we and our Allies must be prepared to fight the war resolutely until a true peace can be won.[4]

Before the war, Chamberlain had taken great pains to avoid bringing Churchill into his government. The press campaigned for his return month after month. An anonymous organisation put up huge posters on 600 sites in London. The biggest was at Piccadilly Circus: 'What price Churchill?'

As the crisis deepened, even before the outbreak of war, Churchill himself approached Chamberlain, saying that it was not a time for mincing words, and that he thought that he could assist the country by joining the government. Chamberlain knew that Churchill's position on the government benches would help him in the Commons, but he was afraid that he would be a hindrance in Cabinet. At a personal level he was not hostile to Churchill, but he had two objections to him. The first was that, like Baldwin who had talked about the bad fairy who denied the baby Churchill the quality of judgement, and for that matter like the majority of mainstream Conservatives, he thought little of Churchill's common sense. In a debate on 7 November 1938 Chamberlain had referred to Churchill in initially flattering tones. Then he went on:

> I remember once asking a Dominion statesman, who held high office for a great number of years, what in his opinion was the most valuable quality a statesman could possess. His answer was judgement. If I were asked whether judgement is the first of my right

honourable friend's many admirable qualities I should have to ask the House of Commons not to press me too far.[5]

The other objection was that given that all Churchill stood for, bringing him into government was the admission of the failure of Chamberlain's policies.

Thus the delay in bringing Churchill in, and thus that further delay between talking of offering him a place in the War Cabinet on the afternoon of 1 September 1939 and following through on the offer. The commitment that afternoon was clear but not specific. Chamberlain's idea was that Churchill would be a member of the War Cabinet but without any departmental responsibilities. That would have involved him in sharing in the direction of the war, but not of interfering too much in other aspects of policy. After Churchill had been left wondering what was happening and reminding Chamberlain of the promise he had made to him, Chamberlain sent for him again on Sunday 3 September 1939. After the declaration of war at 11.00 a.m., the House had met at noon. Churchill made his last backbench speech. When the House adjourned, Chamberlain offered him not just a seat in the War Cabinet, but also the Admiralty.* Churchill chuckled to his personal detective, Inspector Thompson, 'That's a lot better than I thought.'[6]

Churchill and Chamberlain worked fairly well together, and on 13 October, as Churchill wrote in his war memoirs, his 'relations with Mr Chamberlain had so far ripened, that he and Mrs Chamberlain came to dine with us at Admiralty House ... We were a party of four. Although we had been colleagues under Mr Baldwin for five years, my wife and I had never met the Chamberlains in such circumstances before.'[7] It was on this occasion that Chamberlain told Churchill much more than he had formerly known about his time in Andros and Churchill thought to himself what a pity it had been that when Hitler had met Chamberlain and his umbrella at Berchtesgaden, Godesberg and Munich, he had not known that he

---

* The Admiralty's signal to the Fleet of 3 September 1939, 'Winston's back!', is always understood to have conveyed relief and delight. That may not have been the case. He had had an uncomfortable relationship with the navy when he was at the Admiralty from 1911 to 1915 and had a pretty poor opinion of the admirals.

was talking to a hard-bitten pioneer from the outer marches of the British Empire.

Chamberlain was tolerant of the wide-ranging concept of his responsibilities which Churchill took. This had been his habit since his earliest days as an Under-Secretary at the Colonial Office in 1905.* Now too he could find himself so far away from ordering the affairs of the King's navy as for instance to be involved in the formulation of policy for Palestine. He visited Lord Gort at the British Expeditionary Force Headquarters in France. This trip lasted four and a half days and took in visits to the French line and an RAF unit. Churchill's dynamism at the Admiralty was much noticed, and although a new boy in the Cabinet he was also the member who made the biggest public impact.

On 1 October he made the first of a series of Sunday-night radio broadcasts. This one dealt with the general progress of the war at sea, but he did not confine himself to naval matters. Chamberlain went through the motions of trying to rein in his broadcasting career and sent out a Cabinet minute, saying that he had asked Samuel Hoare, the Lord Privy Seal, to exercise a general supervision on broadcasts. Churchill had no intention of clearing his speeches with Hoare of all people and minuted Chamberlain: 'I am of course quite willing to be guided by your wishes on the matter: but I do not think that I should like to address myself to the Lord Privy Seal on such a point.'[8] That was the end of that. Two weeks later, on 15 October, in the course of another Sunday-evening broadcast, he referred to his relationship with Chamberlain in what some Prime Ministers would regard as patronising tones: 'You know that I have not always agreed with Mr Chamberlain; though we have always been personal friends. But he is a man of very tough fibre, and I can tell you that he is going to fight as obstinately for victory as he did for peace.'[9]

The essence of Chamberlain's approach was that *he* presided over the government and allowed Churchill to preside over the war. Churchill was of course in the War Cabinet itself. Chamberlain's War

---

* Given Churchill's extraordinary readiness to barge into other people's areas of responsibility, it is rather delicious that when Bob Boothby in 1940 went to move just the tiniest bit beyond his own departmental brief, Churchill minuted, 'Tell him to mind his own business or he'll have no business to mind.'

Cabinet was a very large one compared to the slimmed down version that Churchill would instigate: far too large in fact. In addition to the Prime Minister there were the departmental chiefs of the three services, and also the Chancellor of the Exchequer, the Foreign Secretary, the Minister for Coordination of Defence, the Minister Without Portfolio (Lord Hankey) and the Lord Privy Seal. A tauter body was required. This was the Military Coordination Committee, which consisted just of the service ministers and a few professional advisers. Initially, the Minister for Coordination of Defence, Admiral Lord Chatfield, who had succeeded Inskip, was the chairman, but Churchill, even when technically deputy chairman dominated it and from the beginning of April 1940 onwards took the chair. Chamberlain was not involved in this important body. With his own 'senior staff officer', General Ismay, Churchill effectively became the Minister of Defence as he would formally be when he became Prime Minister.

The central question for the War Cabinet was to decide how to wage the war. Should Britain be fighting an offensive war, and if so, how? Germany had not yet moved in the west, so the Allies were not looking at a situation like that of August 1914. Should Britain sit tight, awaiting the collapse of the German economy which Chamberlain regarded as inevitable?

Chamberlain might have lasted much longer as Prime Minister if he hadn't started fighting the war. There had been criticism of him and his inactivity in the conduct of the war. Now the government decided, mainly at the instigation of Churchill, focussing on a report from the Ministry of Economic Warfare, that the war could be dramatically shortened by invading Norway and interdicting the supply to Germany of iron ore from Narvik in Norway and Lulea in Sweden. This military initiative was really more an extension of the economic argument.* Chamberlain liked the logic of the argument and thought the Norwegian Campaign might be 'one of the turning points of the war'. For him it was.

---

* It was amateur strategy in conception and incompetent in execution. There was little planning for a joint military and naval campaign, and air support was considered unnecessary. Churchill's involvement was horribly reminiscent of the Dardanelles. He escaped the repercussions only because the Labour Party and elements of the Conservatives were intent on pulling down Chamberlain and concentrated their fire on him.

The debate over the Norway Campaign which brought Churchill to power could equally well have destroyed him. He more than anyone else was responsible for the Campaign; and its naval element, for which he was particularly responsible, had not gone well. There were echoes of Gallipoli. But it was Chamberlain that the government's opponents, on its own benches and on the Labour side of the House, were intent on bringing down.

The story of the debate, a memorable piece of parliamentary theatre, has been told often and will not be rehearsed at length here. Although technically the debate was only one on an adjournment motion, it assumed the character of a vote of confidence. Sir Roger Keyes, the naval hero of the Great War attended, wearing his uniform as an Admiral of the Fleet with six rows of medals to emphasise that he spoke on behalf of the navy. Leo Amery spoke to great effect, for once, quoting Cromwell's dismissal of the Long Parliament. Churchill courageously tried to take a substantial degree of responsibility for what had happened in Norway, but, as he afterwards recalled, he had the exquisite satisfaction of noting that because the House was out to get Chamberlain, every time he tried to shelter his chief someone found some way of exonerating him. Lloyd George told him not to turn himself into an air-raid shelter to protect the Prime Minister.

Above all, Chamberlain did very poorly. He was tired and angry, he spoke badly and seemed to lack confidence. On the second day of the debate, when the opposition announced that it would insist upon a decision, Chamberlain responded with a crass error of judgement, saying that he had friends in the House and he called on them to support him. He was reducing a great national crisis into a purely personal issue.

In the event, a government majority of over 200 was reduced to eighty-one. Forty-one government MPs had voted against their own government and as many again had abstained. Chamberlain said he would go. But even now he was resilient – or obstinate? At 10 o'clock on the following morning, 10 May 1940, Churchill was told that Chamberlain had decided to stay on. But Hitler changed his mind for him. Just as the door to Number Ten appeared to be closing in Churchill's face, Germany launched its offensive on France and the Low Countries.

At 11 o'clock Churchill was summoned to Downing Street for his momentous meeting with Chamberlain and Halifax. This was the occasion mentioned earlier when Churchill chose not to answer the question, 'Can you see any reason, Winston, why in these days a peer should not be Prime Minister?' and turned his back to look out on Horse Guards Parade, leaving Halifax to break the silence. That was the end of Chamberlain as Prime Minister. He had not wanted Churchill as his successor. From a constitutional point of view, Halifax could probably have taken the job. Curzon, as a peer, had only just been ruled out as Prime Minister as recently as 1923, and in the circumstances of the time legislation to return Halifax to the Commons could have been rushed through. But a coalition government was regarded as essential, and it is unlikely that the Labour Party would have been happy with a peer, even if his coronet had been statutorily removed.

A coalition government duly followed. But the idea that there was clean and clear choice between a single party Chamberlain government and a coalition Churchill government is false. Earlier in 1940, Chamberlain had considered bringing Labour into some sort of coalition, and sounded out the party. Three of the party chiefs, A. V. Alexander, Arthur Greenwood, the deputy leader, and Herbert Morrison were prepared to consider coming into government, but Clement Attlee, the leader of the party, would not. The collective decision was to stay apart for the moment; they foresaw that events might allow them to enter in a more critical role later.[10] And well ahead of the Norway Debate and Chamberlain's fall, Churchill was already having secret discussions with Sir Archibald Sinclair,* the leader of the Liberal Party, and with Alexander and Attlee for Labour.

---

* Sinclair had been a close friend of Churchill before the First World War and was indeed talked of as a husband for Clementine Churchill's younger sister. When Churchill was in the trenches during that war Sinclair was his second-in-command and in one way or another remained a sort of aide-de-camp for much of his subsequent career.

*Chapter 30*

# Serving Churchill

Chamberlain didn't look humiliated or disgraced as he made way for Churchill. He did not, as ousted leaders do, issue a Resignation Honours List. He thought he was stepping aside temporarily until the military crisis had been resolved. He remained a government minister, and in no minor, face-saving position.

Until now Churchill had been Chamberlain's number two. Now Chamberlain was Churchill's number two – indeed, if it were possible, somewhere slightly above that ranking. He was Lord President of the Council with a seat in a now smaller, five-member War Cabinet. He remained unequivocally the leader of his party and controlled its apparatus. When he entered the Commons for the first time after his resignation he was greeted with a quite exceptional ovation, very different from Churchill's reception in these days, even after some of the great speeches. He chaired the War Cabinet when Churchill was absent, which was frequently the case as he shuttled back and forward to France. In addition to that, as Lord President he had huge responsibilities in connection with all these domestic matters which were his true preoccupation. The Chancellor of the Exchequer was Kingsley Wood, but as chairman of the Lord President's Committee, Chamberlain continued with the supervisory role in relation to economic matters which had now been his métier for so long. He worked with Margesson to reduce Tory backbenchers' hostility to Churchill and to reconcile them to the new Prime Minister.

The 'temporary' nature of the arrangements was reflected in the fact that Churchill was not the leader of the Conservative Party in fact or in theory. Chamberlain discussed standing down in favour of Churchill, but Churchill felt that as the leader of a national coalition

he should stand above party politics. In any event, he was very doubtful about his appeal to the party and remembered how they had tradi-
tionally regarded him.[1]

Churchill knew how much he was dependent on Chamberlain. He
told him, 'To a large extent I am in yr hands'.[2] He could not throw
aside the appeasement men. He had to make a virtue of embracing his
old enemies in the name of inclusiveness. Even more so, he could not
humiliate their leader. Chamberlain might not have been acceptable
to the Labour Party, but he had far more Conservative supporters than
Churchill. When Churchill entered the Commons, Tory backbenchers received him in silence; the cheers came from the Labour benches.
It wasn't until July 1940, when Churchill told the House about the
destruction of the French fleet at Oran, and Chief Whip Margesson
told them to do so, that the Tories could bring themselves to cheer
their Prime Minister.

Churchill's position was very precarious. It was doubtful whether
he would remain in office for any length of time. Chamberlain
expected to resume the premiership, and he made this clear to his
sisters. The war was not yet a world war or one which would necessarily last long, and when the anomalous circumstances had ended, he,
rather than the mercurial Churchill, would be the man to run the
business of government. It's a remarkable reflection of his self-confidence – his arrogance – that he could imagine that after the circumstances in which he had left office he would ever be invited back – or
indeed that Churchill would return the seals of office to him.

But that's exactly what he did imagine. He told his sisters that he
could expect to resume his role as Prime Minister, and was certainly
not alone in thinking that Churchill was weakly established. On 11
May, J. C. C. Davidson, the former Conservative Party chairman, now
Lord Davidson, wrote to Baldwin, saying, 'The Tories don't trust
Winston. After the first clash of war is over it may very well be that a
sounder Government may emerge.'[3] Later that same day John Colville,
now Churchill's junior private secretary and very recently
Chamberlain's, wrote in his diary, 'There seems to be some inclination
in Whitehall to believe that Winston will be a complete failure and
that Neville will return.'[4] Wishful thinking perhaps: Colville had been
devoted to Chamberlain and had not yet fallen under Churchill's spell
– as he outstandingly did.

In return for Chamberlain's support, Churchill protected Chamberlain against the Labour Party. When they threatened to try to eject him from the government with the assistance of the press, Churchill spoke to Labour colleagues and to the newspaper proprietors, and the confrontation came to nothing.

While Churchill *needed* Chamberlain, needed him to confer respectability and continuity on his regime, there was a bit more to it than that. Chamberlain's support of Churchill, for that matter, went rather beyond the limits of common loyalty. They had worked together for a very long time. Their fathers had been in the Commons together a generation earlier. There was no personal hostility between them. From a practical point of view, Chamberlain could not have worked with Churchill in the pre-war administrations, but he was far from the only Conservative who felt the same way. And for his part, as soon as Churchill was brought into government, he worked very loyally with his chief. To be fair, Chamberlain gave him such a free rein that there wasn't room for a great deal of conflict, but Churchill appreciated being given that free rein. The fact that now as Prime Minister he continued to treat Chamberlain with enormous deference, almost as a senior partner, was not purely the expression of practical necessity.

The bonds that he had established with Chamberlain proved immensely important in the momentous conflict in the War Cabinet at the end of May 1940. Churchill wrote in his war memoirs that the issue of fighting on alone rather than making peace with Hitler was not 'even mentioned in our most private conclaves'.[5] Roy Jenkins described that denial of the discussions which did indeed take place over a series of days as 'the most breathtakingly bland piece of misinformation in all six volumes [of the war memoirs]'.[6]

The drama of these pivotal days in May 1940 has been well told elsewhere.* Briefly, it was far from clear whether Britain could survive on its own. When Churchill was returning from one of his visits to France, where the battle for survival was being lost, General Ismay confidently assured him, 'We will win the Battle of Britain'. Churchill stared at him and said, 'You and I will be dead in three months' time.'[7] That did not mean that Churchill thought Britain would lose the war.

---

* See particularly J. Lukacs, *Five Days in London: May 1940*.

He really did believe that ultimate victory would be achieved, even if it were delivered after his death, perhaps from the Dominions and the United States. But colleagues in the War Cabinet were not all in agreement, or if they were, they did not think that was the kind of war they wanted to fight.

Like Chamberlain, Churchill thought that the German economy was on the verge of collapse and that the Nazi regime was unstable. All the same, there is evidence that even he was not looking for outright victory. He was not averse to a negotiated peace, provided it was not 'destructive of our independence'.[8] Chamberlain quotes him as saying, 'If we could get out of this jam by giving up Malta and Gibraltar and some African colonies he would jump at it.'[9] The difference between Churchill and, in particular, Halifax was that he did not think that the end of May 1940 was the right time for negotiation. He was very strongly for postponing any talks until they could be conducted on more equal terms. On 26 May, pressed by Halifax, he said that he was prepared to discuss terms, 'even at the loss of some territory', provided that matters vital to Britain's independence were unaffected. On the following day he went so far as to say that he could accept the restoration of German colonies and the overlordship of Central Europe; but he did not think that Hitler would settle for that.

What he wanted were negotiations with an economically broken Germany when the Nazis were out of power – very much what Chamberlain had been arguing for at the very beginning of the war. Halifax, on the other hand, was prepared to make immediate concessions to a Germany not yet broken and still under Nazi rule. He was also ready to make immediate concessions to Italy to keep her out of the war. He presented a note to the War Cabinet, suggesting an approach to Mussolini, asking him to act as an intermediary to sound out Germany on peace terms.

The discussions of these days were ultimately to end in a decision which resulted in a long and terrible war from which Britain emerged as a victor, although bankrupt, as opposed to a humiliating peace with a victorious Germany which would certainly have gone on to make further demands. They went on until 28 May. On that day, the discussions began at 11.30 a.m. with a War Cabinet which dealt mainly with operational matters until 4 p.m. when the substantive discussions of the previous days resumed. The meeting was adjourned at 5.30 p.m.

Churchill was not winning the debate, and it had become very heated. The French wanted to meet Hitler, and Halifax could see no objection to that. Churchill accused Halifax of capitulation: '[N]ations that went down fighting rose again, but those which surrendered tamely were finished.' Halifax, very angry, responded by saying that he had said nothing that could be remotely described as capitulation. At this stage there was deadlock. If a vote had taken place, Churchill would have lost it.

The adjournment at 5.30 p.m. took place to allow Churchill to address a meeting of those ministers who were not in the War Cabinet and to whom he had not hitherto been able to speak. He made one of his most powerful speeches, patriotic and effective. Accounts by Dalton and Amery speak of just how persuasive his words were. Dalton says that it contained the phrase, 'If this long island story of ours is to end at last, let it end only when each of us lies choking in his own blood upon the ground.' The reception was ecstatic. He had judged his words and the mood of the meeting marvellously. In a most emotional scene he was thumped on the back.

Sustained and invigorated by the patriotic enthusiasm of the members of the larger body, he returned to confront their more nervous colleagues in the War Cabinet. 'He did not remember', he told them, 'having ever before heard a gathering of persons occupying high places in political life express themselves so emphatically.' It has been said that 'then and there, [Churchill] saved Britain, and Europe and Western civilisation'.[10]

The speech to the larger Cabinet and the way he reported it to the War Cabinet certainly was important, and Churchill was delighted to attribute the fact that the War Cabinet fell in behind him now to his undoubted powers of rhetoric. At least equally important was Chamberlain's position. In the early stages of the discussion, he had been open-minded on the merits of entering negotiations, but by now he had decided that the risks involved in mediation were too great and he was with Churchill. This left Halifax isolated and without support.*

Churchill never again had to face down a negotiated peace and never again was he so exposed in the War Cabinet. He owed his victory to Chamberlain. In return, a couple of months later, he stamped out the so-called 'Under-Secretaries' plot' when the Tory

---

* The War Cabinet at this stage consisted of five members: Churchill, Chamberlain, Halifax, Attlee and Greenwood. The last two, Labour members, were with Churchill throughout these negotiations.

anti-appeasers Amery and Harold Macmillan, along with the Liberal Clement Davies, tried to force Chamberlain out of office.

Churchill was anxious to strengthen his government by bringing in Lloyd George, but he deferred to Chamberlain, who no more wished to work with him in the Second World War than he had enjoyed working with him in the First. Churchill acceded to Chamberlain's wishes but made the request again a month later, promising that if Lloyd George didn't behave properly towards Chamberlain he would be thrown out. Chamberlain agreed to this, but in the event Lloyd George preferred to wait: he was confident that Churchill would not survive and thought that his fall would allow him to become the man who won the war for the second time.

Very soon afterwards, Chamberlain's health began to deteriorate. His gout had been very bad a few months earlier and he had had to be carried from his Downing Street flat into a Cabinet meeting. Now inoperable bowel cancer was detected. After an exploratory operation at the end of July 1940 he moved to Hampshire to recuperate in the house of an aunt. While he was there the Battle of Britain was taking place and, on 15 August, at the height of the conflict, the RAF at last appeared to have more kills than the Luftwaffe. Churchill, capable of immense humanity as well as immense egotism, remembered that Chamberlain was lying in bed unaware of all that was going on. He told his private secretary to phone him with the figures. Chamberlain was touched and overcome with relief. On 9 September, as the Battle of Britain gave way to the Blitz, he returned to Eleven Downing Street.

Now he confided to his diary that he had to adjust himself 'to the new life of a partially crippled man, which is what I am. Any ideas which may have been in my mind about the possibilities of future political activity, and even the possibility of another Premiership after the war, have gone.'[11] Whatever his fantasies, he did not lack grit. Despite his pain he attended the evening meetings of the War Cabinet in the reinforced annexe under St James's Park. Churchill discovered that because Chamberlain needed 'special periodical treatment' which was embarrassing to perform in public, a small, sandbagged area was being converted for him. He went to see Mrs Chamberlain to persuade her that she should take her husband away until he was fit. In the meantime he would send daily telegrams.

Chamberlain went off to the country, never to return to London. He offered to resign, but was pleased Churchill did not accept his resignation. Even now he had a high opinion of his abilities and thought that if he recovered sufficiently he could give Churchill more support than anyone else could. A few months later, at a reshuffle, Churchill changed his mind. Chamberlain was surprised by the speed of the decision but claimed to be pleased that his resignation had been accepted. He received hundreds of sympathetic letters from friends and supporters. His reply to Sir John Simon says what he was all about:

[I]t was the hope of doing something to improve the conditions of life for the poorer people that brought me at past middle life into politics, and it is some satisfaction to me that I was able to carry out some part of my ambition even though its permanency may be challenged by the destruction of war. For the rest I regret nothing that I have done & I can see nothing undone that I ought to have done. I am therefore content to accept the fate that has so suddenly overtaken me.[12]

His resignation took effect on 3 October 1940. On the previous day Churchill offered him the Order of the Garter. Chamberlain declined, remembering his father's attitude to honours. Churchill wrote to him in generous terms: 'You did all you could for peace: you did all you could for victory ... We have been associated, as our fathers were before us, in the ups and downs of politics ... I look back upon the ties of comradeship with feelings of the deepest respect and regard for you.'[13] Now Churchill was finally offered the leadership of the Conservative Party. He was confirmed as leader at Caxton Hall on 9 October, when Halifax proposed a motion that combined approval of Churchill with praise of Chamberlain. Even so, a number of party members abstained. Five days later the Carlton Club, a symbol of Toryism, was destroyed by a German bomb.

Chamberlain, increasingly ill in Hampshire, was sustained by regular letters from Churchill, an appreciated kindness in the midst of the darkest days of the war. Churchill also obtained the King's permission to let Chamberlain continue to see the Cabinet papers. Chamberlain was bitter about the way in which he was vilified in the press, the way in which the *Guilty Men* judgement was accepted and by the fact that

he was ignored by those who had fawned on him.* True to form, he
had no doubts. He wrote to the King: 'I do not feel that I have
anything to reproach myself for in my attempts to avoid the present
war, which might well have succeeded if they had not come up against
the insatiate and inhuman ambitions of a fanatic.'[14] He did not address
the fact that he had failed to recognise these insatiate and inhuman
ambitions. In his diary he wrote that 'Not one [of those who wrote in
the press] shows the slightest sign of sympathy for the man or even
any comprehension that there may be a human tragedy somewhere in
the background. However that is just what I expected.'[15]

He was visited by his son Frank, on leave from the army, and by
others, including the King and Queen. He died on 9 November.
Joseph Chamberlain's third wife, Mary, aged seventy-six, drove from
Odiham on the day of his death. She had a vital, energising effect on
anyone she met, and there was a special bond between her and Neville.
When he heard that she had come he said, 'That is perfect!' His face
lighted and he told her it was lovely to see her. After a few minutes
she saw a change come over his face and she summoned the rest of
the family. She was the last person to whom he spoke.[16]

Churchill wrote to Annie Chamberlain: 'During these long violent
months of war we had come closer together than at any time in our
twenty years of friendly relationship amid the ups and downs of politics. I greatly admired his fortitude and firmness of spirit. I felt when
I served under him that he would never give in: and I knew when our
positions were reversed that I could count upon the aid of a loyal and
unflinching comrade'.[17]

He meant what he said. When he and the Cabinet served as pallbearers at the funeral in Westminster Abbey on 14 November 1940, the tears
ran down his face. Two days earlier Churchill made a masterly speech in
the House of Commons. He talked of Chamberlain's wish to 'die like
his father, plain Mr Chamberlain'. He emphasised not, of course, his
misjudgement of Hitler, but the idealism of Chamberlain's aspirations:

[What] were these hopes in which he was disappointed? What were
these wishes in which he was frustrated? What was that faith that was
abused? They were surely among the most noble and benevolent

* See next chapter.

instincts of the human heart – the love of peace, the toil for peace, the strife for peace, the pursuit of peace, even at great peril and certainly to the utter disdain of popularity or clamour. Whatever else history may or may not say about these terrible, tremendous years, we can be sure that Neville Chamberlain acted with perfect sincerity according to his lights and strove to the utmost of his capacity and authority, which were powerful, to save the world from the awful, devastating struggle in which we are now engaged. This alone will stand him in good stead as far as what is called the verdict of history is concerned.

But did it stand him in good stead and what should the verdict of history be?

## Chapter 31

# The Anatomy of Appeasement

The young accountant who had been apprenticed to Howard Smith, chartered accountants, would have recognised that the interim assessment contained in an earlier chapter was just a trial balance and have realised that a final balance sheet was coming. In any event, his nonconformist background implied a ledger that would have to be squared off to see whether he had lived a useful life. But before we come to a final assessment of that life, I want to explore his involvement in appeasement a little further. Fairly or unfairly, his reputation is so intertwined with it that I must develop a little further the arguments about what appeasement was and what it implied.

The first myth, the first flaw in the analysis lies in the fact that there never was a simple choice between appeasement and belligerence. Redressing grievances was an acknowledged necessity. At the outset, Churchill, for instance, certainly did not disavow the weaknesses in the Versailles settlement and the resentment that they caused in Germany. He referred very specifically to this in his *History of the Second World War*. Rearmament was equally necessary. One was not good and the other bad; they were not alternatives. Equally, each was a matter of degree. Some redressing of grievances was necessary; some preparation for war was equally necessary. There was not a right amount of one or a right amount of the other.

It is far from true 'that the "appeasers" were a narrow circle, widely opposed at the time' by Conservatives united for strenuous resistance to Germany and by a Labour Party clamouring for great armaments. 'On the contrary, few causes have been more popular'.[1]

Robert Blake, in his history of the Conservative Party, acknowledged that Neville Chamberlain's desire to avoid war was an attitude which deserved commendation and not censure. He didn't regard Chamberlain as peculiarly blind to what Hitler was really about.* But the *application* of his policies was more rigid and unyielding and divisive than anything that Baldwin had done and 'left a lasting mark on the Party, not wholly obliterated even as late as 1957'.[2]

Baldwin's appeasement contrasted with Chamberlain's. Roy Jenkins thought the difference was that Baldwin was not characterised by his successor's 'self-righteous energy' and excoriation of his opponents.[3] But although Baldwin disapproved of Chamberlain's foreign policy style (he criticised the Munich Agreement in the House of Lords) he would have been no more disposed to fight for Czechoslovakia in 1938 than he had been to fight against the reoccupation of the Rhineland in 1936.[4]

Chamberlain himself and then Churchill made the issue personal. Chamberlain's egotism pushed him to the forefront of popular attention, and Churchill's egotism created the narrative of a disastrous passage of history from which *he* saved his nation. That narrative oversimplifies events. Difference within the Tory Party over appeasement did not centre round Churchill, despite the strength of his views and the noise that he made. Churchill did not identify with the new spirit of internationalism; he had very few supporters, and he was inconsistent: he did not attack the Japanese invasion of Manchuria or the Italian invasion of Abyssinia. The position of Eden's more numerous supporters, 'the Eden Group' or 'the Glamour Boys', was more important. When Eden resigned in February 1938 and the Labour Party moved a vote of censure against the government, twenty of Eden's supporters abstained, and a slightly bigger number did so again eight months later over Munich. What is particularly notable about the group, however, is that, despite all the plotting, the clandestine meetings, the dinners, its members repeatedly pulled back at the last moment and refused to strike. They embittered the atmosphere without changing the government's direction.

The second flaw in the myth-history relates to Hitler. The myth that developed from the very outbreak of the Second World War was that it had been preceded by a confrontation with a maniac, a maniac who was always intent on war, and whose predetermined desire for a

---

* It's interesting that Lloyd George, so much more emotionally imaginative, got Hitler just as wrong as Chamberlain did.

Great War should have been recognised from the outset. Because of what he did in 1938 and 1939, which were to make a world war necessary, it is assumed that this development was inescapable. Hitler's role has also been misunderstood.

The most informed attack on Chamberlain's foreign policy is contained in Zara Steiner's magnificent account of European history in the years 1933 to 1939, *The Triumph of the Dark*. Greatly though I admire much about her book, in my opinion she adheres to the myth-history. Her take on Chamberlain and his French counterparts is that they just were too dim to see that from the outset Hitler was unvaryingly intent on a major war. She quotes with approval John Ferris: 'A reactive power needs better intelligence than a strong and active one . . . Between 1933 and 1939 the *status quo* powers needed outstanding intelligence. They did not have it.'[5] By 'intelligence' Steiner means not just data, what is now called 'intel', but also the ability to interpret and assess it. This is pretty close to the everyday meaning of intelligence.

With very great respect I cannot accept this argument. I do not see inflexible consistency in Hitler's policies. The intelligence services of the West were far from perfect, but they were infinitely better than those of Germany and Italy, whose acumen was not self-evident. Hitler relied on risk-taking rather than analysis. He went to war in the knowledge that Germany could not match the combined productivity of the combined West. He relied therefore on a very short war, but having failed to defeat Britain he then opened up a long war by attacking Russia. There was nothing rational in the fantasy about fighting Judeo-Bolshevism, and the savagery of anti-Semitism was absurd as well as evil.

Steiner says, 'Western leaders expected their signals would be understood by their opponents; they were not.' Where is the intelligence shortfall here: London or Berlin? She prefaces that remark by saying, 'It would ultimately take the almost archaic romanticism of a Winston Churchill to counter the Führer's visionary ambitions.'[6] Is not archaic romanticism the antithesis of intelligence?

A. J. P. Taylor's thesis now has broad acceptance and I find it persuasive. Hitler did not follow a consistent policy from the moment that he started to write *Mein Kampf*, an inexorable progress towards a second world war in which he would simultaneously confront all the great powers in Europe – and in course the United States beyond the seas. In so far as he had a settled intention, it was to extend German influence in the east of Europe, recovering those areas which it had dominated prior to 1918 by itself and through the Austro-Hungarian Empire. The last thing he wanted was a great war: great wars destroyed great powers. He extemporised to achieve his objects. Indeed, even when he invaded Poland, he appeared to be pursuing a quick and limited war, with his eastern flank protected by his pact with Russia. Had France not unexpectedly and so speedily collapsed, some sort of peace on the lines of 1871 might well have ended hostilities and concluded a war that had never become a world war. France did collapse, and powers just being powers, as Taylor put it, Germany turned on Russia; and Chamberlain thus seemed to have been ineffectually involved in a heroic conflict rather than a Central European squabble. The outbreak of the Second World War was not inevitable. It was the accidental outcome of opportunistic improvisation.

Hitler's aggression was incremental; that was why he got away with it. If it had been foreseeable when he occupied the Rhineland that he would go on to annexe Austria, and then go on to seize Czechoslovakia, if it had been foreseeable when he attacked Czechoslovakia that he would then assault Poland, the case against the appeasers would be much more difficult to answer. But for the Western Allies, who desired at *almost* all costs to avoid a return to 1914–18, there was at each stage – perhaps even until the blitzkrieg attack on France and the Low Countries – an arguable possibility that Nazi aggression would stop.

The way in which Hitler had come to power, the Night of the Long Knives, *Kristallnacht*, the concentration camps, the treatment of the Jews to which Britain extraordinarily managed to turn a blind eye, the culture of the SS and the Gestapo – all of these demonstrated how evil Hitler's regime was, but not what he would finally do. Sir Horace Rumbold, the British Ambassador to Germany from 1928 to 1933 studied *Mein Kampf* in the closest of detail and warned the government in his valedictory dispatch as far back as April 1933 of the true nature of Hitler. But policy would not be governed by gut feelings and personal aversions. Chamberlain too had read *Mein Kampf*, but it was entirely sensible that he did not rush to war on the basis of its turgid prose.

The third skewed perspective is to do with the simplified history which Churchill devised and which a lazy public, enjoying simple dichotomies, bought into and which developed in post-war popular accounts of the conflict and the wonderfully watchable black-and-white films of the period. Churchill defended Chamberlain loyally from the moment he entered his Cabinet until his death, but he made a remark on a number of occasions, in different forms of words, which was entirely accurate: 'Poor Neville, he will come out of history badly. I know, for I shall write the history.' He did write that history in his account of the Second World War. The way he wrote it, its tendentious nature and its unreliability have been well explored by David Reynolds.* Churchill's aim was partly to smooth over some political issues, such as problems with the United States, but above all to establish his own centrality in a heroic battle. He admits to no personal mistakes and minimises the role of other actors. Lord Alanbrooke, the Chief of the Imperial General Staff for most of the war, although a modest man, never forgave Churchill for the way in which his critical role as co-author of British strategy was ignored.

It was an easy war to portray in apocalyptic terms in the sense that more than any other war in modern times it was a fairly clear-cut battle between good and evil (if you don't look too closely at what Churchill's Russian ally had been up to). That needn't of course have been the case, and it wasn't the case on Chamberlain's watch. As I have shown, in May 1940 Churchill himself was not averse to a negotiated peace, if it could be arrived at on terms that were not too humiliating. It was only at a press conference in Casablanca in 1943 that Roosevelt, off the cuff, said that the Allies were fighting for unconditional surrender. By 1945 the hesitant way in which Britain began the war had been eclipsed by the drama of events, and the public had little difficulty in buying in to the great narrative which Churchill created.

The 'low case' for Munich, in Roy Jenkins's words, was the practical acceptance that Britain was in no state, particularly in the air, to fight in 1938. France and Russia could not be relied upon. The Dominions, other than New Zealand, were not enthusiastic about a fight. Public

* See David Reynolds, *In Command of History: Churchill Fighting and Writing the Second World War*.

opinion was certainly against intervention. This pragmatic case for Munich is supported by the frenzy of activity of rearmament, particularly in the air, and civil defence which now took place. From March 1939 particularly, Chamberlain's policy became particularly robust, described as New Appeasement. Here negotiation was accompanied by giving guarantees to Poland, Turkey, Romania and Greece.

It's important to remember that it was always accepted in the interwar years that Britain could not simultaneously defend herself and her Eastern Empire. The Chiefs of Staff repeated this at regular intervals. Chamberlain was aware, more than most of his colleagues, of the fact that a choice had to be made between East and West. The armed services believed that Britain could only win a long war in which the resources of the Empire could be brought to bear. The Treasury on the other hand said that the economy was strong enough only for a short war.

We now know that Germany was not ready for total war at the time of the Munich crisis.[7] With eight divisions, it faced the Western Powers who possessed twenty-three, with the potential for another thirty, and who had mastery of the seas; but the Western powers weren't aware of this superiority. It didn't help, but certainly wasn't Chamberlain's fault, that before the war people like J. F. C. Fuller and Charles Lindbergh hugely overestimated German strength, 'hypnotised' as Victor Davis Hanson has put it, 'by Nazi braggadocio and pageantry rather than [by] examination of precise armament output and relative quality of weapons'.[8]

In addition to these objective factors, there were factors which, though subjective, were not capable of being ignored. The horrors of the First World War were recently and vividly imprinted on the collective memory: anything was worth trying if it might avoid another bloodbath. Plunging back into the abyss was unconscionable to public opinion at home and throughout the Empire.

Britain and even more France, because of the scale of her losses in the First World War, were conditioned by the impact of that war, the war fought to end wars. No one was untouched by the calamities of the First World War, and there was a strong feeling that the sacrifices could only be justified by avoiding a rerun. This pacific spirit, if not pacifism, pervaded the country and affected the electorate as well as political leaders. Those leaders believed that public opinion would not tolerate another war for vague principles or indeed the integrity of far-away states.

Their interpretation of public opinion was reinforced by the extraordinary support that Chamberlain received after Munich. It was certainly true that quite soon afterwards there was a turnaround. Political figures sensed that their reaction to the surrender of Czechoslovakia had been ignoble. There was a reaction of shame and in the public at large there appears to have been a switch from the fear of war to acceptance of its inevitability. This developed increasingly after Hitler broke all his promises and invaded Czechoslovakia in March 1939. This change was remarkable, and one creditable development in a shabby period.

But the point is that this new realism, so far as it existed, and there is not a lot of evidence to show that it did exist widely beyond an elite, was a sudden change from a long period of opposition to war. It's sometimes argued that the government failed to guide public opinion and could have done so by spelling out the true horrors of Nazism.[9] There is a lot of hindsight in that argument. Chamberlain's clique wanted – perhaps wanted too hard – to believe in Hitler. They thought that Britain's interests could best be served by an accommodation with him, and they certainly manipulated the press to avoid spreading information that discredited the German regime. But in truth neither they nor the vast bulk of informed opinion had any true understanding of the unbelievable depravity of Hitler and his creed. It was only after the war and the Nuremberg Trials that the full extent of that depravity was revealed. It was *unbelievable* and those who tried to reveal it before the war or even in its first months were frequently and genuinely thought to be communist propagandists spreading atrocity stories.

The British public was not internationalist. It was insular and blinkered and resistant to cooperation for the benefit of states in the east of Europe of which they knew little and cared less. There is a famous story that at the time of the military occupation of the Rhineland, Eden was in a taxi whose driver's take on the matter was, 'I suppose Jerry can do what he likes in his own back garden.' The Rhineland *was* Jerry's back garden; for that matter Austria was more or less part of Germany and the *Anschluss* was a nicety; the problem of the

Sudetenland was an unfair consequence of the Treaty of Versailles. It was only with the occupation of Czechoslovakia six months before the outbreak of war that Hitler ran out of plausible excuses.

Opinion polling was only beginning to emerge as a scientific discipline in these years, but data from the end of 1938 onwards provides a reasonably accurate record of what people actually thought about appeasement.[10]

The world into which these polls takes us is a very different one from our own. In November 1938 almost 30 per cent of those polled thought that a woman should be barred from any form of employment simply because she was married. In the same month, Chamberlain had an approval rating of 47.72 per cent. In 1939 it was even higher: in February of that year it was 55.86 per cent. There was a surprisingly strong desire to seek better relations between Britain and Soviet Russia – 86.21 per cent in March 1939. On the other hand, almost 60 per cent did not think that Britain should be inevitably involved if Germany were at war with a third party. As late as May 1939 – that is, after the occupation of Prague – 58.26 per cent of those polled thought that the risk of war had decreased since Munich.

What have historians made of appeasement? Even in his lifetime, in July 1940, four months before his death, the first and perhaps the most savage attack on Chamberlain's reputation emerged with the publication of *Guilty Men*. This devastating short book was written under the pseudonym 'Cato' which very ineffectively concealed the identity of three journalists in Beaverbrook's pay – Peter Howard, Frank Owen and Michael Foot. The book was written at great speed, and is a brilliant piece of polemic. The guilty men were above all Chamberlain, but also Sir Horace Wilson 'and a small group of sycophantic ministers'. Its success was not just in indicting Chamberlain himself, but in creating the feeling of a conspiracy engineered in secret by a small group of doctrinal extremists.

*Guilty Men* was journalism – not higher journalism but brilliant special pleading. It was hardly going to be contested during the war and it was not: far from it. Whether it created the mood of the time or tapped into that mood is difficult to say, but as London and the country suffered under the Blitz and the V-1 and V-2 flying bombs, no one was going to argue the case for Chamberlain. He was burned in effigy on bonfires. As he had promised, Churchill's history was scarcely kind to the thirties and appeasement. He was not vicious towards his predecessor: his strongest vitriol was reserved for Baldwin. But he attacked the whole mood with which he characterised the thirties, 'the years which the locust hath consumed', and the Churchill/ *Guilty Men* narrative passed its way into popular acceptance, perhaps never to be dislodged. Not only popular acceptance: Martin Gilbert and Richard Gott published *The Appeasers* in 1964 and argued and gave intellectual credence to the myth.

Subsequent serious histories have gone some way to rehabilitate aspects of Chamberlain's career. Some have argued fairly wholeheartedly for Chamberlain's policy on the basis that war was bound to be a disaster for all involved in it, as of course proved to be the case. Some have said that Chamberlain was rearming as fast as he possibly could and that victory, particularly victory in the air in 1940, could not have been achieved without all that he did. Others have acknowledged that he did rearm, but maintained that he could have armed much more.

Many historians argue that there is no sustainable argument for an out and out rejection of appeasement. A. J. P. Taylor claimed not to be revisionist but was one of the first historians to try to understand the appeasers: 'Historians do a bad day's work when they write the appeasers off as stupid or as cowards. They were men confronted with real problems, doing their best in the circumstances of their time, trying to put a powerful Germany into Europe, as later generations found they too had to do, fearing that the defeat of Germany would be followed by Russian domination, as later experience showed to be the case.'[11]

Perception of appeasement and of Chamberlain's role has moved on. Martin Gilbert described the defensible version of appeasement as being 'rooted in Christianity, courage and common sense' and he took a much less critical view in his *The Routes of Appeasement* in 1966 than he had in *The Appeasers* in 1963.*

The fiftieth anniversary of 1938 opened the archives and the view of appeasement has become more nuanced. 'Appeasement' seems less simple than it had appeared in, say, 1940. 'Economic appeasement',

---

* He acknowledged, for example, that Chamberlain had not inaugurated the policy and that it was not a policy of one-sided capitulation.

'military appeasement', 'political appeasement' and 'social appease-ment' became visible as separate policies. Those who supported one of these strands could be violently opposed to others. Negotiation rather than confrontation continued to be pursued by politicians long after Chamberlain's time, and the awareness of that fact made it more diffi-cult to characterise him in black and white terms. In the same way, the nature of victory in 1945 is now seen as something much more complicated than the glorious outcome of a battle between good and bad in which Britain stood for so long alone. In fact, 1945 saw Soviet Russia, Churchill's historic bogeyman, pre-eminent in the European continent, and Britain bankrupt and increasingly dependent on America. Churchill himself was accused of appeasing Moscow and Washington.[12]

# The Reckoning

For a start, can we discard the downright silly criticisms, such as Larry Fuscher's description of Chamberlain as 'a pathetic old man, one of the great losers of history'? And throw out the ridiculous nicknames, including 'the undertaker' and 'the coroner', both of which were frequently applied to him?

Success engenders admiration and failure engenders ridicule. Churchill's dress, his hats particularly, was archaic in his time. He often affected unusually broad-brimmed Homburgs and stove-pipe hats not very different from those of the Regency. His very broad spotted bow tie was also a nod to the nineteenth century. The walking cane and cigar were conscious affectations of an earlier age. Chamberlain was well aware that his umbrella was a prop. He joked about the number of umbrellas he would be presented with after a popular speech. When Chamberlain was rapturously received on his way from Heston to London he was cheered as the man of the moment, and the get-up was endearing, not pathetic.

Secondly, I hope it can be agreed that an objective assessment of a statesman's achievements does not depend on whether he was likeable. I have already made my views about how likeable or unlikeable I find Chamberlain pretty clear.

Turning to more serious matters, first, to his domestic policies, not a lot need be added to what has been said already. His practical achievements were far greater than anything Joe or Austen had done. In his time at the Ministry of Health and the Exchequer he moved his country from the grudging charity of the nineteenth century and its workhouses to the very brink of the welfare state. It was he who did it: his views were not those of orthodox Conservatives with whom he never felt truly at home.

He brought to his task a *passion*: he was prepared to burn himself out in mastering the detail of his reforms and personally pushing them through. Although he was loath to show his emotions, he was in truth consumed by a burning desire to improve the practical lot of his fellow men, to be *useful*. He was not seized by intellectual visions. He worked for practical ends. He burned to see the ordinary people of the country comfortably off, provided with pensions, living in comfortable houses, served by clean water and effective sewage systems. This wasn't a romantic vision. It involved hard dogged work that allowed ordinary men and women dignity and fulfilment. When Chamberlain became Prime Minister, Anthony Eden said that he had 'had the makings of a really great Prime Minister'.[1] That ambitious assessment was based on what Chamberlain had done as a radical domestic reformer.

In a number of polls, professional historians have chosen Clement Attlee as Britain's best peacetime Prime Minister of the twentieth century. If there had been no Hitler, no war and Chamberlain had died in 1940 instead of resigning, he would have been regarded as second to Attlee.

But there was a war, and Chamberlain's standing has to be assessed on the basis of his foreign as well as his domestic policy. The crucial question here is to know precisely what is alleged against him.

In foreign policy, just as much as in his domestic policy, Chamberlain was a passionate man. Here his passion arose from a totally rational reaction to what had happened in the First World War, an experience that had a general dimension as well as that very personal one in relation to Norman. All that Norman's generation had done would be wasted effort if the world were plunged into another war. Further, his attitude to foreign policy flowed from his awareness of what war would do to his aims for a fairer and better society.

Against that background his foreign policy seems not incomprehensible and, if wrong, not grotesquely so. Of course there are aspects to his appeasement policy which are deeply unappealing. His bullying, arrogance, the self-righteous conviction that he knew best and that those who criticised him were fools or knaves – all of these, more marked as he got older, were particularly evident in relation to foreign policy.

There was too an intolerable self-satisfaction in the delusion that
he had a personal and unique gift for negotiation. For all that he
would say about how much he disliked Nazism and the German leadership, until Germany breached Munich and entered Prague, he
continued to delude himself that Hitler could be trusted: he refused
to admit that he had simply been wrong. In spite of all the evidence,
his overweening self-confidence refused to let go of the fanatical
conviction that he had a secret which would always win Hitler over.

So he was flawed. But I repeat that we must be clear what the charge
against him is. The question remains: Was he a fool and a dupe who
failed to face up to the threat from Hitler and Fascist Germany *so as
to imperil the safety of his country*? That is what is alleged, implicitly or
unconsciously, and the answer is that he was not.

While he entertained his delusive fantasies, he prepared for war all
the same. Britain and France might have stopped Hitler in his tracks
in 1936, but it was nothing to do with Chamberlain that neither
country would think of going into a war with Germany which would,
at that time, have in any case seemed a disproportionate reaction to
events. It was Chamberlain who created a Britain strong enough in
1940 to withstand the Nazi onslaught which destroyed the other
democracies of Europe, and a Britain which was capable of moving
on to victory in 1945.

The aircraft that won the Battle of Britain had been funded,
planned and, for the most part, constructed on his watch. At the
beginning of July 1940 there were forty-four Spitfire and Hurricane
squadrons in Fighter Command; by the end of the year, despite the
losses in August and September, there were seventy-one. The navy
which interdicted German invasion was the strong navy for which
Chamberlain had campaigned since before the First World War.
Without his intervention in the Cabinet debates in May 1940,
Churchill might well have fallen and Halifax would have sued for an
ignominious peace. It is too much to say that he won the Second
World War, but without him it would have been lost.

On the simple stone that commemorates him in the village church-
yard at Heckfield in Hampshire, after the bare record of his name and
of the fact that he had been Prime Minister from 1937 to 1940, the
words he chose to appear were: 'Write me as one that loves his fellow

men'. The quotation is from 'Abou Ben Adhem' by Leigh Hunt. His love was certainly not a touchy-feely love, but the Victorian world in which almost half his life had been spent would have understood the concept of *useful* love. His life was devoted to practical concern for the welfare of his fellow countrymen in war as well as in peace. They have denied him their gratitude.

# Acknowledgements

One of the constant delights associated with writing history is the camaraderie that exists within the republic of scribblers. Old friends and new friends are generous with their time and knowledge. I have incurred many debts, and should like to thank, amongst others, Patricia Clavin, FBA, Professor of International History at the University of Oxford; John Hussey, the laurels of the Templer Prize for *The Campaign of 1815* still green on his brow; and Robert Lyman, who generously diverted attention from the final stages of writing his account of the war in the Far East, *A War of Empires*.

For help with picture research I'd like to thank particularly Francis Chamberlain, Neville's grandson; Helen Fisher, Archivist at Birmingham University; Jason Lee Gelder; Claire and Rick Simpson (Claire's account of Neville's time on Andros, *Neville's Island*, based on research done while she and Nick lived there, supplies detail on this episode); and Caroline Squire, Austen Chamberlain's great-grand-daughter and Neville's great-niece. It deserves mentioning that Francis Chamberlain and Caroline Squire were unreservedly helpful despite experience of how biographers have treated their ancestor – and without knowledge of my take on him, and certainly without seeking to influence my approach. I hope they may feel that this book will develop an informed appreciation of a man who was far from two-dimensional.

James Tilley, Professor of Politics at the University of Oxford, and Kathleen Joyce Weldon of the Center for Public Opinion Research at Cornell were very helpful in relation to opinion polls in the Chamberlain era, and David Greenyer shed light on the interpretation of economic data.

James Rose was a sensitive and perceptive editor with whom it was a pleasure to work. At Birlinn Hugh Andrew and Andrew Simmons, respectively Managing Director and Editorial Director, were as always much involved and great fun to work with. My assistant, Gwen McKerrell, turned confusion into an elegant typescript with efficiency and uncomplaining good humour.

What new to say of Janet, with whom I celebrated the fiftieth anniversary of our wedding during the course of writing the book, and to whom I owe by far the greatest debt of all? Nothing very novel, I fear, but heartfelt all the same: just that life would not be half the fun, nor this book written, nor many other things attempted without her love and support.

WR
Kennacraig, Argyll

# Notes

## CHAPTER I: ANDROS

1 Hyde, H. M., *Neville Chamberlain*, p.14.
2 The Reverend F. B. Matthews to Archdeacon Wakefield, 28 February 1894, quoted Feiling, K., *The Life of Neville Chamberlain*, p.25.
3 Ibid., p.21.
4 Twenty-seven signatories to NC, 25 December 1891.
5 Neville to Hilda, 10 July 1891.
6 JC to NC, 17 September 1891.
7 JC to NC, 27 September 1891.
8 NC to Mary E. Chamberlain, 26 November 1891.
9 JC to NC, 4 January 1892.
10 NC to EC, 29 January 1892.
11 NC to BC, 26 November 1894.
12 JC to NC, 13 December 1894.

## CHAPTER 2: THE COST OF A DREAM

1 NC to BC, 14 January 1898.
2 JC to NC, 30 March 1896.
3 NC to AC, 24 March 1895.
4 The Reverend F. B. Matthews to Archdeacon Wakefield, 28 February 1894, quoted Feiling, K., *The Life of Neville Chamberlain*, p.30.
5 Churchill, W. S., *The Second World War, Volume 1: The Gathering Storm*, pp.388–9.

## CHAPTER 3: RADICAL JOE

1   Churchill, W. S., *Great Contemporaries*, p.47.
2   Joseph Chamberlain, *Notes on the Families of Chamberlain and Harben*, privately printed, copy at Birmingham University Library.
3   Lady Cecily Debenham to Mrs Neville Chamberlain, 11 September 1941.
4   Broadcast by Hilda Chamberlain, 15 September 1953. BBC Archives.
5   Churchill, W. S., *Great Contemporaries*, p.48.
6   Ibid., p.53.
7   Quoted, Asa Briggs, *Victorian Cities*, pp.139–40.
8   Ibid., pp.232–3.
9   Dilks, D., *Neville Chamberlain*, vol. 1, p.9.
10  Austen Chamberlain, *Politics from Inside*, p.15.
11  Neville Chamberlain's memoir of his father, 6 July 1914, quoted Dilks, D., *Neville Chamberlain*, vol. 1, p.14.
12  Whitehill-Laing, D., *Mistress of Herself*, p.226.


## CHAPTER 4: A PARTY DISABLED

1   Lucy, H. W. (ed.), *Speeches of the Right Hon Joseph Chamberlain MP 1885*, p.41.


## CHAPTER 5: ANOTHER PARTY BLOWN TO BITS

1   Churchill, W. S., *My Early Life*, p.387.
2   Quoted Bright, J., and Thorold Rogers, J. E. (eds), *Speeches and Questions of Public Policy by Richard Cobden*, vol. 1, p. 40.
3   Quoted in *Better Times: Speeches by the Right Hon D. Lloyd George MP Chancellor of the Exchequer*, p.43.
4   Jay, R., *Joseph Chamberlain: A Political Study*, p.18.
5   *Birmingham Daily Post*, 10 July 1906.
6   *The Times*, 14 February 1902.


## CHAPTER 6: THE GROWING BOY AND THE SHADES OF THE PRISON HOUSE

1   Undated letter, Chamberlain papers 15/17.
2   Feiling, K., *The Life of Neville Chamberlain*, p.9.
3   Quoted Feiling, K., *The Life of Neville Chamberlain*, p.10.
4   Ibid., p.12.
5   Ibid., pp.12–13.
6   Ward, R., *The Chamberlains: Joseph, Austen and Neville 1836–1940*, p.109.

## CHAPTER 7: A MODEL STATESMAN

1 Jenkins, R., *The Chancellors*, p.112.
2 Vansittart, R., *The Mist Procession*, p.549.
3 Hilda Chamberlain, 'Portrait of the Three Chamberlains and my Elder Sister Beatrice, July–November 1956', see Dilks *op cit*, vol. 1, p.589.
4 Jenkins, R., *The Chancellors*, p.143.
5 Ibid., p.124.
6 Ibid., p.111.
7 Barnes, J., and Nicholson, D. (eds), *The Leo Amery Diaries, Vol 2: The Empire at Bay 1929–1945*, p.437.

## CHAPTER 8: BACK HOME AND INTO HARNESS

1 Letter, 30 October 1897, to Arthur Greenwood, quoted Feiling, K., *The Life of Neville Chamberlain*, p.38.
2 Letter, 7 October 1900, to Arthur Greenwood, quoted Feiling, K., *The Life of Neville Chamberlain*, p.33.
3 Quoted in Dilks, D., *Neville Chamberlain: Volume one, Pioneering and reform, 1869–1929*, p.144.
4 Oxford Dictionary of National Biography.
5 Diary, 22 March 1915.
6 Quoted in Dilks, D., *Neville Chamberlain: Volume one, Pioneering and reform, 1869–1929*, p.182.

## CHAPTER 9: THE DOMESTIC COCOON

1 Letter, 25 December 1901, to Arthur Greenwood.
2 NC to MC, 28 October 1903.
3 NC to Father Matthews, 19 October 1902.
4 HC to NC, 16 March 1909.
5 NC to Annie Vere Cole, December 1910.
6 Smart, N., *Neville Chamberlain*, p 47.
7 NC to BC, 10 May 1911.
8 NC to IC, 19 February 1916.
9 Dilks, D., *Neville Chamberlain: Volume one, Pioneering and reform, 1869–1929* p.175.

## CHAPTER 10: EARNEST ENGAGEMENTS

1 Dilks, D., *Neville Chamberlain: Volume one, Pioneering and reform, 1869–1929* p.91.
2 Ibid., p.85.

3 Quoted Dilks, D., *Neville Chamberlain: Volume one, Pioneering and reform, 1869–1929*, p.107.

4 Quoted Feiling, K., *The Life of Neville Chamberlain*, p.42.

5 *Birmingham Daily Post*, 10 November 1915.

6 Quoted Feiling, K., *The Life of Neville Chamberlain*, p.52.

7 NC to MC, 8 November 1915.

8 NC to HC, 12 December 1915.

9 Quoted Feiling, K., *The Life of Neville Chamberlain*, p.85.

10 Ibid., p.48.

11 Ibid.

12 Memorandum, January 1942, Mr Chamberlain and a Midland Union of Conservative and Unionist Associations, quoted Dilks, D., *Neville Chamberlain: Volume one, Pioneering and reform, 1869–1929*, p.139.

13 NC to BC, 24 March 1916.

14 Lloyd George Papers, C/14/9, cited Dilks, D., *Neville Chamberlain: Volume one, Pioneering and reform, 1869–1929*, p.145.

## CHAPTER 11: AN EXTRAORDINARY DISPLAY OF DISCOURTESY

1 Quoted Dilks, D., *Neville Chamberlain: Volume one, Pioneering and reform, 1869–1929*, p.191.

2 Ibid., p.202.

3 Hansard, 27 February 1917.

4 Amery Diaries, p.143.

5 Hankey Diary, 14 January 1916.

6 Addison, C., *Politics from Within*, vol. II, p.119.

7 NC to Lloyd George, 29 June 1917, Lloyd George Papers F/7/1/8.

8 Quoted Dilks, D., *Neville Chamberlain: Volume one, Pioneering and reform, 1869–1929*, p.228.

9 NC to Mary Carnegie, 14 August 1917.

10 Diary, 21 October 1917.

11 Diary, 17 December 1917.

## CHAPTER 12: THE MOST INTIMATE FRIEND I HAD

1 Chamberlain, N., *Norman Chamberlain, A Memoir*, p.45.

2 Norman Chamberlain to NC, 24 April 1916, Chamberlain Papers.

3 Norman Chamberlain to NC, 19 August 1917, Chamberlain Papers.

4 Neville Chamberlain, *Norman Chamberlain, A Memoir*, p.162.

5 Quoted in Feiling, K., *The Life of Neville Chamberlain*, p.78.

6 Quoted in Dilks, D., *Neville Chamberlain: Volume one, Pioneering and reform, 1869–1929*, p.288.

## CHAPTER 13: AN INTERIM ASSESSMENT

1 Smart, N., *Neville Chamberlain*, p.xiv.
2 Ibid., p.xii.
3 Cannadine, D., *Pleasures of the Past*, p.306 *et seq.*
4 Macleod, I., *Neville Chamberlain*, p.23.
5 Dilks, D., *Neville Chamberlain: Volume one, Pioneering and reform, 1869–1929*, p.450.
6 Self, R., *Neville Chamberlain: A Biography*, p.358.
7 Parker, R.A.C., *Chamberlain and Appeasement. British Policy and the Coming of the Second World War*, p.2.
8 Ibid., p.8.

## CHAPTER 14: INESCAPABLE DESTINY: WESTMINSTER

1 Jenkins, R., *The Chancellors*, p.335.
2 Quoted, Self, R., *The Neville Chamberlain Diary Letters, Vol 1: The making of a Politician 1915–1920*, p.282.
3 NC to HC, 3 August 1918.
4 Self, R., *The Austen Chamberlain Diary Letters. The Correspondence of Austen Chamberlain with his Sisters Hilda and Ida, 1916–1937*, p.239.
5 Feiling, K., *The Life of Neville Chamberlain*, p.97.
6 Said to his son-in-law Steven Lloyd, see Dilks, D., *Neville Chamberlain*, p.295.

## CHAPTER 15: AT THE CENTRE

1 NC to IC, 3 March 1922.
2 Ramsden, J., *The Age of Balfour and Baldwin, 1902–1940*, p.295.
3 Taylor, A.J.P., *Beaverbrook*, pp.136–7.
4 Diary, 11 November 1923.
5 Hansard, 21 January 1924
6 Diary, February 9 1924.
7 Feiling, K., *The Life of Neville Chamberlain*, p.197.
8 Ibid., p216.

## CHAPTER 16: A RADICAL AT THE HEART OF THE TORY PARTY

1 Diary, 9 August 1925.
2 NC to IC, 8 May 1926.
3 Memorandum by Chief General Inspector Ministry of Health 11 December 1928, appended to a memorandum by Chamberlain of 3 December, CAB 27/381.

4  NC to Mary E Carnegie, 1 June 1929.

5  Diary, 22 March 1930.

6  Smart, N., *Neville Chamberlain*, p.148.

7  Diary, 22 March 1930.

8  Diary, 26. July 1930.

9  Diary, 23 February 1931.

10  Feiling, K., *The Life of Neville Chamberlain*, p.180.

11  Diary, 23 August 1931.

12  Feiling, K., *The Life of Neville Chamberlain*, p.193.

13  Stewart, G., *Burying Caesar: Churchill–Chamberlain and the Battle for the Tory Party*, p.92.

14  Hyde, H. M., *Neville Chamberlain*, p.66.

15  Feiling, K., *The Life of Neville Chamberlain*, p.196.

16  Diary, 8 March 1935.

## CHAPTER 17: THE HEALTH OF THE NATION

1  Austen Chamberlain to Mrs Austen Chamberlain, 5 November 1924.

2  Dilks, D., *Neville Chamberlain*, p.375.

3  Ibid., p.398.

4  Ibid., p.421.

5  Ward, R., *The Chamberlains: Joseph, Austen and Neville 1836–1940*, p.135.

6  Dilks, D., *Neville Chamberlain*, p.416.

7  Feiling, K., *The Life of Neville Chamberlain*, p.128.

8  Dilks, D., *Neville Chamberlain*, p.327.

9  Feiling, K., *The Life of Neville Chamberlain*, p.129.

10  Attlee, C., *As it Happened*, p.31.

11  NC to IC, 19 June 1927.

12  Diary, 18 March 1928.

13  Hansard, 26 November 1928.

14  Diary, 1 December 1928.

15  Jenkins, R., *The Chancellors*, p.339.

16  Macleod, I., *Neville Chamberlain*, p.114.

17  *Sunday Times*, 24 May 1925.

18  Taylor, A. J. P., *English History 1914–1945*, p.256.

19  Reekes, A., *More than Munich: The forgotten legacy of Neville Chamberlain* (Alcester: West Midlands History Ltd, 2018), epub.

## CHAPTER 18: SECOND IN COMMAND: CHANCELLOR OF THE EXCHEQUER

1  Diary, 8 March 1934.

2  Stewart, G., *Burying Caesar: Churchill–Chamberlain and the Battle for the Tory Party*, p.61.

3   *The Daily Post*, 18 January 1907, quoted Macleod, I., *Neville Chamberlain*, p.50.
4   Dilks, D., *Neville Chamberlain*, p.546.
5   Hansard, 261.296.
6   Jenkins, R., *The Chancellors*, p.348.
7   James, R. R., *Bob Boothby, A Portrait*, p.175.
8   Dawson to NC, 8 November 1940, Dawson Papers 81/48.
9   Cato, *Guilty Men*, p.86.
10  Gilbert, M., 'Horace Wilson, Man of Munich:', in *History Today*, 32/10 (1982), pp.3–9.
11  Bouverie, T., *Appeasing Hitler: Chamberlain, Churchill and the Road to War*, p.218.
12  Ibid.
13  Ibid., p.219.

## CHAPTER 19: GOLD PATCHES IN THE MIST

1   Quoted Jenkins, R., *The Chancellors*, p.353.
2   Diary, 4 December 1934.
3   Quoted Rose, K., *King George V*, p. 183.
4   Rhodes James, R., *A Spirit Undaunted*, p.138.
5   Diary, 25 April 1937.

## CHAPTER 20: PRIME MINISTER

1   Hyde, H. M., *Neville Chamberlain*, p.3.
2   Self, R., *The Neville Chamberlain Diary Letters Volume 4 : The Downing Street Years 1934–1940*, pp. 269–270.
3   Ibid., p.435. See also Stewart, G., *Burying Caesar: Churchill–Chamberlain and the Battle for the Tory Party*.
4   NC to IC, 8 December 1935.

## CHAPTER 21: CHAMBERLAIN'S PRESS

1   Margach, J., *The Abuse of Power: The War between Downing Street and the Media from Lloyd George to Callaghan*, p.50.
2   Ibid.
3   Cockett, R., *Twilight of Truth: Chamberlain, Appeasement and the Manipulation of the Press*, p.105.
4   Margach, J., *The Abuse of Power: The War between Downing Street and the Media from Lloyd George to Callaghan*, p.52.
5   Rhodes James, R. (ed.), *Memoirs of a Conservative. J. C. C Davidson's Memoirs and Papers 1910–1937*, p272.

6 Cockett, R., *Twilight of Truth: Chamberlain, Appeasement and the Manipulation of the Press*, p.11.

7 *The Diaries and Letters of Harold Nicolson*, vol. 2, 28 July 1941.

8 Margach, J., *The Abuse of Power: The War between Downing Street and the Media from Lloyd George to Callaghan*, p.59.

9 Ibid.

## CHAPTER 22: A FOREIGN OFFICE QUARTET

1 Minute, 6 May 1933, Vansittart MSS.

2 Hyde, H. M., *Neville Chamberlain*, p.99.

3 Dilks, D. (ed.), *Diaries of Sir Alexander Cadogan O.M. 1938–1945*, 27 April 1937.

4 Ibid., p.14.

5 Henderson, N., *Failure of a Mission: Berlin 1937–1939*, p.168.

6 Ibid., p.13.

7 Henderson and the Foreign Office, 24 February 1938, quoted Cockett, R., *Twilight of Truth: Chamberlain, Appeasement and the Manipulation of the Press*, p.52.

## CHAPTER 23: FOREIGN AFFAIRS: THE LANDSCAPE AND THE FOG

1 Earl of Avon, *The Eden Memoirs: Facing the Dictators*, p.445.

2 Diary, 24 March 1934.

3 Diary, 28 July 1934.

4 Self, R., *Neville Chamberlain: A Biography*, p.214.

5 Smart, N., *Neville Chamberlain*, p.229.

6 Nicolson, N. (ed.), *Harold Nicolson: Diaries and Letters 1930–1939*, 9 March 1936.

7 Bouverie, T., *Appeasing Hitler: Chamberlain, Churchill and the Road to War*, p.88.

8 Quoted Bouverie, T., *Appeasing Hitler: Chamberlain, Churchill and the Road to War*, p.91.

9 Quoted Feiling, K., *The Life of Neville Chamberlain*, p.329.

10 Crozier, A. J., *Appeasement and Germany's Last Bid for Colonies*, p.225.

11 Henry Channon, Diary, 5 March 1938.

12 Smart, N., *Neville Chamberlain*, p.230.

13 Douglas, R., quote Chamberlain and Eden, *Journal of Contemporary History* (1978), 13, 113.

## CHAPTER 24: TALKING OF PEACE
## AND PREPARING FOR WAR

1 For a reference for the contrary view see Smart, N., *Neville Chamberlain*, p.220.
2 Hyde, H. M., *Baldwin*, p.568.
3 Hansard, 12 November 1936.
4 Quoted Macleod, I., *Neville Chamberlain*, pp.176–7.
5 NC to HC, 28 July 1934.
6 Quoted Howard, M., *The Continental Commitment*, p.110.
7 Feiling, K., *The Life of Neville Chamberlain*, pp.261–2.
8 Jenkins, R., *The Chancellors*, p.354.
9 'Note by the Chancellor of the Exchequer on the report of the DRC', 20 June 1934, CAB 16/111.
10 Ward, R., *The Chamberlains*, p.145.
11 Hyde, H. M., *Neville Chamberlain*, p.80.
12 Official History of British War Production, p.109.
13 Ferguson, N., *The War of the World: History's Age of Hatred*, p.236, and Dutton, D., *Neville Chamberlain*, p.50.
14 For an analysis of the statistics, see Davis Hanson, V., *The Second World Wars*.
15 Hyde, H. M., *Neville Chamberlain*, p.169.
16 Macleod, I., *Neville Chamberlain*, p.206.

## CHAPTER 25: THE DARKENING
## OF THE EASTERN SKY

1 Hansard, 5c, 333.1406–6.
2 Feiling, K., *The Life of Neville Chamberlain*, pp.347–8.
3 NC to HC, 13 March 1938.
4 Bouverie, T., *Appeasing Hitler: Chamberlain, Churchill and the Road to War*, p.211.
5 *The Times*, 19 March 1938.
6 Butler Papers, quoted Bouverie, T., *Appeasing Hitler: Chamberlain, Churchill and the Road to War*, p.194.
7 Bouverie, T., *Appeasing Hitler: Chamberlain, Churchill and the Road to War*, pp.195–6.
8 Barnes, J., and Nicholson, D. (eds), *The Leo Amery Diaries, Vol 2: The Empire at Bay 1929–1945*, p.508.
9 Wheeler-Bennett, J. W., *Munich, Prologue to Tragedy*, p.77.

## CHAPTER 26: BERCHTESGADEN: FLY, FLY, AND . . .

1 Feiling, K., *The Life of Neville Chamberlain*, p.357.
2 Bouverie, T., *Appeasing Hitler: Chamberlain, Churchill and the Road to War*, p.240.

3  Ibid., p.246.

4  Hyde, H. M., *Neville Chamberlain*, p.118.

5  Baldwin Papers, quoted Bouverie, T., *Appeasing Hitler: Chamberlain, Churchill and the Road to War*, p.43.

6  Dilks, D. (ed.), *Diaries of Sir Alexander Cadogan O.M. 1938–1945*, p.105.

7  Ibid., p.107.


## CHAPTER 27: . . . FLY AGAIN

1  Douglas-Home, A., *The Way the Wind Blows*, pp.64–5.

2  Thorpe, D. R., *Alec Douglas-Home*, p.83.

3  Douglas-Home Papers, 'Notes on Munich', quoted Bouverie, T., *Appeasing Hitler: Chamberlain, Churchill and the Road to War*, p.279.

4  Quoted Cockett, R., *Twilight of Truth: Chamberlain, Appeasement and the Manipulation of the Press*, p.81.

5  Liddell Hart, B. H., *The Memoirs of Captain Liddell Hart*, vol. 2, p.228.

6  Rhodes James, R., *Bob Boothby*, p.187.

7  See Harold Nicolson, *Diaries and Letters, 1939–45*, p.71.

8  Jenkins, R., *Churchill*, p.583.

9  Dilks, D. (ed.), *Diaries of Sir Alexander Cadogan O.M. 1938–1945*, p132.


## CHAPTER 28: AFTER MUNICH

1  Hyde, H. M., *Neville Chamberlain*, p,134.

2  Ibid., p.133.

3  Ibid.

4  Cockett, R., *Twilight of Truth: Chamberlain, Appeasement and the Manipulation of the Press*, pp.89–90.

5  Colvin, I., *The Chamberlain Cabinet*, p.188.

6  Dilks, D. (ed.), *Diaries of Sir Alexander Cadogan O.M. 1938–1945*, 30 March 1939.

7  Cadogan to Colgin, 20 January 1964, quoted Dilks, D. (ed.), *Diaries of Sir Alexander Cadogan O.M. 1938–1945*, pp.166–7.

8  Smart, N., *Neville Chamberlain*, p.257.

9  Harvey, J. (ed.), *The Diplomatic Diaries of Oliver Harvey 1937–1940*, p.257.

10  Smith, A. (ed.), *Hostage to Fortune: The Letters of Joseph P. Kennedy*, p.362.


## CHAPTER 29: THE CONTINUATION OF
## DIPLOMACY BY OTHER MEANS

1  The *Spectator*, 1940.

2  House of Commons, 12 October 1939.

3  MC to IC, 5 November 1939.

4  Buccleuch Papers, quoted Bouverie, T., *Appeasing Hitler: Chamberlain, Churchill and the Road to War*, pp.389–90.

5  Hansard, 5th Series, vol. 341, col. 1196.

6  Thompson, W. H., *I was Churchill's Shadow*, p.20.

7  Churchill, W. S., *Second World War*, vol.I, p.388.

8  *War Papers*, vol. I, p.304.

9  *War Papers*, vol. I, p.358.

10 McKinstry, L., *Attlee and Churchill: Allies in War, Adversaries in Peace*, p.184.

## CHAPTER 30: SERVING CHURCHILL

1  Reynolds, D., 'Churchill and the British "decision" to fight on in 1940', in Langhorne, R. (ed), *Diplomacy and Intelligence During the Second World War: Essays in Honour of FH Hinsley* (Cambridge, Cambridge University Press, 1985).

2  Churchill to Chamberlain, 10 May 1940, quoted Reynolds, D., *From World War to Cold War*, p.77.

3  Baldwin Papers, quoted Gilbert, M., *Winston S. Churchill*, vol. v, p.237.

4  Colville Diary, 11 May 1940.

5  Churchill, W. S., *The Second World War*, vol. II, p.157 *et seq.*

6  Jenkins, R., *Churchill*, p.610.

7  Ismay to Robert Sherwood, quoted Reynolds, D., *In Command of History*, p.172.

8  Halifax, Diary, 6 June 1940, quoted, Reynolds, D., *From World War to Cold War*, p.82.

9  Diary, 26 May 1940.

10 Lukacs, J., *Five Days in London: May 1940*, p.2.

11 Diary, 9 September 1940.

12 Self, R., *Neville Chamberlain, A Biography*, p.446.

13 Churchill to Chamberlain, 2 October 1940, Chamberlain Papers.

14 Chamberlain to King George VI, 30 September 1940, quoted Feiling, K., *The Life of Neville Chamberlain*, p.452.

15 Diary, 4 October 1940.

16 Whitehill-Laing, D., *Mistress of Herself*, p.214.

17 Quoted, Self, R., *Neville Chamberlain: A Biography*, p.447.

## CHAPTER 31: THE ANATOMY OF APPEASEMENT

1  Taylor, A. J. P., *The Origins of the Second World War*, p.25.

2  Blake, R., *The Conservative Party from Peel to Churchill*, pp.239–40.

3  Jenkins, R., *Baldwin*, p.23.

4  Ibid., p.24.

5  Ferris, J., 'Intelligence', in Boyce, R., and Maiolo, J. A. (eds), *The Origins of World War Two: The Debate Continues*, pp.322–3.

6 Steiner, Z., *The Triumph of the Dark*, p.1051.

7 Bouverie, T., *Appeasing Hitler: Chamberlain, Churchill and the Road to War*, p.415.

8 Davis Hanson, V., *The Second World Wars*, ch.2.

9 Bouverie, T., *Appeasing Hitler: Chamberlain, Churchill and the Road to War*, p.417.

10 The data referred to in this section are taken from British Institute of Public Opinion Polls 1938 SN2037 and British Institute of Public Opinion Polls 1939 SN2038.

11 Taylor, A. J. P., *The Origins of the Second World War*, p.25.

12 Robbins, K., *Appeasement*, pp.7–8

## EPILOGUE: THE RECKONING

1 Harvey, J., *The Diplomatic Diaries of Oliver Harvey*, pp.33–4.

# Select Bibliography

Barnes, J. and Nicholson, D. (eds), *The Leo Amery Diaries. Vol. 1, 1896–1929* (London: Hutchinson, 1980)

——, *The Empire At Bay: The Leo Amery Diaries: 1929–1945* (London: Hutchinson, 1988)

Berry, G., *Aftermath: 1918–1924: Years that Shaped the Twentieth Century* (London: Austin Macauley, 2017)

Blake, R., *The Conservative Party from Peel to Churchill* (London: Eyre & Spottiswoode, 1970)

Bouverie, T., *Appeasing Hitler: Chamberlain, Churchill and the Road to War* (London: The Bodley Head, 2019)

Boyce, R. and Maiolo, J. A. (eds), *The Origin of World War Two: The Debate Continues* (Basingstoke: Palgrave Macmillan, 2003)

Briggs, A., *Victorian Cities* (Berkeley and Los Angeles: University of California Press, 1963)

Bright, J. John and Thorold Rogers, J. E. (eds), *Speeches and Questions of Public Policy by Richard Cobden, PM, Volume 1* (London: Fisher Unwin, 1908)

Cato, *Guilty Men* (London: Victor Gollancz Ltd, 1940)

Chamberlain, N., *Norman Chamberlain, A Memoir* (London: John Murray, 1923)

Charmley, J., *Chamberlain and the Lost Peace* (London: Hodder and Stoughton, 1989)

Churchill W. S., *My Early Life: A Roaming Commission* (London: The Reprint Society, 1930)

——, *Great Contemporaries* (London: Reprint Society, 1941)

——, *The Second World War, Volume 1: The Gathering Storm* (London: Cassell and Co, 1948)

Cockett, R., *Twilight of Truth: Chamberlain, Appeasement and the Manipulation of the Press* (London: Weidenfeld and Nicolson, 1989)

Crozier, A. J., *Appeasement and Germany's Last Bid for Colonies* (London: Palgrave Macmillan, 1988)

Dilks, D. (ed.), *Diaries of Sir Alexander Cadogan O.M. 1938–1945* (London: Cassell, 1971)

——, *Neville Chamberlain: Volume one, Pioneering and reform, 1869–1929* (Cambridge: Cambridge University Press, 1984)

Douglas-Home, A., *The Way the Wind Blows* (London: Collins Sons & Co Ltd, 1976)

Dutton, D., *Neville Chamberlain* (London: Arnold/Hodder Headline Group, 2001)

Eden, A., Earl of Avon, *The Eden Memoirs: Facing the Dictators* (London: Cassell and Company Ltd, 1962)

Feiling, K., *The Life of Neville Chamberlain* (London: Macmillan & Co Ltd, 1946)

Fuchser, L. W., *Neville Chamberlain and Appeasement: A Study in the Politics of History* (New York: W. W. Norton, 1982)

Gilbert, M., *The Roots of Appeasement* (London: Weidenfeld and Nicolson, 1966)

——, and Gott, R., *The Appeasers* (London: Houghton Mifflin Company, 1963)

George, D. L., *Better Times: Speeches by the Right Hon D. Lloyd George MP Chancellor of the Exchequer* (London: Hodder & Stoughton, 1910)

Griffiths, R., *Fellow Travellers of the Right: British Enthusiasts for Nazi Germany 1933–9* (London: Constable, 1980)

Harvey, J. (ed.), *The Diplomatic Diaries of Oliver Harvey, 1937–40* (London: Collins, 1970)

Hyde, H. M., *Neville Chamberlain* (London: Weidenfeld and Nicholson, 1976)

James, R. R., *A Spirit Undaunted: The Political Role of George VI* (London: Abacus, 1998)

Jay, R., *Joseph Chamberlain: A Political Study* (Oxford: Oxford University Press, 1981)

Jenkins, R., *Baldwin* (London: Collins, 1987)

——, *The Chancellors* (London: Macmillan, 1998)

——, *Churchill* (London: Pan Macmillan, 2002)

Langhorne, R. (ed.), *Diplomacy and Intelligence During the Second World War: Essays in Honour of F. H. Hinsley* (Cambridge: Cambridge University Press, 1985)

Lucy, H. W. (ed.), *Speeches of the Right Hon Joseph Chamberlain MP* (London: George Routledge & Sons, 1885)

Lukacs, J., *Five Days in London: May 1940* (New Haven and London: Yale University Press, 1999)

Macleod, I., *Neville Chamberlain* (London: Frederick Muller Limited, 1961)

Margach, J., *The Abuse of Power: The War between Downing Street and the Media from Lloyd George to Callaghan* (London: W. H. Allen, 1978)

Neville, P., *Neville Chamberlain: A Study in Failure?* (London: Hodder & Stoughton, 1992)

Nicolson, N. (ed.), *Harold Nicolson: Diaries and Letters 1930–1939* (London: Collins, 1966)

Olson, L., *Troublesome Young Men: The Rebels who Brought Churchill to Power in 1940 and Helped to Save Britain* (London: Bloomsbury, 2007)

Parker, R. A. C., *Chamberlain and Appeasement: British Policy and the Coming of the Second World War* (London: Macmillan, 1993)

Ramsden, J., *The Age of Balfour and Baldwin, 1902–1940* (London: Longman, 1978)

Reeks, A., *More Than Munich: The Forgotten Legacy of Neville Chamberlain* (Alcester: West Midlands History Ltd, 2018)

Reynolds, D., *In Command of History: Churchill Fighting and Writing the Second World War* (London: Random House, 2004)

Robbins, K., *Appeasement* (Oxford: Blackwell Publishers, 1988 and 1997)

Rose, K., *King George V* (London: George Weidenfeld & Nicolson Ltd, 1983)

Self, R., *The Sir Austen Chamberlain Diary Letters. The Correspondence of Austen Chamberlain with his Sisters Hilda and Ida, 1916–1937* (Cambridge: Cambridge University Press, 1995)

——, *The Neville Chamberlain Diary Letters. Volume 1: The Making of a Politician, 1915–1920* (Aldershot: Ashgate, 2000)

——, *The Neville Chamberlain Diary Letters. Volume 2: The Reform Years, 1921–1927* (Aldershot: Ashgate, 2000)

——, *The Neville Chamberlain Diary Letters. Volume 4: The Downing Street Years, 1934–1940* (Aldershot: Ashgate, 2005)

——, *Neville Chamberlain: A Biography* (Aldershot: Ashgate, 2006)

Shakespeare, N., *Six Minutes in May: How Churchill Unexpectedly Became Prime Minister* (St. Ives: Penguin Random House UK, 2017)

Smart, N., *Neville Chamberlain* (Abingdon: Routledge, 2010)

Steiner, Z., *The Triumph of the Dark: European International History 1933–1939* (Oxford: Oxford University Press, 2011)

Stewart, G., *Burying Caesar: Churchill–Chamberlain and the Battle for the Tory Party* (London: Phoenix, 2000)

Taylor, A. J. P., *The Origins of the Second World War* (London: Hamish Hamilton Ltd, 1961; 1963, and subsequent editions, contain an important Foreword, 'Second Thoughts')

——, *Beaverbrook* (London, Hamish Hamilton Ltd, 1972)

Thorpe, D. R., *Alec Douglas-Home* (London: Sinclair-Stevenson, 1996)

Todman, D., *Britain's War: Into Battle 1937–1941* (St. Ives: Penguin Random House UK, 2017)

Ward, R., *The Chamberlains: Joseph, Austen and Neville 1836–1940* (Stroud: Fonthill Media Limited, 2015)

Watt, D. C., *Too Serious a Business: European Armed Forces and the approach to the Second World War* (London: Temple Smith, 1975)

——, *How War Came: The Immediate Origins of the Second World War, 1938–1939* (London: Heinemann, 1989)

Wheeler-Bennett, J. W., *Munich, Prologue to Tragedy* (London: Macmillan, 1948)

Whitehill-Laing, D., *Mistress of Herself* (Barre Massachusetts: Barre Publishers, 1965)

# Index